INTRODUCTION
CYBER SECURITY

GUIDE TO THE WORLD OF CYBER SECURITY

ANAND SHINDE

INDIA • SINGAPORE • MALAYSIA

Notion Press

No. 8, 3rd Cross Street
CIT Colony, Mylapore
Chennai, Tamil Nadu – 600004

First Published by Notion Press 2021
Copyright © Anand Shinde 2021
All Rights Reserved.

ISBN 978-1-63781-642-4

This book has been published with all efforts taken to make the material error-free after the consent of the author. However, the author and the publisher do not assume and hereby disclaim any liability to any party for any loss, damage, or disruption caused by errors or omissions, whether such errors or omissions result from negligence, accident, or any other cause.

While every effort has been made to avoid any mistake or omission, this publication is being sold on the condition and understanding that neither the author nor the publishers or printers would be liable in any manner to any person by reason of any mistake or omission in this publication or for any action taken or omitted to be taken or advice rendered or accepted on the basis of this work. For any defect in printing or binding the publishers will be liable only to replace the defective copy by another copy of this work then available.

CONTENTS

INTRODUCTION

1.1 CYBER SECURITY - THE NEED OF THE HOUR

1.1.1 It's a virus attack, literally!

The word 'Virus' is used in a specific context in the world of computers, software, and the internet. It is an unwanted set of commands designed to unsettle the operating system of users' devices. No one knows who makes the viruses and what exactly the makers want in return. But anyone and everyone using electronic devices are under constant threat of a virus attack. Of course, there are several proactive and corrective measures that can be taken to minimise the damage; but none of them can promise a complete protection or complete recovery.

All of this now sounds relatable like never before. Despite centuries of research and advancement in medical science, humankind is still under the threat of some unknown virus attack. The recent outbreak of Coronavirus (COVID-19) has challenged our belief that we can predict the future and plan our own lives. This unwanted virus has unsettled the routine operations of every nation across the world. Not a single sector is left unaffected, thanks to this global health crisis. To be specific, all businesses and markets were abruptly shut down after the Government(s) decided to restrict human contact by declaring a nation-wide LockDown!

Schools, colleges, offices, and all other establishments were closed. Travel within and outside the cities, villages, and states was restricted, rather stopped for perhaps the longest duration in history. Public transport facilities such as buses, trains, and air travel were discontinued with immediate effect. Colonies and areas were sealed to contain the spread of Coronavirus. The world, it seems, was not at all prepared for such a virus attack.

1.1.2 The Health Crisis and The Internet

The outbreak of Coronavirus brought with it several surprises. The effects of COVID-19 were as unpredictable as the virus itself. For example, who would have imagined that a virus could change the way we use the internet in our routine life? Until recently, e-mails were considered to be a 'corporate' mode of communication; social media was considered to be youth's domain; and even corporates and young executives were not so comfortable with virtual meetings for official purposes.

The sudden outbreak of Coronavirus and subsequent lockdown situation in a way forced people to rely on the internet like never before. The family members stuck at different locations in the country or world resorted to video calls for staying in touch with each other. The printing and distribution of newspapers came to a halt and people started accessing news portals and social media websites for latest updates and news. Schools and colleges were closed and the teachers had to conduct online sessions for the students who might be attending from locations as good as hundreds of miles away from each other. The local grocery shop started accepting orders on Whatsapp and the restaurants switched from dine-in to home delivery service facilitated by third party online platforms.

1.1.3 Changing Landscape of Cyber Security and Cyber Crimes

In the pre-COVID era, the corporates were too conscious about handling and security of their data. However, the Government-imposed restrictions on physical movement left them with no other option than allowing their employees to work remotely. The concept of 'Work From Home' (WFH) has become the order of the day as we sail through these Corona times. The businesses and individuals across the globe have become more dependent on the internet due to this Work From Home style of working.

The pandemic and the lockdown forced more and more people to use the internet for both personal and official purposes. Several people from all age groups and all sections of the society were suddenly exposed to the Cyber World during this period. There was no time or provision or resources available to train them on the goods and the bads of this world. Not surprisingly, these naive users became easy targets for the cyber criminals already laying traps on the web. These cyber criminals found a new way of targeting large organizations through their employees accessing the otherwise secure systems while working from home.

On one hand, the world at large was busy dealing with the unforeseen challenges posed by the pandemic, while on the other hand, the cyber criminals took the opportunity to develop and boost their attacks at an alarming pace. The unstable social and economic situation created fear and uncertainty among people, which were further exploited by the cyber criminals. Along with the working habits of people and businesses, the modus operandi of cyber-crime has also changed during this lockdown period. The increasing dependency of people upon the internet and online transactions is also creating new opportunities for the cyber criminals. With many businesses and individuals not ensuring their cyber defences, the Work From Home model is now becoming an opportunity for the cyber criminals to exploit people through e-mail scams, hacking passwords, phishing, ransom attacks, online sexual harassment, etc.

1.1.4 Cyber Crimes to Cyber Warfare - Everybody Is At Risk!

When we think about Cyber Security, the first thing that comes to our mind is Cyber Crimes. This is a global problem and its threat is growing immensely, especially during this pandemic and lockdown period. Before talking about Cyber Security, let's try to understand the what's and how's of Cyber Crime.

Although it is difficult to guess the number of ways cyber-crimes are committed, we can discuss a few common patterns here to start with. For example, some of the cyber criminals take advantage of unattended bugs to break into systems. When they use a new unknown bug, it is called a zero-day attack. In other cases, they break in using known bugs that the developers or users have not bothered to 'patch' or fix. Another example many of us might know (or might have even experienced) is that of cyber attackers simply tricking people into handing over login credentials or One Time Passwords (OTPs). In many cases, the cyber attackers break into the system by installing harmful software, known as malware, in the user's device.

Cyber criminals usually target individuals or companies, with an intention of stealing money or company secrets. But in a few cases, a cyber-attack might be targeted at a larger group - say, an entire country. In such cases, certain information and privacy are not the only things at risk. Some cyber-attacks are aimed at creating chaos and causing unrest among the public, leading to destruction and damage at a large scale. If some country directs such an attack at another country, it is considered to be an act of Cyber Warfare. This includes hacking the Government websites with an intention to malign the country's image on global level. Cyber warfare also aims at stealing confidential information, especially regarding the armed forces and defence strategies of the target country.

With the raging COVID-19 pandemic, an evident crisis of Coronavirus-related cyber-attacks has also proliferated since March 2020. Cyber attackers are exploiting the fears and uncertainties around the virus by spreading fake news and using click baits in the name of Coronavirus vaccine, Government schemes, etc. Phishing scams, Ransomware and Trojan attacks have seen a dramatic rise over the last six months, adding to the financial frauds and duping cases across the globe.

1.1.5 Cyber Security - The Need of the Hour

Every industry - from manufacturing to finance - and every entity in the market - from Government to private - are growing more and more dependent on Information Technology. The IT services encompass every aspect - from business communication to marketing to financial transactions - of any company. Cyber Security plays an important role in the field of information technology. Securing the information and transactions has emerged as one of the biggest challenges in the current times.

The use of the Internet has increased considerably over the past decade. From ordering food to shopping and from education to entertainment, everything has become online. While on one hand, this technological revolution has proved to be a boon, on the other hand, the internet and its users have become more vulnerable to cyber-attacks. This has indeed created a bigger need for cyber security awareness in order to protect the users from online frauds and cyber-crimes. These articles are intended to provide an introduction to the concept and create basic understanding of Cyber Security.

With the technological advancement in the field of the internet, Cyber Security is emerging as one of the most lucrative career options available today, and the demand for Cyber Security professionals is increasing day by day. Let's take this opportunity to grow personally and professionally while helping the society at large. Let's join hands to fight against the viruses - real as well as virtual - and make the internet space safer and more useful for now and forever!

1.2 HISTORY OF INTERNET

Internet is among the most important inventions of the century. The Internet has revolutionized the computer and communications world like nothing before. The invention of the telegraph, telephone, radio, and computer set the stage for this unprecedented integration of capabilities. Its history is complex and involves many aspects – technological, organizational, and community. While the complete history of the Internet could easily fill a book, we will look at few key milestones and events related to the growth and evolution of the Internet. There are several events that help shaped the Internet we see and use today. So let's take a brief look at the history of the Internet.

The Internet started in the 1960s as a way for government researchers to share information. Computers in the '60s were large and immobile and in order to make use of information stored in any one computer, one had to either travel to the site of the computer or have magnetic computer tapes sent through the conventional postal system. Another catalyst in the formation of the Internet was the heating up of the Cold War. The Soviet Union launched the world's first satellite named SPUTNIK into the space on 4th October, 1957. This was clearly the victory of Russia over the space.

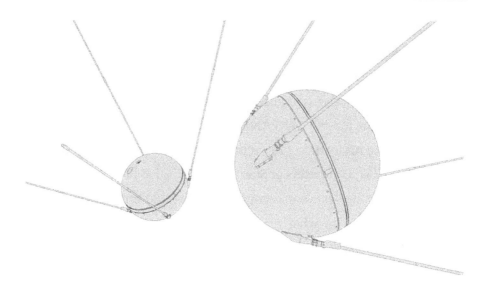

▲ **Sputnik Satellite**

This spurred the U.S. Defense Department to consider ways information could still be distributed even after a nuclear attack from Soviet Russia. This eventually led to the formation of the ARPANET (Advanced Research Projects Agency Network) in early 1960's. The network that ultimately evolved into what we now know as the Internet. ARPANET was a great success but membership was limited to certain academic and research organizations who had contracts with the Defense Department. In response to this, other networks were created to provide information sharing.

The concept of data communication through an electromagnetic medium such as radio or an electric wire – pre-dates the introduction of the first computers. Communication systems like electromagnetic medium such as radio or an electric wire were typically limited to point to point communication between two end devices. Telegraph system machines can be considered early precursors of this kind of communication. Fundamental theoretical work in data transmission and information theory was developed by Claude Shannon, Harry Nyquist, and Ralph Hartley.

In late 1966 DARPA (Defense Advanced Research Projects Agency) started to develop the computer network concept and quickly put together his plan for the "ARPANET", publishing it in 1967. Arpanet was the first real network to run on packet switching technology. On the October 29, 1969, computers at Stanford and UCLA (The University of California, Los Angeles) were connected for the first time. In effect, they were the first hosts on what would one day become the Internet. The first message sent across the network was supposed to be "Login", but reportedly, the link between the two colleges crashed on the letter "g". By December 1969, a four-node network was connected by adding the University of Utah and the University of California, Santa Barbara. In the 1970s there was no single global Internet as we know it today. There were lots of different networks like the government's big ARPANET, satellite networks and little community operations. But they all had their own different format and they connected to each other in different ways. The world needed a common language a standard set of protocols that would allow all these networks to talk to each other. The internet got the common language it needed thanks to two pioneering scientists Vint Cerf and Bob Kahn who worked for years to solve the problem of connectivity.

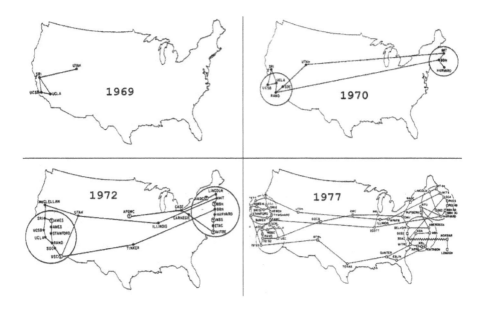

After the ARPANET had been up and running for several years, ARPA looked for another agency to hand off the network to. ARPA's primary mission was funding cutting edge research and development, not running a communications utility. Eventually, in July 1975, the network had been turned over to the Defense Communications Agency, also part of the Department of Defense. The networks based on the ARPANET were government funded and therefore restricted to non-commercial uses such as research; unrelated commercial use was strictly forbidden. This initially restricted connections to military sites and universities. During the 1980s, the connections expanded to more educational institutions, and even to a growing number of companies such as Digital Equipment Corporation and Hewlett-Packard, which were participating in research projects or providing services. Several other branches of the U.S. government, the National Aeronautics and Space Administration (NASA), the National Science Foundation (NSF), and the Department of Energy (DOE) became heavily involved in Internet research and started development of a successor to

ARPANET. In the mid-1980s, all three of these branches developed the first Wide Area Networks based on TCP/IP. NASA developed the NASA Science Network, NSF developed CSNET and DOE evolved the Energy Sciences Network or ESNet.

January 1, 1983 is considered the official birthday of the Internet. Prior to this, the various computer networks did not have a standard way to communicate with each other. A new communications protocol was established called Transfer Control Protocol/Internetwork Protocol (TCP/IP). This allowed different kinds of computers on different networks to "talk" to each other. ARPANET and the Defense Data Network officially changed to the TCP/IP standard on January 1, 1983, hence the birth of the Internet. All networks could now be connected by a universal language.

1.2.1 First Email

Raymond Samuel Tomlinson was an American computer engineer was born in Amsterdam, New York. Soon after his birth his family moved to the Broadalbin, New York. Raymond attended Broadalbin Central School. Later he attended Rensselaer Polytechnic Institute (RPI) in Troy, New York where he participated in the co-op program with IBM. He received a Bachelor's degree in Electrical Engineering from RPI in 1963. After graduation, Raymond entered the Massachusetts Institute of Technology (MIT) to continue his electrical engineering. At MIT, Raymond worked in the Speech Communication Group and developed an analog-digital hybrid speech synthesizer as the subject of his thesis for the master's degree in Electrical Engineering, which he received in 1965.

In 1971, Ray Tomlinson was a recent MIT graduate was hired to help build the earliest components of Advanced Research Projects Agency Network (ARPANET), the precursor to the internet. Tinkering on his own, he decided to build a networked messaging program. Most computers at the time allowed users to message one another, but back then few computers were networked. There was little reason to send messages across computers. The first email was sent on the ARPANET system and the first person to send an email was Ray Tomlinson. The idea of using a computer to send another person a message was nothing new in 1971. It had been done for years. But there are a couple key reasons why the world considers Ray Tomlinson to be the inventor of email. A lot of the conventions that he put in place in 1971 and his first email are still in place today. At the time; In order to send an email to somebody else on a different computer user needed that person's name such as Ray and also needed to know what computer they were on. One had to separate these two pieces of information by using the @ symbol. Something that we still use to this day. So what did that very Raymond's first email say? According to Ray Tomlinson "These test messages were entirely forgettable and I have therefore forgotten them. Most likely the first message was QWERTYIOP or something similar." Over the next few years world started to see email grow and evolve into what we know today. In 1972 programs that can sort messages and allow users to reply and forward them was developed. On in 1981 ASCII encoding becomes the standard the way of representing text within an email. By 1985 email was becoming commonplace in government and educational institutions. In 1989 the first dial-up internet services started popping up. 1991 the first email was sent from space 1992. File attachments feature was born in 1998.

Tomlinson died at his home in Lincoln, Massachusetts, on March 5, 2016, from a heart attack. He was 74 years old. Before this death he was inducted into the Internet Hall of Fame by the Internet Society (ISOC).

1.2.2 First Website

Timothy Berners-lee was born in London on June the 8th 1955. His parents were members of the team at Manchester University which developed the mark one Computer. One of the first stored-program computers. In 1973 Berners-lee went to study physics at Oxford. As a student he built his first computer using a soldering iron transistor an early microprocessor and an old television set. After graduating Berners-lee worked as a programmer. In 1980 he spent six months in Switzerland as an independent contractor with CERN the European Centre for particle physics. At first he had no idea who was responsible for what at CERN and which computer programs they were using. To gain an overview he wrote his own program. It compared documents on staff members their projects and the software they were using. The program checked whether the documents contained certain keywords; if so their locations in the documents were interlinked.

In The first web page went live on August 6, 1991. It was dedicated to information on the **World Wide Web project** and was made by British computer scientist **Sir Timothy John Berners-Lee**. He practically invented the World Wide Web in 1989. The first web page address was http://info.cern.ch/hypertext/WWW/TheProject.html. It outlined how to create Web pages and explained more about hypertext. Here's what it looked like in 1992 (below).

World Wide Web

The WorldWideWeb (W3) is a wide-area hypermedia information retrieval initiative aiming to give universal access to a large universe of documents.

Everything there is online about W3 is linked directly or indirectly to this document, including an executive summary of the project, Mailing lists, Policy , November's W3 news , Frequently Asked Questions .

What's out there?
    Pointers to the world's online information, subjects , W3 servers, etc .
Help
    on the browser you are using
Software Products
    A list of W3 project components and their current state. (e.g. Line Mode ,X11 Viola , NeXTStep . Servers . Tools . Mail robot . Library)
Technical
    Details of protocols, formats, program internals etc
Bibliography
    Paper documentation on W3 and references.
People
    A list of some people involved in the project.
History
    A summary of the history of the project.
How can I help ?
    If you would like to support the web..
Getting code
    Getting the code by anonymous FTP , etc.

Remembering an old-fashioned encyclopedia from his childhood Berners-lee called his program **Enquire**. It was an apt name because with its cross references the program functioned like an encyclopedia. Many entries ended with the recommendation. Enquires links led to a list of other documents with the same keywords. Since the program's links were based on the hypertext principle; Berners-lee called them **hyperlinks**. His program only ran on the computer at CERN and was never published. Nevertheless it formed the basis for the World Wide Web which he developed later. Because Berners-lee didn't just want to interlink documents on one computer, he also wanted to interlink documents on several computers at different locations. It was this concept that resulted in the creation of the World Wide Web. An appropriate network of interconnected computers already existed in the form of the Internet. It was the ideal vehicle for the realization of Berners-Lee's vision.

Berners-Lee has received many awards and honors. On 16 July 2004 He was knighted by Queen Elizabeth II. Time magazine's March 1999 issue listed him among the 100 Most Important People of the 20th century.

1.3 IMPACT OF INTERNET

One cannot accurately fathom the effect Internet has made on the world. Let alone me trying to achieve this in just one chapter. Internet is among the most important inventions of the century. No other technology has impacted humans globally like Internet has. Internet has changed our lived within 3 decades of its existence. Initially people thought that the Internet would be a small and limited project and would not last long. But now there billons of people who use Internet on daily basis. There are millions of new people each year who gain access to the Internet. It is an undeniable fact that both computers and the Internet have become one of the most important achievements of modern society. This brought its own revolution in human daily life (science, education, information, entertainment etc.) eliminating the distances and offering immediate and easily access to information and communication.

In August 1962, an American psychologist and computer scientist Joseph Carl Robnett Licklider, known simply as J. C. R. proposed a new but monumental idea; computers that could talk to one another. A simple idea; but one whose implications resulted in a world changing Network. The first message sent over the Internet which at this time was called the ARPANET was sent from UCLA to Stanford in 1969. Their goal was just to try and find a way to make computing power more efficient. During this time computers were basically huge machines called Mainframes that sat in rooms of buildings doing nothing but handling one task at a time. The ARPANET planned to connect these mainframes to create multiple streams of processing power to improve research. The idea of the Internet at this point was for science. The first message sent was login and it failed. The computer at Stanford only received the L in the O before the system crashed. But it worked and it changed everything. The shift from newspapers to radio was barely anything when compared from the transition from radio to television. People could see and hear people from parts of the world that they had never seen before. Almost immediately the world became connected in a way that was never before imagined. TV changed the way people and our families were entertained.

However the Internet as we know it change the world in ways that make the past 2,000 years of work and technological advancement look like baby steps. A hundred year ago the fastest way to send of mail from one side of the country to the other was by horse riders. He could deliver a letter from Kashmir to Kayakumari over 2,800 kilometers away in only 10 days. Today however user could do that in literally a second. This did not happen overnight. In early 1970s there were huge computers in multiple places. However they really had no way to communicate with each other. Because they had different software's, programs and so on. It made the communication almost impossible. Until TCP/IP came in and it changed everything. It's the foundation of how every computer talks to one another today. TCP/IP allows data to be chopped up into what we call packets sent from one place to another and regardless of how it gets there. It'll display the same information on the other side. Using TCP/IP computers could talk to one another. So this can be considered the beginning of the internet. Except it isn't the same Internet as we know it today. In the 1970s most traffic across the internet was just email. Until Tim Berners-Lee came in 1990s. He saw a way of being able to store information and data on the Internet. At this time the internet was just full of basically documents full of text information. It was boring. But Tim Berners-Lee created something that allows for people anywhere sharing any and all information they had through separate pages and with a specific location to be found. Webs of information a user can reference, certain pages the chapters go back and forth. The year is 1991 and Tim Berners-Lee had just created what we know today as the World Wide Web. After that the connectivity begins to explode more and more, things are being connected to the Internet. With the continuous development of new technologies, the Internet users are able to communicate anywhere in the world to shop online, use it as an educational tool, work remotely and carry out financial transactions with various services offered by banks. Since its creation, the Internet has grown exponentially in terms of numbers of networks connected to it. By 1985, only 100 networks, both public domain and commercial were utilizing TCP/IP protocol suite. Within a couple of years in 1987 the number had grown to two hundred. In 1989, it exceeded five hundred and by the end of 1991, the Internet had grown to include some 5,000 networks in over 36 countries, serving over 700,000 host computers used by over 4,000,000 people. In a matter of very few years, the Internet consolidated itself as a very powerful platform that has changed forever the way we do business, and the way we communicate. Internet has affected everyone's life, even of those who never used it at all.

Two things have immensely contributed to the growth of Internet. First being the invention and growth of Mobile Phone technology and introduction of Social networking. These two innovations have changed the way people use the Internet. With the help of Social networking services people have found a new way to communicate with each other. Since its creation in year 2004, Facebook has grown into a worldwide network of over 2,70,00,00,000 (2.7 Billion) active users as of August 2020. Mobile technology has made possible a much greater reach of the Internet, increasing the number of Internet users globally. The numbers are still growing day by day. Almost every phone sold today has some sort of access to the Internet. Internet is making its way into every piece of technology that we use today. The things that used to be average items like Television, Fridge, and Wrist-watch are now being connected to the Internet. From Smart TVs, Smart Cars, Smart watches, Smart washing machines are now replacing the old mechanical things. Refrigerators for some reason are able to connect to the Internet, so our washers and dryers and blenders.

1.3.1 Positive Impact of Internet

Learning: One aspect of Internet that has had a great impact on society is how it affects learning. Internet has made learning more interactive and collaborative. This has helped people better engage with the material that they are learning. Also, it gets students better access to resources. With the creation of the internet, it gives students access to information at a twenty-four-hour rate. Students have access to almost anything online. In addition, it allows students to get work done easier. Students can take quizzes and exams more easily, and teachers being able to hold online classes effectively. Internet has expanded the boundaries of the classroom, encouraging self-paced learning. College students and even outsiders can access learning through YouTube and social media. This helps students learn better than sitting down for lectures and reading from textbooks. These technological advancements made learning more fun and convenient.

After the outbreak of Covid-19 (Corona Virus) the schools, colleges and other educational institutes were closed to stop the outbreak. But the learning did not stop. The world quickly adapted to the new challenge. The Internet provided a way to attend the classes from the comfort of the home. Classes started online. Prestigious universities like Harvard have made their most famous professor's lectures available on YouTube. People now have access to high quality education at a fraction of cost than that of collage fees.

Communication: Despite the presence of thousands of language globally, now the internet has provided a platform for everyone to come together and connect to each other. Internet does not respect the boundaries. It has reached every corner of the world, including Antarctica. Even the Astronaut around orbit of the earth in space has access to internet. The rover exploring the surface of planet Mars have access to internet. The internet has revolutionized all forms of communication since the beginning of its existence. The world has now become 'smaller' or more like a 'global village', so to speak. The Internet makes communication easier and faster, and makes modes of communication more diverse.

With the Internet, people can stay in touch with friends and family regardless of time and location. This helps foster intimacy and togetherness in an increasingly spread-out, mobile world. Another way technology has impacted society is through communication, how we talk and communicate with one another worldwide. Technology brought many new methods of electronic communication. For example, there are emails, social networking, user can face time a person that lives on the other side of the world, and then there's video conferencing where users can have conferences electronically. Internet also creates more opportunities for strangers to meet because of common interests, and for new friendships and other relationships to develop between random acquaintances. With the Internet ordinary people have more power to grow their networks of contacts and thereby expand their reach.

Social Networks: The human being is often considered as a Social being. We humans have been living in societies even before we started walking on two legs. It is no surprise that the Internet is also used for Social interactions. Internet has positively transformed from a simple tool for publishing information to a mean of social interaction and participation. Social networks can be defines as online services that allow individuals to create a public profile which is visible to the entire world. Additionally, users publish a list of other users with whom they share a connection and view. A user can exchange their own lists of connections and those who are created by others. Social networks are a set of interactions and relationships of individuals. The term is also used today to describe services that allow interactions between users sharing their views, photos and other information. The most famous of these websites are Facebook, Twitter, My Space, LinkedIn, and Tumblr. These services have helped form virtual communities where people can communicate and develop contacts through them.

Social media use has skyrocketed over the past decade and a half. The rise of social media means it's unusual to find an organization that does not reach its customers and prospects through social media platforms. Companies see the importance of using social media to connect with customers and build revenue. Businesses have realized they can use social media to generate insights, stimulate demand, and create targeted product offerings. This is important in traditional businesses, and, obviously, in the world of e-commerce. Many studies suggest implementing social networks within the workplace can strengthen knowledge sharing. The result is to improve project management activities and enable the spread of specialized knowledge. Fully implementing social technologies in the workplace removes boundaries, eliminates silos, and can raise interaction and help create more highly skilled and knowledgeable workers.

Health Care: With the help of Internet the technological advancements that were made within the health care industry too. Positive effects of Internet as health information have enhanced patient confidence in dealing with doctors, better health choices and decision making, improved understanding of health conditions, and improved communication with medical staff. Improved information access through Internet health information, given the information is clinically relevant, accurate, and validated, has been linked to improved outcomes.

Internet has helped keep people safe and healthy. There are many innovate apps on phones that guides people to watch their weight, how many calories they intake, heart-rate and other health properties any time of the day. There's increased accessibility of treatment available. There is the change in healthcare that adds benefits for the elderly, and hospitals using advanced technology within their surgical rooms. Health information gained from internet provides a sense of empowerment, purpose, and control, and patient empowerment can lead to better treatment and higher levels of patient satisfaction.

Medical research was once a somewhat modular field, wherein universities and hospital networks were working independently from each other. Thanks to the internet, medical researchers around the globe are now able to collaborate in ways which were simply not feasible even as recently as 25 years ago. Doctors, insurers, and other distinct sections of healthcare can pass information back and forth without investing in time-consuming and costly methods of secured manual transfer. The internet has undoubtedly changed just about every industry on the planet. Healthcare has been no exception. Amid the greater evolution of information technology happening all around us, it's easy to overlook the ways in which it's altered the healthcare industry.

Business: The majority of businesses use the internet for marketing and selling. Businesses are using social media platforms such as YouTube, Twitter, and Instagram; along with websites, and blogs to promote products and services directly to the end users on the internet. Digital Marketing tools help all kinds of businesses to communicate the marketing message and brand values with the people. Businesses are growing attracting more customers with engaging campaigns, digital content, and by using online marketing methods to their online stores. Today the consumers expect the revolutionized products and services. Internet user's priorities, expectations, desires, and styles have changed. Consumers are now connected with Internet. Due to the availability and higher speed of information, knowledge, and opinions, it's changing the decisions and priorities of customers, consumers, companies that provide various services. The fact is that now a day it's impossible to conduct business without using the internet. Business use internet in every aspect; from idea to management, production to marketing, selling, and purchasing and accounts management to tax filing. One can see that the internet has impacted the traditional methods far more that any other revolution has done in history.

There are big opportunities for everyone on the internet to start the business. The Internet created opportunities to start and operate a business online. Anyone can start an online business from home. Such as Ecommerce, affiliate marketing, publishing, content creation, designing, and web/app development, blogging and digital marketing, etc. Businesses have big opportunities on the internet. There are thousands of people and companies doing business online and making a big profit in a shorter time.

Entertainment: Entertainment is an activity, which provides a diversion or permits people to amuse themselves in leisure time. Entertainment industry is a part of tertiary sector of the economy and includes a large number of sub industries devoted to entertainment. It is also known as showbiz. Internet sector has also influenced the entertainment sector. Due to safe e commerce environment and digitalization of content, the entertainment industry has new face now. This industry consists of several areas like music, movies, television, games, sports, broadcasts and much more. The combination of music, films, ads and games etc. enables completely new product and services to be created. The internet has played a significant role in entertainment. It has changed the way that entertainment is viewed, consumed and also the way in which it's received. Many years ago, entertainments were primarily enjoyed in real time and live. Now, we are able to watch things live and also watch replays of entertainment thanks to the provision of the internet. As with everything, this has many implications for the entertainment industry and has helped artists globally. It has also created an avenue for other sub-forms of entertainment to emerge as a result. Social media platforms, like YouTube, Facebook, Instagram, Tik-Tok etc. have made many entertainers more influential than they may have been without its existence.

Jobs and Employment: Technological advances have often come at the expense of certain categories of jobs. This was evident in the industrial revolution and recent digital revolution. But with the invention of Internet, the world has witnessed a paradigm shift. Internet certainly has affected some businesses, but globally it has created thousands and thousands of new professions which never existed before. Jos, skills, techniques which were unheard of is emerging day by day. Internet has provided an opportunity to work from home during the outbreak of Covid-19. The internet is a tool that gives access to resources that individuals can use to develop businesses with potential to grow and even to generate employment. It offers a means of accessing new business opportunities – through the development of new products, new services and new markets.

1.3.2 Negative impacts of Internet

The internet has received much negative news coverage in recent years. While the social and economic benefits of the internet cannot be denied. The internet has been on the receiving end of much negative news coverage in recent years. The focus has been on major privacy scandals and security breaches, the proliferation of fake news, rampant harmful behaviors such as Cyber-bullying, Cyber-theft, Revenge porn, Sextortion, the exchange of child porn and internet predation, internet addiction, and the negative effects of the internet on social relations and social cohesion. There are several significant harmful social and cultural effects associated with internet use. Let's look at them briefly.

Internet addiction: In a world in which Digital Technology usage has been growing, there is no debate whether Internet addiction exists or not. How people have been using the Internet has changed substantially since the advent of mobile phone technology. The internet has become an integral part of modern day life. Over the past few years, correlation between excessive internet use and mental disorders has grown. Internet addiction is a behavioral addiction in which a person becomes dependent on use of the Internet, or other online devices. Internet addiction is becoming widely recognized and acknowledged, particularly in developed countries where it is affecting large numbers of people. Internet addicts develop an emotional attachment to on-line friends and get addicted to activities they have created, such as YouTubers, Instagramers, Tik-Tokers and other social media influencers. People suffering from Internet addiction use the virtual fantasy world to connect with real people through the Internet, as a substitution for real-life human connection, which they are, fail to achieve normally. Symptoms of Internet addiction include Feeling guilty, ashamed, anxious, or depressed as a result of online behavior, Failed attempts to control behavior, Neglecting sleep to stay online, Weight gain or loss, backaches, headaches, carpal tunnel syndrome. Internet addiction is a harmful. Lack of control over one's internet consumption that can lead to a decrease in physical and psychological wellbeing, with associated symptoms of distress, anger, loss of control, social withdrawal, familial conflict, and others.

Though internet addiction is not officially recognized as a distinct behavioral disorder yet but in context of rapidly growing internet use, the internet addiction is been recognized as a global concern. The addiction is especially growing among teens and youths. Young people are spending most of their time in online activities including pornography, gambling, online video games, excessive chatting, Cyber bullying and Cyber-crimes etc. India has the youngest population in the world but it's our responsibility to inculcate the right habits among next generation so we don't lose the power of our young just in surfing online.

Information Overload: We're living in a world of information overload. A theory that has recently been developed to address the intake of too much data due to the widespread use of digital devices, massive amounts of new information and the ability to transmit this information quickly. It's fascinating is that average internet user spend half of their year consuming information. The average person spending 32 hours online a month. Over 4 million blog posts are published every day. There are more than 800,000 podcasts and more than 30 million podcast episodes available. Countless emails land in our inbox daily with 'COVID-19' or 'webinar' somewhere in the subject line. But too much of anything is simply too much, and trying to keep up with all of this information can be exhausting. A Yahoo survey found that In terms of emails the average professional receives at least 100 emails a day. The average professional checks their inboxes 30 to 40 times an hour. In a college lecture students open twice as many distracted windows on their laptops as productive windows. For every 100 productive windows students also opened 27 email windows 33 surfing and entertainment windows 43 instant messaging windows. 87 operation system windows and 19 miscellaneous windows. But the survey also found that average user only remembers 10% of what they see on the internet.

Managing information in daily life is no longer restricted to a wealthy elite but is a problem which faces nearly everyone. Social media, e-mail, webpages, mobile apps, etc. all spill data into our lives daily. Information overload is a real phenomenon which prevents people from taking decisions or actions because they feel they have too much information to consume. Current research suggests that the surging volume of available information—and its interruption of people's work—can adversely affect not only personal well-being but also decision making, innovation, and productivity. With the information floodgates open, content rushes at us in countless formats: Text messages and Twitter tweets on our cell phones. Facebook friend alerts and voice mails. There are even claims that the relentless cascade of information lowers people's intelligence.

Harmful effects on Social relationships: Internet has drastically changed the cultural norms and behavior of individuals. Use of excess

Internet has resulted less face-to-face interaction within societies. This is in consequence of addiction to which the frequent access of internet is preferable not only for leisure time but also on behalf of most activities to undertake. Thus people tend to playing gadget and being introvert. Youths are more inclined towards using mobile phones for activities other than communication than older generation. Because in adolescence stage, people are more susceptible to changing fashion trends and style, building them more Tech savvy this creates certain behavioral disorders. The fame of the mobile phones is followed by an alarm towards the detrimental effects of cell phone radiation, fatigue, headache, decreased concentration and local irritation and burning are the major effects of excessive usage of mobile phones. One potential negative effect of increasing internet use is that it will undermine and degrade social relationships and reduce the quality of social interaction. As users spend more time online, they tend to neglect existing social relationships and be less likely to form new relationships. For example, users might, due to their (excessive) internet use, act in ways that actively damage the relationship. Some might neglect the necessary maintenance of the relationship due to internet use. There is a considerable amount of evidence linking internet use, particularly social media use, to loneliness and social isolation. The harm that internet use causes to romantic relationships is best documented in relation to pornography. Given the number of internet users that regularly watch pornography use has the potential to harm relationships in a variety of ways. Adolescents who watch pornography have lower degrees of social integration, more delinquent behavior and decreased emotional bonding with caregivers. Certainly, one can argue that online communication is not yet the dominant form of communication among young people, but it's gaining popularity day by day. The more spread it achieves the higher its impact is going to be on the personal and social relationship.

Harmful effects on knowledge and belief: Significant harm is also done by false information and disinformation on the internet, and by the phenomenon of echo chambers. Here the ideas are reinforced through repetition in a closed system that does not allow for alternative viewpoints. Empirical evidence suggests that the internet contains much false and misleading information, and that users have difficulty distinguishing accurate from inaccurate information. Fake news poses a particular problem. Misinformation can cause significant harms to the health and wellbeing of individuals and to the proper functioning of society. Including the functioning of democratic institutions. Echo chambers appear to be more pervasive, and may separate those with more extreme and partisan political and ideological positions from the rest of society. Thereby undermining possibilities for civil discourse and tolerance. This supports radicalization. Misinformation can be very difficult to correct and may have lasting effects even after it is discredited. One reason for this persistence is the manner in which people make causal inferences based on available information about a given event. As a result, false information may continue to influence beliefs and attitudes even after being debunked; if it is not replaced by an alternate causal explanation. The spread of anti-vaccination misinformation on social media, (and its implications for public health and the global fight against COVID-19) is a textbook example of how misinformation can have serious real world.

Cyber Crimes: These days Cyber Crime is a fast-growing area of crime. As, the technology is advancing man is becoming dependent on internet for all his needs as it gives easy access to do shopping, gaming, online studying, social networking, online jobs etc. everything at one place. Like developed countries, India is also not far where the rate of incidence of Cyber-crime is increasing day by day. Criminals are mostly exploiting the speed, convenience and anonymity of the internet, commit various criminal activities and pose real threat to victims all over the world. These crimes can be phishing, Fraud due to credit card, debit card, bank robbery, illegal downloading, child pornography, distribution of viruses etc.

Loss of privacy: Internet is changing the world we are living in. As the internet growing at a rapid pace, its users are losing the privacy. With internet's growth Rapid developments and globalization have brought new challenges towards personal data protection. Internet has started to influence on every aspect of our life. So whenever a user navigates in Internet, makes a phone call or uses different technology tools users' privacy becomes vulnerable. Although these technologies are helping us in various ways, we are losing our privacy to these technologies. Protection of personal data in relation to current developments in technology is one of the subtle challenges of the global information society. There is no doubt that the proliferation of numerous activities within the use of information technology and use of new forms of communication present difficulties. Often people use their personal camera for entertainment purposes or the cultural ones; transmitting images in which other people can also be part. What can infringe private life is not their holding in "safe" places, but their distribution in the third persons, online or other without the consent of those persons.

1.4 INTERNET IN INDIA

The history of internet in India began with the launch of the Educational Research Network (ERNET) in 1986. ERNET was initiated by the Department of Electronics (DoE), with funding from the Government of India and United Nations Development Program (UNDP), involving eight premier institutions as participating agencies—NCST Bombay, Indian Institute of Science, five Indian Institutes of Technology (Delhi, Mumbai, Kanpur, Kharagpur and Chennai) and the DoE in New Delhi.

The year 1986 saw a dial-up link running UUCP for email exchange being established between NCST and IIT-Bombay. 1987 saw IIT-Madras and IIT-Delhi connecting to the NCST VAX 8600 by dial-up. This machine became the dial-up hub named shakti.ncst.ernet.in. Very soon all ERNET partners were on dial-up ERNET email and hundreds of Indian academics in these institutions started using email to talk to colleagues all over the world, using a dial- up link between Shakti at NCST and a router at the Centrum voor Wiskunde en Informatica (CWI) in Amsterdam.

The first leased line of 9.6 kbit/s was installed in January 1991 between Delhi and Mumbai. ERNET was allotted Class B IP address 144.16.0.0 by InterNIC in 1990. Subsequently, Class C addresses were allotted to ERNET by APNIC. All IITs, IISc Bangalore, DOE Delhi and NCST Mumbai were connected by 9.6 kbit/s leased line by 1992. In the same year, 64 kbit/s Internet gateway link was commissioned from NCST Mumbai to UUNet in Virginia, United States. NICNet was established in 1995 for communications between government institutions. The network was operated by the National Informatics Centre.

India went online on 15 August 1995—actually the day before, so the announcement could happen on Independence Day. The first publicly available internet service in India was launched by State-owned Videsh Sanchar Nigam Limited (VSNL) on August 15, 1995. At the time, VSNL had a monopoly over international communications in the country and private enterprise was not permitted in the sector. The internet service, known as the Gateway Internet Access Service (GIAS), provided a speed of 9.6 kbit/s speed. GIAS was available immediately from Mumbai, Delhi, Kolkata and Chennai.

It was made available in Pune and Bangalore by the end of 1995. The first commercially launched internet service in India offered dial-up speeds of up to 9.6 kbit/s in 1995. With the advent of better modems, the network speed was increased to 14.4. kbit/s, followed by 28.8 and 33.4 kbit/s accesses by 1998. Dial-up was later upgraded to provide speeds up to 56 kbit/s on analog lines. The service was plagued by several hardware and network issues. B.K. Syngal, then chairman and managing director of VSNL, publicly apologized and took responsibility for the issues. Syngal stated that the company had not conducted any survey of the potential demand for the service. The modems used by VSNL were of poor quality, and often would make a beeping sound every three minutes and subsequently disconnect. VSNL's internet service garnered 10,000 subscribers within the first 6 months of the launch. In 2004, the government formulated its broadband policy which defined broadband as an always-on Internet connection with download speed of 256 kbit/s or above. From 2005 onward, the growth of the broadband sector in the country accelerated. Initially tariffing too was obscene: ₹25,000 per month for a corporate account, ₹15,000 for an individual account, ₹5,000 for a shell account (only text, no visuals). Quite simply, the charges were too high, and in this case, the quality of the service Indian ISP were providing in exchange was poor. In 2010, the government auctioned 3G spectrum followed by an equally high-profile auction of 4G spectrum that set the scene for a competitive and invigorated wireless broadband market. In January 2019, Daily News and Analysis reported that DoT officials planned to raise the minimum broadband speed to 2 mbps initially and then to 5 mbps, as part of its new "Broadband for All" policy. Connection speeds from 40 Mbit/s to 1 Gbit/s provided through optical fiber are now common in cities of India.

Today, Indians typically get internet at 4G speeds and at the world's cheapest rate of about Rs. 20 per GB of data. From zero users in 1995, India now has about 600 million internet users — the second highest in the world. The internet is probably the most important technology of our era.

INTRODUCTION TO CYBER SECURITY

2.1 WHAT IS CYBER SECURITY

In the 1950s, the word "Cyber" used to refer to Cybernetics – The scientific study of control and communication in the animal and the machine. This was followed by "Cyber" standing for "computerized." The term Cyber security is disputed. The definition changes from one organization to other organization, from one nation to another nation. Even within a nation the definition varies from one government department to the next. The Education department may have a different definition than the Defense division. This vagueness means it can cover an almost endless range of different issues such as privacy or human rights. "A New America Foundation" study from 2014 which found over 400 different Cyber Security definitions. Most of the definitions were developed over years by research and development institutes, training institutes, Businesses, intelligence and military actors focuses on the security of digital information and the network infrastructure that stores and transmits this information.

One might wonder why we are spending so much time talking about definitions. After all it's just words, isn't it? Well "The devil is in the detail". Small differences in the emphasis of Cyber-security definitions can have big implications for human rights and actions. Definitions create the norms and rules on which policies are based and the narratives which justify them. If the definitions are too broad or focused on systems they can be used to justify a wide range of measures both legitimate and illegitimate.

There are several bodies that have helped to shape the International definition of Cyber Security. Technical bodies such as Internet Engineering Task Force (IETF), The Internet Corporation for Assigned Names and numbers (ICANN) and the International Telecommunications Union (ITU) are also active in developing their own definitions of Cyber-security. Broadly speaking the widely accepted international definition as defined by ISO 27000 standards is "**Cyber-security** is the **Preservation through policy technology** and **Education** of the **Availability, Confidentiality** and **Integrity** of **Information** and its **Underlying Infrastructure** so as to **Enhance** the **Security** of **Persons** both **Online** and **Offline.**

2.2 C I A TRIAD

In order to define the Cyber Security one needs to have Understanding of the significance of the three foundational information security principles: Confidentiality, Integrity, and Availability, otherwise known as the *CIA Triad*. The concept of the CIA triad formed over time and doesn't have a single creator. Confidentiality it may have been first proposed as early as 1976 in a study by the U.S. Air Force. Likewise, the concept of integrity was explored in a 1987 paper titled "A Comparison of Commercial and Military Computer Security Policies." The paper recognized that commercial computing had a need for accounting records and data correctness. Even though it's not as easy to find an initial source, the concept of availability became more widespread one year later in 1988. By 1998 people saw the three concepts together as the CIA triad.

- Confidentiality – information is not disclosed to unauthorized individuals.

- Integrity – ensuring accuracy and completeness of data.
- Availability – users must have information when they need it.

The CIA Triad is a central tenant of ISO/IEC 27001:2013 (ISO 27001), the international standard that describes best practice for an ISMS (information security management system). ISO 27001 neatly summarizes Information security as the maintenance of confidentially, availability and integrity of the confidential assets of an organization

CIA Triad is a model designed to guide policies for information security. It provides us with a reference to evaluate and implement secure information systems, independently of the underlying technologies. Each one has specific requirements and processes. CIA Triad is aimed at protecting the organization's digital assets against the ever-growing Cyber-attacks. This can be ensured by deploying appropriate security controls to provide several security features such as deterrent, prevention, and detection of Cyber-crimes. In this context, confidentiality is a set of rules that limits access to information, integrity is the assurance that the information is trustworthy and accurate, and availability is a guarantee of reliable access to the information by authorized people. Lets look at components of CIA Triad individually.

2.2.1 Confidentiality

Confidentiality is roughly equivalent to privacy. Confidentiality ensures privacy to the sensitive information while it is in transit over a network. Proactive measures undertaken to ensure confidentiality are designed to prevent sensitive information from unauthorized people / processes, while making sure that only authorized people and only to the intended parties have access to it. The malicious actors must not intercept the data to use it for nefarious purposes. It is common for data to be categorized according to the amount and type of damage that could be done should it becomes accessible to authorized people / processes. There are various implementations which can be incorporated to ensure the confidentiality of data. Safeguarding data confidentiality involves special trainings for those needs to access and work on sensitive data. These training would typically include understanding of security risks that could compromise the Confidentiality. Training can help users to get familiarize with risk factors and how to safeguard against common attacks. Further aspects of training should include password-related best practices and information about social engineering methods, to prevent users from bending data-handling rules with good intentions and potentially disastrous results.

An example of methods used to ensure confidentiality is an account number or token number when banking online. Cryptography is the best solution in this regard. Data encryption is one of the most common and robust method of ensuring confidentiality. The encryption mainly ensures the confidentiality of sensitive data. It converts the plaintext of data into the Cipher-text, which is an unreadable form for humans. Cipher text can only be understood by the authorized entities. Encryption might involve one of the two vital security controls either Symmetric Encryption or Asymmetric Encryption. User IDs and passwords constitute a standard procedure; two-factor authentication is also being implemented in most online banking transactions. Other options include biometric verification and security tokens, soft or hardware tokens. Users can also take precautions to minimize the number of places where the information appears and the number of times it is actually transmitted to complete a transaction. Extra measures might be taken in the case of extremely sensitive data, such as storing only on air gapped computers and networks, disconnected storage devices for highly sensitive information, in hard copy form only. In addition, user can also use Steganography to hide data into another type of data such as images, audio, or video files. Hidden sensitive data in large media files is much difficult to compromise.

Confidentiality should ensure that

- Data should be handled based on their required privacy.
- Data should be encrypted, with a form of two-factor authentication to reach it.
- Keeping access control lists and other file permissions up to date.

2.2.2 Integrity

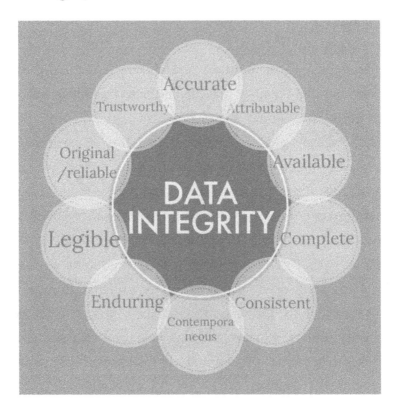

Integrity involves maintaining the consistency, accuracy, and trustworthiness of data over its entire life cycle. Integrity refers to preventing data from being tampered with, modified, or altered in malicious way to achieve malicious goals. That means data which is sent must be received intact and unaltered by an authorized party. Data must not be changed in transit, and steps must be taken to ensure that data cannot be altered by unauthorized people (a breach of confidentiality). Integrity is essential for data whether it is in transit or it is in a storage media. Data integrity is crucial for E-commerce and business websites. These measures include file permissions and user access controls. Version control may be used to prevent erroneous changes or accidental deletion by authorized users from becoming a problem. Various attacks that compromise data integrity include a Man-In-the-Middle (MITM) attack, penetrating into the web server, and introducing malicious code in databases.

In addition, some means must be in place to detect any changes in data that might occur as a result of non-human-caused events such as an electromagnetic pulse (EMP) or server crash. Use of Hashing Algorithms such as MD5 and SHA1 are normally provided by developers in order to check the integrity of data. Other techniques include certificates, digital signatures, and non-repudiation. Some data might include checksums, even cryptographic checksums, for verification of integrity. Backups or redundancies must be available to restore the affected data to its correct state.

Integrity should ensure that

1. Employees are knowledgeable about compliance and regulatory requirements.
2. Use a backup and recovery software.
3. To ensure integrity, make use of version control, access control, data logs and checksums.

2.2.3 Availability

Availability is also a security service which ensures the constant availability of resources and services to only authorized parties in a timely manner. Availability is best ensured by rigorously maintaining all hardware, performing hardware repairs immediately when needed and maintaining a correctly functioning operating system environment that is free of software conflicts. Reliable hardware must be maintained in order to provide constant services to a large number of customers in any organization. There must be less downtime during upgrades and backup of sensitive data in external drives will be helpful in case of data loss. It's also important to keep up with all necessary system upgrades. Providing adequate communication bandwidth and preventing the occurrence of bottlenecks are equally important. Quick disaster recovery plans should be followed in worst case scenarios. Other important security controls for availability include data backup, patching, and redundant systems. Redundancy, failover, RAID even high-availability clusters can mitigate serious consequences when hardware issues occur.

Fast and adaptive disaster recovery is essential for the worst-case scenarios; that capacity is reliant on the existence of a comprehensive Disaster Recovery Plan (DRP). Redundancy ensures fault tolerance. It means, when a primary system fails to perform, the secondary system is available to continue the delivery of functions and services. In this case, security analysts redirect all traffic or workload to a backup system. Safeguards against data loss or interruptions in connections must include unpredictable events such as natural disasters and fire. To prevent data loss from such occurrences, a backup copy may be stored in a geographically-isolated location, perhaps even in a fireproof, waterproof safe. Extra security equipment or software such as firewalls and proxy servers can guard against downtime and unreachable data blocked by malicious denial-of-service (DoS) attacks and network intrusions.

Availability

- Use preventative measures such as redundancy, failover and RAID. Ensure systems and applications stay updated.
- Use network or server monitoring systems.
- In case of data loss, ensure a Data Recovery and Business Continuity plan is in place.

2.3 REASONS OF CYBER CRIMES

One of the worst acts a man can perform is committing a crime. Crimes represent violations of the moral laws and ethical norms and they can be explained by various sociological, environmental, psychological and political approaches. One of the first questions asked by law enforcement officials after a crime is committed is "What was the motive?" The advancement of technology has made man dependent on Internet for all his needs. Internet has given man easy access to everything from the comfort of our homes. Social networking, online shopping, gaming, online studying, online jobs, every possible thing can be done through the internet. With the development of the internet and its related benefits also developed the concept of Cyber-crimes. Cyber-crimes are committed in different forms. Initially there was lack of awareness about the Cyber-crimes that could be committed. In the matters of Cyber-crimes, India is also not far behind the other countries where the rate of incidence of Cyber-crimes is also increasing day by day. As people increasingly conduct business and live their lives online, more and more criminals are leveraging the internet to steal. So let's look at some of the reasons why Cyber Crime is on Rise globally.

2.3.1   Ease of Committing Crime

Today, fewer skills than ever are required to commit a Cyber-crime. Cyber criminals do not need to be a computer or programming expert to know how to hack. A variety of low-cost hackers' tools are available online for Cyber criminals. There are hundreds of tutorials and digital manuals available on YouTube / Facebook and other social platforms that explain step by step how to use these hacking tools. The sad part is that movies and videos portray Cyber Criminals in glamorous ways. That affects the mindset of adolescent kids. They try to copy these behaviors of Cyber Criminals. Many of the videos, tutorials and websites linked to teen-oriented content on social media. One more lucrative aspect of Cyber-crime is that the Cyber-criminal can target the entire globe from the comfort of his home. As a result Cyber Crime has skyrocketed. Cyber Criminals can also target multiple locations simultaneously locally and globally.

2.3.2   Reward to Risk Ratio

Cyber-crimes are not hazardous as other types of crimes are. Reward to risk ratio is very high in Cyber-crime cases. Forces acting against such crimes are still technologically lagging as compared to people implementing the crime; thus, the risk of criminals getting caught is lowered. Another temptation for criminals is the earnings to cost ratio, which is also soaring high. The technology and skills required for such acts can be easily availed and are cheap, but the profits of criminals are much higher than the cost. Just hacking into a single account can fetch Cyber-criminals a lot of money, resources, and information about the user, which can be used to extort compromised user. The risk of Cyber Criminal getting caught is very low, making cyber Crimes one of the most lucrative field for criminals.

2.3.3 Anonymity

An increasing number of Cyber criminals are using the encrypted part of the internet that cannot be tracked — to shop for software that helps them remain anonymous while carrying out their crimes. The most significant feature of the Internet is that the identity of its users can be kept hidden and cannot be tracked, which is why Cyber Criminals are harder to tack. The traditional means of tracking using IP address can easily be avoided using VPN or Onion routing which is a technique for anonymous communication over a computer network. A Cyber Criminal can commit most heinous crime and stay undetected forever. MyDoom is the most devastating computer virus to date, which caused more than $38 billion in damage. Microsoft offered $2,50,000 reward for information leading to the arrest and conviction of the person responsible for releasing MyDoom worm. Till date no one has claimed that award. This shows that it's almost impossible to catch a Cyber-criminal.

2.3.4 Espionage

After land, sea, air and space, warfare has entered the fifth domain: Cyber-space. President Barack Obama has declared America's digital infrastructure to be a "strategic national asset". Cyber spying is the act of engaging in series of attacks that let an unauthorized user view classified / secret information / data. It's an action by a nation-state to penetrate another nation's computers or networks for the purposes of causing damage or disruption. The goal is typically to acquire intellectual property of an organization or government secrets. Attacks can be motivated by greed or profit, and can be used in conjunction with a military operation or as an act of terrorism. Cyber espionage attacks can result in damaged reputations and stolen data, including personal and private information. Cyber-attacks targeted at the government may cause military operations to fail, and can also result in lives lost due to leaked classified information.

In December of 2009, Google began to notice persistent Cyber-attacks aimed at acquiring information specific to Gmail accounts. The accounts were held by Chinese human rights activists, and Google wasn't the only target. To the search engine giant's credit, they quickly informed at least 20 other companies that they too were being targeted through a vulnerability in Microsoft Internet Explorer. Preventive measures were taken, and McAfee Labs identified the problem in early 2010 and code-named it 'Aurora'. Similarly; A very sophisticated Cyber espionage virus targeting computers in the Middle East and discovered in 2012. A very large and complex virus that uses various methods to hide itself and spoof antivirus software, Flame was designed to grab local and network data, including Skype video sessions. Also called "Flamer" and "SkyWiper," unlike Stuxnet, which was targeted at industrial controllers, Flame is a general-purpose virus for Windows PCs that can be remotely commanded to perform countless surveillance tasks.

2.3.5 Hacktivism

As the name suggests a form of activism involving the hacking of computers and computer networks. This is done in order to protest against acts of injustice or tyranny. The term was coined in 1994 by a cult of "The Dead Cow" member known by his online handle Omega. The cult of the dead cow is a computer hacker and media organization that was founded in 1984 in Lubbock Texas. This was one of the earliest hacking organizations formed. Hacktivism has been brought into the spotlight in recent years with more hacktivists active online than ever before. Anonymous a loosely associated ever-changing group of hacktivists composed of people from all walks of life united by their love of computer systems and their love for fighting the system and passion for human rights. Anonymous can be thought of as the faceless do-gooders of the web. The anonymous movement grew from the online community 4-Chan. Anonymous is now a world renowned political movement. Anonymous has fought for a plethora of good causes. For example Operation Darkness was aimed at retaliating against under aged pornographic websites, targeting the digital properties of various hate groups, uncovering Chinese military cyber-attacks against the United States etc. Hacktivists do their online attacks not to make money but to make a political point they're not interested in personal gain. They hack into places leak sensitive information or launch denial of service attacks to make a point to protest.

2.4 WHY WE NEED CYBER SECURITY

Why is Cyber security important all of a sudden? We are living in a far more technologically advanced world than we were before the Covid-19 outbreak. With the outbreak of COVID-19 global pandemic has forced organizations and individuals to embrace remote working. This global pandemic has created an enormous challenge for government and organizations worldwide. It has forced them to continue operating regularly despite massive shutdowns of offices and other important facilities. Overnight, the demands placed on the digital infrastructure have skyrocketed. Most of the organizations asked its IT professionals to connect to office network remotely from home. Many employees who hadn't worked from home in the past. Government and organizations were not fully prepared to adapt to this sudden change. Many organizations struggled to adapt to this drastic change and some are still struggling to adopt to it. While the world is focused on the health and economic threats posed by this pandemic, globally the Cyber criminals are trying to capitalize on this crisis. This outbreak has given Cyber criminals much bigger and more lucrative targets which were hiding behind Organizations' perimeter security. As a result Individuals are compelled to perceive Cyber Security as one of the key component of fighting the opportunities these Cyber criminals trying to encash on. As more and more people are forced to work remotely, this rise in the widespread use of technology brought with it a rise in Cyber-crimes. For hackers, the possibilities increased exponentially over a small period of time, along with the potential rewards. The fact that Cyber-crime now permeates every facet of society shows why Cyber security is crucially important. Thankfully Cyber Security is receiving more attention from the media and society than ever before.

In just a single month, the world became far more digitally connected than it was ever before. It has equally become vulnerable. Before the outbreak in March 2020, organizations always required employees to come to office premises to access the data centers and office network. A location which is physically and Cyber Security wise; highly secure and robust. With the outbreak the organizations were forced to allow its employees to use highly vulnerable and less reliable public Internet. This has highlighted the need for Cyber Security. The risk of Cyber-attack has increased by an order of magnitude, with increased communication and wholesale changes in way organizations conduct online businesses. It has also introduced a wide range of new risks which it has never faced ever before. Organizations' perimeter security is at risk of being breached. Security and risk management leaders now must safeguard their companies on a massive scale, and quickly. They must ensure that their enterprises' online services and digital platforms are resilient against Cyber-attacks. We all live in a technological era, where everything is intertwined with each other. Social media, the Internet, artificial intelligence - all are the product of technologies. It has become practically impossible to live without them. User could not work in an office if user does not have access to the Internet. As information and communication technologies pervade every aspect of our lives – from shopping and banking to education and commerce, they also leave us vulnerable to Cyber-crime. Not having Cyber Security is like not having doors on one's house and no alarm system or security cameras. It would just simply allow anyone into users system and allow them to do anything they want. Enforcing enterprise security policies and controls on the remote workforce is a difficult task. Most controls have limited scalability and require considerable time to deploy. Some organizations had no option but to allow employees to use their personal digital devices to access office networks and resources without any mechanism for enforcing security controls. Many organizations, Business Continuation Plans (BCP) and Incident Response Plans (IRP) are inadequate or even non-existent for dealing with pandemics. The fact is very few organizations were prepared for their workforces to be working remotely in mass. They now realize that secure remote-access capacity and protected access to enterprise systems have become a major constraint.

2.5 DAMAGE TO THE ORGANIZATIONS

In Cyber-space; Data is among the biggest and most valuable asset of any organization. The number attacks are proportional to the value of the assets. Data having the highest value also attacks highest number of attacks. Cyber-attacks have become an inevitable part of business in Cyber Space for organizations of all sizes worldwide. Despite growing awareness of the consequences of a successful attack, many organizations still downplay the risks associated with it, especially when additional spending on security is discussed. But make no mistake – a Cyber-attack can have devastating and long-lasting consequences for the entire organization.

Cyber-attacks can be extremely harmful to organization. Tangible costs range from stolen funds and damaged systems to regulatory fines, legal damages, and financial compensation for affected parties. However, what might hurt even more are the intangible costs - such as loss of competitive advantage due to stolen intellectual property, loss of customer or business partner trust, loss of integrity due to compromised digital assets, and overall damage to an organization's reputation and brand - all of which can send an organization's share price plummeting, and in extreme cases can even drive a company out of business. Let's look at some of the damage a successful Cyber-attack may

Economic Cost: In a world increasingly driven by digital technologies and information, Cyber-threat management is more than just a strategic imperative. It's a fundamental part of doing business. For any organization direct financial costs are perhaps the most obvious consequence of a Cyber Security breach. Fines and damage payments also fall under this category. However, economically all the consequences of Cyber Security breach have their own financial cost and significant impact on organizations bottom line.

A) **Loss of Productivity** - For any organization, every minute of downtime is directly linked with measurable financial losses. If critical systems or data are unavailable for certain period, the business stops making money. Even if organizations core business is not impacted by the Security Breach, the IT security and operations staff will be drawn away from value-added activities to deal with the emergency.

B) **Revenue Loss** - The longer business remain down due to Cyber security breach the higher the loss of business. Business models that rely on being always online, downtime might directly results into business loss. If the online store goes offline, customers can't place orders or buy products. Cyber-attack such as DDoS may result in degraded system functionality, which will adversely consumer experience resulting revenue loss. Also by concerned customers canceling orders or postponing them until the Cyber Security Breach Is under control.

C) **Response and Recovery Cost** - A serious Cyber Security Breach incident is likely to engage most or all of IT personnel of that organization; which otherwise could have been engaged in other productive work. Organizations probably may require to hire external contractors and providers as well, resulting in costly additional man-hours. Depending on organizations environment and setup, restoring backups and performing other recovery operations may mean even more expense.

D) **Investigation Cost** - Post Cyber Security breach forensics and vulnerability analysis may require organization to bring in costly external auditors, consultants, and contractors. There might be a necessity to collect evidences, logs and other artifacts increasing the cost of investigation. Depending on the complexity of the Cyber Security breach the cost may vary significantly.

Below the surface costs: Loss of intellectual property is an intangible cost associated with loss of exclusive control over trade secrets, copyrights, investment plans, and other proprietary and confidential information.

This can lead to loss of competitive advantage, loss of revenue, and lasting and potentially irreparable economic damage to the company. In addition to the economic costs of incident response, there are several intangible costs that can continue to impair a business long after the event itself. The impact of operational disruption tends to be woefully underestimated – especially among firms that have little in the way of formal business resilience and continuity strategies – and small organizations that already struggle to manage cash flow may face crippling rises in insurance premiums or see an increased cost to raise debt.

Reputation Loss: A Cyber Security breach always has an adverse effect on organizations reputation. Serious damage to organizations reputation will eventually lead to less favorable financial forecasts, potentially impacting share value and the company's overall valuation in market. This may also lead to loss of potential customers, Investors and future deals. Company may have to work hard to gain the reputation which it had lost due to Cyber Security breach.

Legal and PR costs: After a major Cyber Security breach, organization may need to finance intensive legal and PR efforts to protect the company image, manage communications with stakeholders and regulators, and prepare for or head off potential legal or regulatory action. In order to uphold these stiff privacy agreements, businesses are required to observe certain laws. Consumers may sue an organization for wrongfully disclosing their personal information, whether due to hacking or employee negligence. Consumers might sue on the ground that they were promised their information would remain secure, but the organization failed to comply. In some cases, a defamation claim may also be involved, in which a data breach resulted in someone's ruined reputation. Organizations may face significant payouts. Organization might even face Criminal Charges for Evading Regulations. Many states have strict regulations regarding Cyber security laws, based on strong privacy principles. As if direct financial losses weren't punishment enough, there is the prospect of monetary penalties for businesses that fail to comply with data protection legislation. Global authorities are considering tougher regulations: one of the most draconian measures proposed by the European Parliament for a privacy breach, applicable from 25 May 2018, is a fine of 20 million euros, or 4% global annum revenues whichever was the higher– a sum that would threaten many growing businesses with insolvency.

2.6 HISTORY OF CYBER CRIME

Digital technology provides connectivity and gives its users many valuable benefits. But at the same time, it provides a rich environment for criminal activity, ranging from vandalism to stolen identity to theft of classified government information, also coined as Hacking. Cyber-crime is the most lucrative crime in today's digital age. It is just too easy and too rewarding, and the chances of being caught and punished are perceived as being too low. As a result the Cyber Crimes have grown exponentially. Lest have a brief look at the history of the Cyber-crimes.

The history of Cyber Crimes pre-dates invention of computers. In 1834 A pair of thieves hack the French Telegraph System and steal financial market information, effectively conducting the world's first Cyber-attack. In 1870 A teenagers hired as a switchboard operator was able to disconnect and redirect calls and use the line for personal usage. In 1878 Two years after Alexander Graham Bell invents the telephone, the Bell Telephone Company kicks a group of teenage boys off the telephone system in New York for repeatedly and intentionally misdirecting and disconnecting customer calls. In 1903 During John Fleming's first public demonstration of Marconi's "secure" wireless telegraphy technology, Nevil Maskelyne disrupts it by sending insulting

Morse code messages discrediting the invention. During world War in 1939 Alan Turing and Gordon Welchman develop BOMBE, an electro-mechanical machine, while working as code breakers at Bletchley Park. It helped to break the German Enigma codes used by German soldiers to securely communicate with each other. In 1955 David Condon whistles his "Davy Crockett Cat" and "Canary Bird Call Flute" into his phone, testing a theory on how phone systems work. The system recognizes the secret code, assumes he is an employee, and connects him to a long-distance operator. She connects him to any phone number he requests for free.

After the invention of the computer in MIT in 1962, MIT had set up the first computer passwords, for student privacy and time limits. Student Allan Scherr makes a punch card to trick the computer into printing off all passwords and uses them to log in as other people after his time runs out. He also shares passwords with his friends, leading to the first computer "troll." They hack into their teacher's account and leave messages making fun of him. In 1969 an anonymous person installs a program on a computer at the University of Washington Computer Center. The inconspicuous program makes copies of itself (breeding like a rabbit) until the computer overloads and stops working. At the beginning of the 1970s, criminals regularly committed crimes via telephone lines. The perpetrators were called Phreakers and discovered that the telephone system in America functioned on the basis of certain tones. They were going to imitate these tones to make free calls. John Draper was a well-known Phreaker who worked on it daily; he toured America in his van and made use of public telephone systems to make free calls. Steve Jobs and Steve Wozniak were inspired by this man, and even joined him. Of course they all ended up on the right path: Steve Jobs and Wozniak founded Apple, the well-known computer company.

2.6.1 Evolution of Cyber-crimes

The history and evolution of Cyber-crime are easy to track and coincide with the evolution of the Internet itself. The first crimes were of course simple hacks to steak information from local networks. As the Internet became more established so too did the attacks. Because of the early and widespread adoption of computers and the Internet in the United States, most of the earliest victims and villains of Cyber-crime were Americans. As the computer became more and more popular, this attracted attention of the ordinary criminals. They started using computers to commit crimes.

The exact origin of Cyber-crime, the very first instance in which someone committed a crime across a computer network, is impossible to know.

1971 – John Draper, a phone phreak, discovers that a whistle given out as a prize in boxes of Cap'n Crunch Cereal produced the same tones as telephone switching computers of the time. Phone phreak is a term used to describe computer programmers obsessed with phone networks, the basis of modern day computer networking. He built a "blue box" with the whistle that would allow him to make free long distance phone calls, and then published instruction on how to make it. As a result the instances of wire fraud rose significantly.

1973 – A teller at a local New York bank used a computer to embezzle over $2 million dollars.

1978 – The first electronic bulletin board system came online and quickly became a preferred method of communication for the Cyber world. It allowed fast, free exchange of knowledge including tips and tricks for hacking into computer networks.

1981 – Ian Murphy, known as Captain Zap to his fans, was the first person convicted of a Cyber-crime. He hacked into the AT&T network and changed the internal clock to charge off-hours rates at peak times. He received 1,000 hours of community service and 2.5 years of probation, a mere slap on the wrist compared to today's penalties, and was the inspiration for the movie Sneakers.

1982 – Elk Cloner, a virus, is written as a joke by a 15 year old kid. It is one of the first known viruses to leave its original operating system and spread in the "wild". It attacked Apple II operating systems and spread by floppy disk.

1983 – The movie War Games is released and brings hacking to the mainstream. The movie depicts a teenage boy who hacks into a government computer system through a back door and nearly brings the world to World War III.

1986 – Congress passes the Computer Fraud and Abuse Act, making hacking and theft illegal.

1988 – Robert T. Morris jr, a graduate student at Cornell, released a self-replicating worm onto the Defense Department's APRANET. ARPANET is the precursor to the Internet as we know it today. The worm gets out of hand, infects more than 600,000 networked computers and lands Mr. Morris with a $10,000 fine and 3 years' probation, another slap on the wrist.

1989 – The first large-scale case of Ransomware is reported. The virus posed as a quiz on the AIDS virus and, once downloaded, held computer data hostage for $500. At the same time another group is arrested stealing US government and private sector data and selling it to the KGB.

1990 – The Legion Of Doom and Masters Of Deception, two Cyber-based gangs, engage in online warfare. They actively block each other's connections, hack into computers and steal data. These two groups were large-scale phone phreaks famous for numerous hacks into telephone mainframe infrastructure. The proliferation of the two groups, along with other Cyber gangs, led to an FBI sting cracking down on BBS's promoting credit card theft and wire fraud.

1994 – The World Wide Web is launched, allowing black hat hackers to move their product info from the old bulletin board systems to their very own websites. A student in the UK uses the information to hack into Korea's nuclear program, NASA and other US agencies using only a Commodore Amiga personal computer and a "blue boxing" program found online.

1995 – Macro-viruses appear. Macro-viruses are viruses written in computer languages embedded within applications. These macros run when the application is opened, such as word processing or spreadsheet documents, and are an easy way for hackers to deliver malware.

1996 – CIA Director John Deutsch testifies to Congress that foreign based organized crime rings were actively trying to hack US government and corporate networks. The US GAO announced that its files had been attacked by hackers at least 650,000 times, and that at least 60% of them were successful.

1997 – The FBI reports that over 85% of US companies had been hacked, and most don't even know it. The Chaos Computer Club hack Quicken software and are able to make financial transfers without the bank or the account holder knowing about it.

1999 – The Melissa Virus is released. It becomes the most virulent computer infection to date and results in one of the first convictions for someone writing malware. The Melissa Virus was a macro-virus with the intention of taking over email accounts and sending out mass-mailings. The virus writer was accused of causing more than $80 million in damages to computer networks and sentenced to 5 years in prison.

2000 – The number and types of online attacks grows exponentially. Music retailer CD Universe is extorted for millions after its clients' credit card information was published online. Denials of Service (DDoS) attacks are launched, numerous times, against AOL, Yahoo! Ebay and many others. Fake news causes shares of Emulex stock to crash nearly 50%. The "I Love You" Virus spreads across the Internet.

2002 – Shadow Crew's website is launched. The website was a message board and forum for black hat hackers. Members could post, share and learn how to commit a multitude of Cyber-crimes and avoid capture. The site lasted for 2 years before being shut down by the Secret Service. 28 people were arrested in the US and 6 other countries.

2003 – SQL Slammer becomes the fastest spreading worm in history. It infected SQL servers and created a denial of service attack which affected speeds across the Internet for quite some time. In terms of infection speed, it spread across nearly 75,000 machines in less than 10 minutes.

Most Prominent Cyber Security Breaches till date.

Compromised Company	Records Exposed	Discovered
Quest Diagnostics	11.9 million	2018–2019
Marriott	500 million	2014–2018
Equifax	145.5 million	2017
Facebook	50 million	2017
MySpace	360 million	2016
Uber	57 million	2016
Yahoo	500 million	2014
Ebay	145 million	2014
Yahoo	3 billion	2013
Target	110 million	2013
Linkedin	100 million	2012
TJX	94 million	2003–2004

2.6.2 Cyber Crime Classification

One of approach to defining Cyber-crime is to develop a classification scheme that links crimes with similar characteristics into appropriate groups similar to the traditional crime classifications. Several schemes have been developed over the years. One of the common schemes is that there are only two general categories: Active and Passive computer crimes. An active crime is when someone uses a computer to commit the crime, for example, when a person obtains access to a secured computer environment or telecommunications device without authorization (hacking). A passive computer crime occurs when someone uses a computer to both support and advance an illegal activity. An example is when a narcotics suspect uses a computer to track drug shipments and profits.

Classification based on computer's relationship to the crime:

1. Computers, Networks, Data or Cyber Infrastructure as a Target: Crimes such as Hacking into a restricted network, creating Malwares to disrupt the normal function of computers, stealing data such as customer data, banking detail, or stealing classified information etc.

2. Computer as the Instrumentality of the Crime: Unlawful use of automated teller machine (ATM) cards and accounts, theft of money from accrual, conversion, or transfer accounts, credit card fraud, fraud from computer transaction (stock transfer, sales, or billing), and telecommunications fraud.

3. Computer Is Incidental to Other Crimes: Money laundering and unlawful banking transactions, organized crime records or books, and bookmaking.

4. Crime Associated with the Prevalence of Computers: Software piracy/ Counterfeiting, Copyright violation of computer programs, Counterfeit equipment, Black market computer equipment and programs, and theft of technological equipment.

Classification based on the target of the Cyber Attack.

1. **Against Individuals:** This is the one that directly affects any person or their properties. Examples of this type of Cyber-crime include Harassment via electronic mails, Dissemination of obscene material, Cyber-stalking, Defamation, Indecent exposure, Cheating, Unauthorized control/access over computer system, Email spoofing, Fraud.

2. **Against Companies / Organizations:** This is one of the most common types of Cyber-crime today. When a company's online presence or any of its products are hacked, it becomes a serious problem that can result in a big number of consequences for the company, as well as their employees, associates and customers. Examples include data breaches, Cyber extortion and Distribution of Pirate software etc.

3. **Against Society:** This one affects society as a whole, for example: Child pornography, Indecent exposure, Sale of illegal articles such as drugs, Trafficking, Forgery, Online gambling etc.

4. **Against Government:** This types of Cyber-crime known as Cyber Terrorism, and includes such activities as breaking into government systems and networks, defacing and shutting down military websites, and spreading propaganda.

2.7 TYPES OF CYBER CRIMES

2.7.1 Phishing Scams

Phishing is a Cyber-attack where attackers trick users into doing something that is harmful to the victim in various ways. Phishing is also a method of trying to gather personal information using deceptive e-mails, Social media posts and websites. This Cyber-attack uses disguised email as a weapon. The goal is to trick the user into believing that the message is something helpful or they want or need for instance, a request from their bank, or a person, or government entity, or a note from someone in their company — and to click a link or download an attachment or to share banking information, or to share personal details. The Cyber attackers masquerade as a trusted entity of some kind, often a real or plausibly real person, or a company the victim might do business with, or they might trust. It's one of the oldest types of Cyber-attacks, dating back to the 1990s, and it's still one of the most widespread and pernicious, with phishing messages and techniques becoming increasingly sophisticated.

"Phish" is pronounced just like it's spelled, which is to say like the word "fish" — the analogy is of an angler throwing a baited hook out through the Cyber space and hoping the target takes a bite. The term arose in the mid-1990s among hackers aiming to trick AOL users into giving up their login information. The "ph" is part of a tradition of whimsical hacker spelling, and was probably influenced by the term "phreaking," short for "phone phreaking," an early form of hacking that involved playing sound tones into telephone handsets to get free phone calls. The first phishing lawsuit was filed in 2004 against a Californian teenager who created the imitation of the website "America Online". With this fake website, he was able to gain sensitive information from users and access the credit card details to withdraw money from their accounts.

Common characteristics of Phishing attacks are:

Too Good To Be True – Lucrative offers and eye-catching or attention-grabbing statements are designed to attract people's attention immediately. For instance, many Phishing attacks claim that user have won a lottery, a new Phone, or some other prizes through lucky draw. User's need to keep in mind that if any offer seems to be too good to be true, it probably is!

Sense of Urgency – A favorite tactic amongst Cyber-criminals is to ask users to act fast because the super deals are only for a limited time. Attacker often will even tell users that they have only a few minutes to respond. Sometimes, they will tell user that their account will be suspended unless users update their personal details immediately. Most reliable organizations and services give ample time before they terminate an account and they never ask user to update personal details over the Internet.

Hyperlinks – A link may not be all what it appears to be. Hovering over a link shows user the actual URL where it will be directed upon clicking on it. It could be completely different or it could be a popular website with a misspelling, for instance www.Amazon.com - the 'O' is actually an 'U'.

Attachments – The goals of phishing emails or website is to compel the victim to download the attachment, or execute a program.

If there is an attachment in an email user weren't expecting or that doesn't make sense, don't open it! They often contain payloads like Ransomware or other viruses. The only file type that is always safe to click on is a. txt file.

Unusual Sender – The phishing attacks are designed to look and feel legitimate source. The look of the email, Social media post, text message is from someone user doesn't know or someone user might know. The message is designed to look nothing out of the ordinary, unexpected, out of character or just suspicious in general. The attacker might even pretend to know the suspect in order to gain trust.

Phishing statistics – Phishing is one of the oldest and still among the most successful method of Cyber Attack. Phishing attack has created a major threat to those who use the internet, with millions of users getting affected every day. Let's look at some of the statistics of this attack.

a. Nearly one-third of all data breaches in 2019 involved phishing.

b. One in every 25 branded emails is a phishing email. Two most popular brands phishers pose as are Microsoft (42%) and Amazon (38%).

c. Globally 76% of organizations were targeted by phishing in 2019.

d   91% of Cyber-attacks in 2012 began with a spear phishing email.

e. URL phishing detections increased 269% in 2018.

2.7.2 Cyber Bullying

The simplest definition is "Cyber-bullying is bullying with the use of digital technologies". Cyber-bullying takes place over digital devices like Cell phones, Computers, and Tablets. Cyber-bullying can occur through SMS, Text, and apps, or online in social media forums, or Online gaming etc. where people can view, participate in, or share content. Cyber-bullying includes sending, posting, or sharing negative, harmful, false, or mean content about someone else. It can include sharing personal or private information about someone else causing embarrassment or humiliation. Some Cyber bullying crosses the line into unlawful or criminal behavior.

2.7.2.1 Forms of Cyber Bullying

1) **Exclusion:** This can happen in several ways. A victim might be deliberately excluded from online activities conversations or social media tags. Victims who don't have the latest technology or gadgets such as a mobile phone or gaming devices are prone to exclusion.

2) **Harassment:** This is sustained and intentional bullying comprised of abusive or threatening messages sent to victim or to a group. This can severely affect victim's mental well-being.

3) **Outing:** This is the act of publicly humiliating a child or group through the online posting of private or embarrassing information; without consent of the targeted victim.

4) **Cyber Stalking:** This is a dangerous form of Cyber-bullying in which attackers harass victims through online communications like email or social media. It also refers to adults using the Internet to contact and meet young people for abusive purposes.

5) **Fraping:** A 'Frape' or 'Fraping' (a combination of 'Facebook' and 'rape') is when someone uses victim's Facebook account without

permission and destroys comments or pictures, or created new and offensive comments and pictures pretending to be the victim. It's when an attacker uses victim's social media account and impersonates them posting inappropriate content in their name. Remember everything rude or otherwise posted online may never be fully gone even if deleted.

6) **Fake Profiles:** Can be created by someone to hide their real identity with the intention of Cyber-bullying the victim. The Cyber bully may also use someone else's email or mobile phone to harass victim.

7) **Dissing:** is sending or posting cruel information about the victim online to damage their reputation or friendships. It also includes posting damaging photos screenshots, videos online.

8) **Trickery:** Involves gaining victim's trust so that secrets can be shared publicly online. A Cyber-bully will befriend the victim leading them into a false sense of security before sending their private information to others.

9) **Trolling:** means deliberately provoking a response through the use of insults on online forums and social media sites. A troll will personally attack the victim aiming to make them angry and provoke a response.

10) **Cat fishing:** involves stealing online identities and recreating social networking profiles for deceptive purposes. Cat fissures often copy or mimic victims profile and take information to create a fake persona similar to victim. This could involve using personal information potentially damaging victim's online reputation.

2.7.2.2 Cyber bullying places:

Text messaging and messaging apps on mobile, tablet or similar devices.

- Instant messaging, direct messaging, and online chatting over the internet.

- Online forums, chat rooms, and message boards, such as Reddit.
- Social Media, such as Facebook, Instagram, Snapchat, and Tik Tok.
- Email.
- Online gaming communities.

2.7.2.3 Effects of Cyber Bullying:

Cyber bullying affects people from any age or walk of life, including children, teens and adults who all feel very distressed and alone when being bullied online. Cyber bullying can make victims feel totally overwhelmed which can result in victim feeling embarrassed that they are go through such a devastating time, and not knowing what support is available to them. Many children feel unable to confide in an adult because they feel ashamed and wonder whether they will be judged, told to ignore it or close their account which they might not want to do. For many Cyber bullying affects their everyday lives and is a constant source of distress and worry. With mobile technology being so freely available it is an ongoing issue and one that is relentless. Not only does it go on after school, college or work has finished, but it then carries through into the next day and the cycle continues. The Cyber bullying effects can last a long time and affect a person in following ways:

- Mentally — feeling upset, embarrassed, stupid, even angry
- Emotionally — feeling ashamed or losing interest in the things users love
- Physically — tired (loss of sleep), or experiencing symptoms like stomach aches and headaches

2.7.3 Identity Theft

Identity theft, also called identity fraud, use of an individual's personally identifying information by someone else (often a stranger) without that individual's permission or knowledge. This form of impersonation is often used to commit fraud, generally resulting in financial harm to the individual and financial gain to the impersonator. In the context of identity theft, identity refers to information intrinsic to a specific individual. Publicly available information, such as a person's telephone number and home address, as well as confidential information, such as a person's Adhar card number, mother's maiden name, and credit card numbers, contribute to a person's identity. By acquiring access to that information, an identity thief can impersonate someone else to commit online frauds. While identity theft is often associated with financial gain, it can also be used to acquire unauthorized entry, privileges, or benefits. It sometime used to Cyber bully someone else too. The stolen information can be used to run up debt purchasing credit, goods and services in the name of the victim or to provide the thief with false credentials.

Identity theft is an insidious crime to combat because the repercussions often don't happen immediately. It can take months for the effects to be noticed, and some people don't find out for years. Identity theft crimes are on rise. The data on Identity theft crimes found that the Cyber criminals are becoming increasingly sophisticated, gaining toeholds into poorly secured social media accounts as a way to access more important segments of the victim's financial life. The data suggest that in 2019, 14.4 million consumers became victims of identity fraud — that's about 1 in 15 people. Overall, 33 percent of U.S. adults have experienced identity theft, which is more than twice the global average. Statistics say that identity theft occurs every 2 seconds, and a third of the time it's not even an individual's fault. In 2017 there were 1,579 data breaches which exposed 179 million personal records from companies. One in five victims of identity theft has experienced it more than once. Over 1 million children in the U.S. were victims of identity theft in 2017, costing families $540 million in out-of-pocket expenses. There's a new victim of identity theft every 2 seconds. Identity theft is the most common consequence of a data breach, occurring 65% of the time.

Types of Identity theft: There are many different examples of identity theft. The 6 major types are as below.

Financial Identity Theft: This is the most common type of identity theft. Financial identity theft seeks economic benefits by using a stolen identity. When someone uses another person's information for financial gain. Senior citizens may be particularly vulnerable to identity theft because they may be more trusting and less able to recognize a scam. For instance, a fraudster may use user's bank account or credit card numbers to steal money or make purchases, or use user's Social Security number to open a new credit card. However, credit card fraud is just the tip of the iceberg. With enough of victim's personal information, criminals could successfully apply for new credit cards and loans in victim's name, drain victim's bank account, and receive a bogus income tax refund

Criminal Identity Theft: All identity theft is criminal, but this particular type means someone who is arrested provides victims information to law enforcement. Victim wouldn't be able to detect this until consequences arise. Such as a speeding ticket goes unpaid, and a judge issues a bench warrant for victims arrest. Criminals sometimes back this up with containing stolen credentials. If this type of exploit is successful, the victim is charged instead of the thief. This type of ID theft is low is number as compared to other ID thefts. But it can be difficult for the victim of a criminal identity theft to clear their record. The victim might need to locate the original arresting officers and prove their own identity by some reliable means such as fingerprinting or DNA testing, and may need to go to a court hearing to be cleared of the charges.

Child Identity Theft: This ID theft occurs when someone uses a child's Social Security number or other identity information to commit fraud. The impostor can be a family member, a friend, or even a stranger who targets children. That might include opening credit accounts, obtain driver's licenses, taking out loans or applying for government benefits or a job. The crime can go undetected for years. Victims of child identity theft often discover it when they're older. Not only are children in general big targets of identity theft but children who are in foster care are even bigger targets. This is because they are most likely moved around quite frequently and their identity information is being shared with multiple people and agencies.

Medical Identity Theft: Medical identity theft occurs when someone steals user's personal information and uses it to obtain medical services, treatment or drugs. It can also occur when criminals use user's personal information to fraudulently bill insurance providers or government programs for medical goods and services never provided. In other cases of medical identity theft, a doctor or other medical provider might submit insurance claims for services not provided.

Identity cloning: In this situation the identity thief impersonates someone else in order to conceal their own true identity. Identity thieves may use victim's information to get a job or pass a background check. Examples are illegal immigrants hiding their illegal status, people hiding from creditors or other individuals, and those who simply want to become "anonymous" for personal reasons. Unlike identity theft used to obtain credit which usually comes to light when the debts mount, concealment may continue indefinitely without being detected, particularly if the identity thief is able to obtain false credentials in order to pass various authentication tests in everyday life.

Synthetic identity theft: In synthetic identity theft, fraudsters can create fake identities using fake or real information, or a combination of the two. For instance, an identity thief might use a real Social Security number but use a name that's not associated with that number. Children and deceased people can be vulnerable since their Social Security numbers typically aren't actively used. Usually, this type of theft is difficult to track because the activities of the thief are recorded files that do not belong to a real person.

Identity Theft Techniques: Before the Cyber criminals can impersonate a victim they need to get the victims personal or identifying information. There are few common ways a Cyber criminals can achieve this. Following are few techniques used by Cyber criminals to get the desired information from the victims.

Dumpster diving: Retrieving personal paperwork and discarded mail from trash dumpsters is an easy way for an identity thief to get victims information. Dumpster diving is salvaging personal or identifying information from the items discarded by their owners. This may include unshredded mails, Credit Card receipts, Bank statements, Phone bills. Many a times users and organizations do not wipe clean the data before their PCs, servers, PDAs, mobile phones, USB memory sticks and hard drives that have been disposed of carelessly at public dump sites, given away or sold. A cyber-criminal may be able to salvage useful information from the poorly disposed devices.

Mail Theft: Mail theft is a non-technological identity theft technique, as it merely involves a thief removing sensitive information from users' mailbox. Through mail theft, someone else can obtain information about users from credit card bills, bank statements and other personal materials that can be used to assume users identity. The main motive behind Mail theft is to gain the victims information before actual identity theft can be mounted.

Shoulder surfing: This happens when the thief gleans information as the victim fills out personal information on a form, enter a passcode on a keypad or provide a credit card number over the telephone. In this attack the attacker has to be physically in the vicinity of the victim and should be able to observe victim while he shares this information. Likely hood of this is pretty low, but not zero. The attacker might get Common-knowledge questioning schemes that offer account verification, such as "What's users mother's maiden name?", "what was users first car model?", or "What was users first pet's name?" etc.

Phishing: Attacker might trick the victim to voluntarily share the personal information. Such as advertising bogus job offers in order to accumulate resumes and applications typically disclosing applicants' names, home and email addresses, telephone numbers and sometimes their banking details. Phishing might also lead to stealing personal information from computers using breaches in browser security or malware such as Trojan horse keystroke logging programs or other forms of spyware Hacking computer networks, systems and databases to obtain personal data, often in large quantities.

2.7.4 Cyber Stalking

Stalking is unwanted obsessive attention to a specific person. Physical stalking can involve following, secret surveillance, persistent and manipulative calling and texting, and other means of approaching the victim unexpectedly. Cyber-stalking is a crime in which the attacker harasses a victim using electronic communication, such as e-mail or instant messaging (IM), or messages posted to a Web site or a discussion group. A Cyber-stalker relies upon the anonymity afforded by the Internet to allow them to stalk their victim without being detected. Cyber-stalking messages differ from ordinary spam in that a Cyber-stalker targets a specific victim with often threatening messages, while the spammer targets a multitude of recipients with simply annoying messages.

Cyber-stalking can take many different forms, but in the broadest sense, it is stalking or harassment that takes place via online channels such as social media, forums or email. It is typically planned and sustained over a period of time. The Case of Cyber-stalking can often begin as seemingly harmless interactions. Sometimes, especially at the beginning, a few strange or perhaps unpleasant messages may even amuse the target. However, eventually then become systematic, it becomes annoying and even frightening to the victim.

WHOA (Working to Halt Online Abuse), an online organization dedicated to the Cyber-stalking problem, reported that in 2001; 58% of Cyber-stalkers were male and 32% female. In some cases the perpetrator's gender is unknown as the stalker is able to remain anonymous. In a variation known as corporate Cyber-stalking, an organization stalks an individual. Corporate Cyber-stalking is usually initiated by a high-ranking company official with a grudge, but may be conducted by any number of employees within the organization. Cyber-stalking began with e-mail messages most often, followed by message boards and forums messages, and less frequently with chat. In some cases, Cyber-stalking develops from a real-world stalking incident and continues over the Internet. However, Cyber-stalking is also sometimes followed by stalking in the physical world. People put so much of their lives online that it has become extremely easy for someone to stalk a victim. Victim's interests, events they're attending, places they visit, their workplace, email, and even their phone number can be found with just a little bit of digging.

Cyber-stalking is common — at least 40% of adults report experiencing some sort of harassment online, including stalking, with the majority of targets being women. Whether she is a college student, working professional or housewife get stalked on a regular basis. Let's explore the kinds of Cyber-stalking that till now has been reported worldwide.

Cat fishing: In Cat fishing, Stalkers create a fake profile on social media to approach victims. Sometimes they copy the existing user's profile with photos to look it like a real one.

Monitoring location check-ins: Stalkers keep an eye on the activities of a victim from their check-ins on social media such as Facebook and Instagram. This is an easier job for a stalker to gauge a victim's behavioral pattern quite accurately. Social media platforms like Facebook, Instagram, Twitter usually also include the location from where the content was posted by user. A stalker can easily "Follow" the victims by check-ins recorded by these aps.

Online Maps: If a stalker discovers the victim's address, then it is not hard to find the area, neighborhood, and surroundings by using online maps such as Google maps, Google Earth or Street View. Stalker can discover the victim's place from the posts or photos posted on social media. In September 2019, a Japanese man was arrested for reportedly stalking a pop star and attacking and groping her at her home. This man found the victim's woman's home by studying photos she posted on social media, observing a train station reflected in her eyes, finding that train station using Google Street View, waiting for her at the train station, and following her home.

Hijacking webcam: Computer's webcam hijacking is one of the most disturbing methods of Cyber-stalking to invade the victim's privacy. Stalkers push malware-infected files into the victim's computer which gives them access to the webcam. In June 2016 Chief Executive Officer of Facebook Mark Zuckerberg posted a photo of himself celebrating Instagram's latest user numbers. In this picture his laptop was also visible. Strangely the Camera and mic-jack of his laptop were covered with Tape. The taped-over camera and microphone jack are intended to protect against hackers using users' laptop camera to take covert pictures or videos or accessing users' microphone to eavesdrop on conversations – a possibility once users' device has been accessed through "ratting."

Installing Stalker-ware: One more method that is increasing its popularity is the use of Stalker-ware. It is a kind of software or spyware which keeps track of the location, enable access to text and browsing history, make an audio recording, etc. And an important thing is that it runs in the background without any knowledge to the victim. These Stalker-ware can track users' message on any social media platform, emails, content like photos and videos saved on the device. The hacker can remotely switch on the victims camera, microphone to eavesdrop on the victim.

Geo-tags to track location: - Most digital pictures contain geo-tags which is having information like the time and location of the picture in the form of metadata. Geo-tags come in the EXIF format embedded into an image and is readable with the help of special apps. In this way, the stalker keeps an eye on the victim and gets the information about their whereabouts which are shared by the victim.

2.7.5 Hacking

Hacking is identifying weakness in computer systems or networks to exploit its weaknesses to gain unauthorized access. A Hacker is a person who finds and exploits the weakness in computer systems and/ or networks to gain unauthorized access. Hackers are usually skilled computer programmers with knowledge of computer security. Although the term hacker predates computers and was used as early as the mid-1950s in connection with electronic hobbyists. In early 1960s most hackers were young people driven by intellectual curiosity; many of these people later have gone on to become computer security architects. However, as some hackers sought notoriety among their peers, their exploits led to clear-cut crimes. In particular, hackers began breaking into computer systems and then bragging to one another about their exploits, sharing stolen documents as trophies to prove their boasts. These exploits grew as hackers not only broke into but sometimes took control of government and corporate computer networks.

The scale of hacking crimes is among the most difficult to assess because the victims often are not aware of the Hack that has happened. Most of the recent hackers prefer not to let their presence noticeable to the victim. These hackers quietly steal the data, financial information from the victim and then erase any trace of their presence before existing. This makes it almost impossible for the victim to know the scale of hack. Some victims prefer not to report the crimes—sometimes out of embarrassment or fear of further security breaches. Same goes with Organizations. They fear that announcing the hack may damage the reputation and even face loss of business and fine. One of the largest known case of computer hacking was discovered in late March 2009. It involved government and private computers in at least 103 countries. The worldwide spy network known as GhostNet was discovered by researchers at the University of Toronto, who had been asked by representatives of the Dalai Lama to investigate the exiled Tibetan leader's computers for possible malware.

Classification of Hackers: Hackers are classified according to the intent of their actions. The following list classifies hackers according to their intent. These different terms come from old Spaghetti Westerns, where the bad guy wears a black cowboy hat and the good guy wears a white hat.

White Hat Hackers: White Hat hackers are also known as Ethical Hackers. They never intent to harm a system, rather they try to find out weaknesses in a computer or a network system as a part of penetration testing and vulnerability assessments. Ethical hacking is not illegal and it is one of the demanding jobs available in the IT industry. There are numerous companies that hire ethical hackers for penetration testing and vulnerability assessments of the company infrastructure.

Black Hat Hackers: Black Hat hackers, also known as crackers, are those who hack in order to gain unauthorized access to a system and harm its operations or steal sensitive information. Black Hat hacking is always illegal because of its bad intent which includes stealing corporate data, violating privacy, damaging the system, blocking network communication, etc.

Grey Hat Hackers: Grey hat hackers are a blend of both black hat and white hat hackers. They act without malicious intent but for their fun, they exploit a security weakness in a computer system or network without the owner's permission or knowledge. Their intent is to bring the weakness to the attention of the owners and getting appreciation or a little bounty from the owners.

Miscellaneous Hackers: Apart from the above well-known classes of hackers, there are few categories of hackers based on what they hack and how they do it –

Red Hat Hackers: Red hat hackers are again a blend of both black hat and white hat hackers. They are usually on the level of hacking government agencies, top-secret information hubs, and generally anything that falls under the category of sensitive information.

Blue Hat Hackers: A blue hat hacker is someone outside computer security consulting firms who is used to bug-test a system prior to its launch. They look for loopholes that can be exploited and try to close these gaps. Microsoft also uses the term BlueHat to represent a series of security briefing events.

Elite Hackers: This is a social status among hackers, which is used to describe the most skilled. Newly discovered exploits are usually circulated among these hackers.

Script Kiddie: A script kiddie is a non-expert who breaks into computer systems by using pre-packaged automated tools written by others, usually with little understanding of the underlying concept, hence the term Kiddie.

Neophyte: A neophyte, "n00b", or "newbie" or "Green Hat Hacker" is someone who is new to hacking or phreaking and has almost no knowledge or experience of the workings of technology and hacking.

Hacktivist: A hacktivist is a hacker who utilizes technology to announce a social, ideological, religious, or political message. In general, most hacktivism involves website defacement or denial of-service attacks.

2.7.6 Logic Bombs

Logic Bomb is a set of instructions secretly incorporated into a program so that if a particular condition is satisfied, they will be carried out, usually with harmful effects. It's a malicious program that is triggered when a logical condition is met; such as after a number of transactions have been processed, or on a specific date (also called a time bomb). Logic Bombs – also known as slag code – are dormant until/unless those conditions are satisfied. While their uses are typically malicious – think a disgruntled employee leaving a present after being let go. Logic bombs can also be used in trial software to end free access after a certain period. A virus can act as a logic bomb if by example the virus waits until a specific date to run its destructive payload. Happy Birthday Joshi was a boot sector virus from 1990 that is able to infect hard drives. On January 5 of any year, the screen will turn green and the text "TYPE HAPPY BIRTHDAY JOSHI" will appear. The system will not respond until "HAPPY BIRTHDAY JOSHI" is typed. The 2003 CSI/FBI Computer Crime and Security Survey reports that disgruntled employees is the second likely source of attacks (77%), preceded only by hackers (82%). From 1980 to 1985, some software developers imbedded logic bomb into their software, set to destroy the software itself if the license was not renewed. Of course, today this practice is illegal, but people are still using logic bombs in other contexts to achieve their ends.

Triggering: The triggering is what relates this type of code to a real bomb. When setting up a bomb attacker would like to have some time to run away before it explodes. This could be done by setting a timer or by sending a radio signal to the bomb when attacker is out of danger. The same principle applies to a logic bomb. Attacker may plant a slag code somewhere in the financial system and tell it to "explode" 6 months from the current date. If attacker stills an employee at the target organization, then the attacker can add another 6 months to the counter, but if attacker been fired then the destructive payload will be unleashed. The most common triggers are

Specific date/time: The payload will be executed when the system clock is equal or higher than the specified date/time.

Countdown: This Works like the specific date/time trigger but does not rely on the system clock. Instead the trigger implements its own timer bases on the number of seconds elapsed since the logic bomb was activated. This is somewhat harder to implement, but also harder to diffuse. Most slag codes relying on a specific date/time trigger can be tricked by changing the internal clock of the system. This trick doesn't really diffuse the bomb but can buy the defuse some time to find a way to actually disable it. In this case, changing the internal clock won't alter the timer implemented into the slag code, so it won't do any good. ·

Third party triggering: A time bomb can also be triggered by external scheduler software like Windows Scheduler or the Linux Cron. These kinds of slag codes are particularly easy to make since the triggering code is already available for the attackers. Attacker can, by example, create a batch file that formats the system drive and schedules it to run in a few weeks. ·

Reset: This trigger must be combined with one of the first three triggers. It's simply a way to extend the time before the logic bomb actually goes off. For example in the movie Safe House an ex-government agent played by Patrick Stewart has life threatening information about his former employer. He puts in place a time bomb that sends all the information to different magazines and newspaper if he doesn't enter the correct password each day. ·

State Changing: This one checks for changes on a specific entity before running the payload. If attackers name still in the HR database? If attackers account still active? Etc. It can monitor everything, to registry keys, passwords files, database entry, system configuration, etc. This type of attack can be launched from outside the company if the programmer manages to check an external web site for state changing.

2.7.7 DDoS Attack

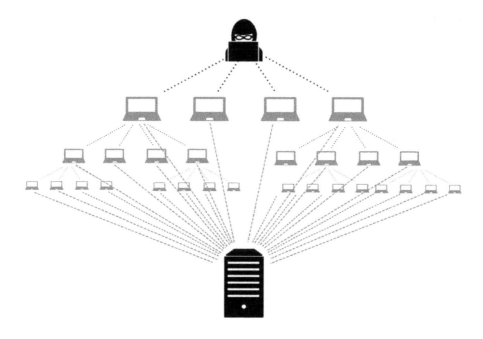

A distributed denial-of-service (DDoS) attack is a malicious attempt to disrupt normal traffic of a targeted server, service or network by overwhelming the target or its surrounding infrastructure with a flood of Internet traffic. Distributed denials of service (DDoS) attacks are a subclass of denial of service (DoS) attacks. Unlike other kinds of Cyber-attacks, DDoS assaults don't attempt to breach users security perimeter. Rather, a DDoS attack aims to make victims website and servers unavailable to legitimate users. DDoS attacks achieve effectiveness by utilizing multiple compromised computer systems as sources of attack traffic. Exploited machines can include computers and other networked resources such as IoT devices. From a high level, a DDoS attack is like a traffic jam clogging up with highway, preventing regular traffic from arriving at its desired destination.

DDoS can also be used as a smokescreen for other malicious activities and to take down security appliances, breaching the target's security perimeter. DDoS attacks can come in short bursts or repeat assaults, but either way the impact on a website or business can last for days, weeks and even months, as the organization tries to recover. The differences between regular and distributed denial of service assaults are substantive.

In a DoS attack, a perpetrator uses a single Internet connection to either exploit software vulnerability or flood a target with fake requests—usually in an attempt to exhaust resources such a RAM, CPU, Bandwidth etc. On the other hand, distributed denials of service (DDoS) attacks are launched from multiple connected devices that are distributed across the Internet. These multi-person, multi-device barrages are generally harder to deflect, mostly due to the sheer volume of devices involved. Unlike single-source DoS assaults, DDoS attacks tend to target the network infrastructure in an attempt to saturate it with huge volumes of traffic. The underlying effectiveness of most DDoS attacks comes from the disparity between the amount of resources it takes to launch an attack relative to the amount of resources it takes to absorb or mitigate one.

Number of Bing web page search results for "denial of service attack"

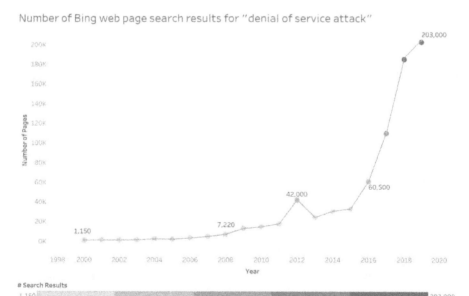

Https://www.comparitech.com/blog/information-security/ddos-statistics-facts/

Types of DDoS attacks: DoS attacks can be divided into two general categories—application layer attacks and network layer attacks. Each of these types of DDoS attacks define certain parameters and behaviors used during the attack, as well as the target of the attack.

Application layer attacks: (a.k.a., layer 7 attacks) can be either DoS or DDoS threats that seek to overload a server by sending a large number of requests requiring resource-intensive handling and processing. Among other attack vectors, this category includes HTTP floods, slow attacks (e.g., Slowloris or RUDY) and DNS query flood attacks. The size of application layer attacks is typically measured in requests per second (RPS), with no more than 50 to 100 RPS being required to cripple most mid-sized websites. While this is still the case with L7 attacks, the efficiency of affecting both the targeted server and the network requires less total bandwidth to achieve the same disruptive effect; an application layer attack creates more damage with less total bandwidth.

Distinguishing between attack traffic and normal traffic is difficult, especially in the case of an application layer attack such as a botnet performing an HTTP Flood attack against a victim's server. Because each bot in a botnet makes seemingly legitimate network requests the traffic is not spoofed and may appear "normal" in origin. With other attacks such as SYN floods or reflection attacks such as NTP amplification, strategies can be used to drop the traffic fairly efficiently provided the network itself has the bandwidth to receive them.

Common application layer attacks are as below:

BGP Hijacking: The Border Gateway Protocol (BGP) is used to direct traffic across the Internet, allowing networks to exchange "reachability information" to facilitate reaching other networks. BGP hijacking is a form of application-layer DDoS attack that allows an attacker to impersonate a network, using a legitimate network prefix as their own. When this "impersonated" information is accepted by other networks, traffic is inadvertently forwarded to the attacker instead of its proper destination.

Slowloris Attack: Slowloris is an application layer DDoS attack which uses partial HTTP requests to open connections between a single computer and a targeted Web server, then keeping those connections open for as long as possible, thus overwhelming and slowing down the target. This type of DDoS attack requires minimal bandwidth to launch and only impacts the target web server, leaving other services and ports unaffected.

Slow Post Attack: In a Slow Post DDoS attack, the attacker sends legitimate HTTP POST headers to a Web server. In these headers, the sizes of the message body that will follow are correctly specified. However, the message body is sent at a painfully low speed. These speeds may be as slow as one byte every two minutes. Since the message is handled normally, the targeted server will do its best to follow specified rules. The server will subsequently slow to a crawl. When attackers launch hundreds or even thousands Slow POST attacks at the same time, server resources are rapidly consumed, making legitimate connections unachievable.

Slow Read Attack: A slow read DDoS attack involves an attacker sending an appropriate HTTP request to a server, but then reading the response at a very slow speed, if at all. By reading the response slowly – sometimes as slow as one byte at a time – the attacker prevents the server from incurring an idle connection timeout. Since the attacker sends a Zero window to the server, the server assumes the client is actually reading the data and therefore keeps the connection open. A Slow Read attack is characterized by a very low number for the TCP Receive Window size, while at the same time draining the attacker's TCP receive buffer slowly. This in turn creates a condition where the data flow rate is extremely low.

HTTP Flooding Attack: An HTTP flood attack utilizes what appear to be legitimate HTTP GET or POST requests to attack a web server or application. These flooding attacks often rely on a botnet, which is a group of Internet-connected computers that have been maliciously appropriated through the use of malware such as a Trojan horse. These types of DDoS attacks are designed to cause the targeted server or application to allocate the most resources possible in direct response to each request. In this way, the attacker hopes to overwhelm the server or application, "flooding" it with as many process-intensive requests as possible. HTTP POSTs are often used because they involve complex server-side processing, while HTTP GET attacks are easier to create, thus lending themselves to botnet attacks which rely on scale to achieve the desired disruption.

Large Payload Post Attack: This is also referred to as "Oversize Payload Attacks" or "Jumbo Payload Attacks." A Large Payload Post is a class of HTTP DDoS attack where the attacker abuses XML encoding used by webservers. In this type of attack, a webserver is sent a data structure encoded in XML, which the server then attempts to decode, but is compelled to use an excessive amount of memory, thus overwhelming the system and crashing the service.

Mimicked User Browsing: A Mimicked User Browsing DDoS attack involves botnets that pose as legitimate users attempting to access a website. A sufficiently high volume of these bots will ultimately overwhelm the target website causing it to crash, or making it impossible for legitimate traffic to get through. This attack is designed to replicate the activity of a legitimate human browsing, it is difficult to detect. The website will quickly become heavily loaded as the bots outnumber the actual users, making it difficult to service legitimate requests.

Low and Slow Attack: also known as a slow-rate attack, involves what appears to be legitimate traffic at a very slow rate. This type of state exhaustion attack targets application and server resources and is difficult to distinguish from normal traffic. Common attack tools include Slowloris, Sockstress, and R.U.D.Y. (R U Dead Yet?), which create legitimate packets at a slow rate, thus allowing the packets to go undetected by traditional mitigation strategies. Detecting a low and slow attack can be accomplished by performing network behavioral analysis during normal operations and then comparing this data to periods when an attack might be occurring.

Network layer attacks: (a.k.a., layer 3–4 attacks) are almost always DDoS assaults set up to clog the "pipelines" connecting users network. Attack vectors in this category include UDP flood, SYN flood, NTP amplification and DNS amplification attacks, and more. L3 DDoS attacks typically accomplish this by targeting network equipment and infrastructure. There are a few important differences between layer 3 DDoS attacks and attacks at the higher layers:

Layer 3 attacks target the network layer, not transport layer or application layer processes (as layer 4 and layer 7 DDoS attacks do)

- Layer 3 attacks do not have to open a TCP connection with the target first
- Layer 3 attacks do not target a specific port

Types of Network Layer Attacks:

- **Ping flood:** In a ping flood DDoS attack, the attacker sends thousands or even millions of ping requests to a server at once.
- **Smurf attack:** ICMP has no security or verification measures in place, making it possible for an attacker to spoof an IP address in an ICMP request. In a Smurf DDoS attack, the attacker sends out ping requests to thousands of servers, spoofing the target's IP address in the ping requests so that the responses go to the target, not the attacker. Most modern networking hardware is no longer vulnerable to this attack.

- **Ping of death:** In an ICMP ping of death attack, an attacker sends a ping request that is larger than the maximum allowable size to the target. Routers along the way to the target will fragment the ping into smaller packets, so that the target accepts them, but when it tries to reassemble the large packet from the smaller fragments, the packet size exceeds the maximum and crashes the target. Like Smurf attack; Modern devices are not vulnerable to this attack as well.

2.7.8 Salami Attack

"Salami Slicing Attack" or "Salami Fraud" is a technique by which Cyber-criminals steal money or resources a bit at a time so that there's no noticeable difference in overall size. The perpetrator gets away with these little pieces from a large number of resources and thus accumulates a considerable amount over a period of time. The essence of this method is the failure to detect the misappropriation. The most classic approach is "collect-the-round off" technique. Salami Attack consists of merging bits of seemingly inconsequential data to produce huge results. A simple example is when an attacker/forger removes Rs. 0.01 (1 paise) from each bank account. No one will notice such a tiny mismatch. But when one paise is deducted from all account holders of that bank; it produces a huge amount. Computer computations many a times rounded off to nearest small fractions. It is while doing such corrections many bankers tries to rob money. A small attack that transform into a large attack is known Salami attack. It is sometimes called Salami slicing, because the attack goes almost unnoticed by the victims due to the nature of the attack. In general, Salami slicing is defined as anything that is reduced interested in minor activities or segments. Most calculations are carried out in a particular currency are rounded off up to the nearest number. If a programmer decides to collect these excess fractions of money to a separate account, no net loss to the system seems apparent. This is done by carefully transferring the funds into the perpetrator's account. Attackers insert a program into the system to automatically carry out the task. Logic bombs may also be employed by unsatisfied greedy employees who exploit their know-how of the network and/or privileged access to the system. In this technique, the criminal programs the arithmetic calculators to automatically modify data, such as in interest calculations.

Stealing money electronically is the most common use of the Salami slicing technique, but it's not restricted to money laundering. The Salami technique can also be applied to gather little bits of information over a period of time to deduce an overall picture of an organization. This act of distributed information gathering may be against an individual or an organization. Data can be collected from web sites, advertisements, documents collected from trash cans, and the like, gradually building up a whole database of factual intelligence about the target. Since the amount of misappropriation is just below the threshold of perception, organizations need to be more vigilant. Careful examination of company assets, transactions and every other dealing including sharing of confidential information with others might help reduce the chances of an attack by this method.

2.7.9 Email Bombing

An email bomb or "mail bomb" is a malicious act in which a large number of email messages are sent to a single email address in a short period of time. The purpose of an email bomb is typically to overflow a user's inbox. An email bombing is an attack on victim's inbox that involves sending massive amounts of messages to victim's address. Sometimes these messages are complete gibberish, but more often they'll be confirmation emails for newsletters and subscriptions. In the latter case, the attacker uses a script to search the internet for forums and newsletters and then signs up for an account with victims email address. Each forum and newsletter will send victim a confirmation email asking to confirm victims email address. This process repeats across as many unprotected sites as the script can find.

The term "email bombing" can also refer to flooding an email server with too many emails in an attempt to overwhelm the email server and bring it down. But that could not be real goal of attacker. Instead of a denial-of-service (DOS) attack against the email servers victims are using, the onslaught of messages is a distraction to hide the attacker's true intentions. An attack's intensity can range from an inconvenience to a complete interruption of service. Some email bombs are accidental or self-inflicted, such as when automatic replies sent to a distribution list cause a cascade of emails. Additionally, Cyber-criminals sometimes use email bomb attacks to mask other attacks and prevent users from receiving notices about account activity.

Types of Email Bombs:

Mass mailing: This attack occurs when someone intentionally or unintentionally sends large quantities of email traffic to targeted email addresses.

List linking: These attacks involve malicious actors signing targeted email addresses up to numerous email subscription services. Many of these services do not ask for verification or if they do, they send confirmation requests via email. This type of attack is difficult to prevent because the traffic originates from various legitimate sources.

ZIP bomb: These attacks consist of attacker sending malicious archived files designed to decompress to very large sizes. When the email server decompresses the file, significant server resources are consumed, potentially causing the server to slow down or stop responding.

Attachments: This attacks occur when malicious attacker send multiple emails with large attachments, intending to overload the storage space on a server and cause the server to stop responding.

Reply-all email bombs: These attacks occur when distribution list members reply to all members of the list; instead of just the original sender. This floods inboxes with a cascade of emails, which are compounded by automated replies, such as out-of-office messages. This type of attack also occurs when a malicious actor spoofs an email and the automatic replies are directed toward the spoofed address.

2.7.10 Piracy

In old days Piracy meant the practice of attacking and robbing ships at sea. Piracy has changed very little over the years. Only the mode has changed. Instead of a boat, now users have a computer, instead of the high seas, users now have the Internet and instead of stealing gold; people now steal software, music, movies, books etc. In spring 2009 four Swedish internet pirates were being sentenced to pay more than three million dollars in fines and serve a year in the jail. Their crime was running the Pirate Bay portal. One of the web's most visited file-sharing communities. The Pirate Bay is a part of the trend of peer-to-peer technologies used to illegally share music, videos and application. Public sites such as Pirate Bay, ISOhunt and Mininova indexed and track BitTorrent files which allow computers to connect and download content. People go to these sites to search for and grab illegal software, books, music and videos. However these web sites were not the first of their kind. In fact there's been a long lineage of illegal file sharing websites. The first and most infamous was Napster. It was the first peer-to-peer (P2P) file-sharing network of its kind. In October of 2000 it had been reported that Napster had over 32 million users and it was estimated that there were about 800,000 people using it at any one time. At the same time site membership was also growing at a rate of 1 million users per week. In its initial years Napster was not illegal. This is mainly because the concept of Napster was so original and so new that laws had not yet been created to say that it was violating copyright laws. Consequently many people who would otherwise avoid illegal actions took part in Napster because it wasn't yet illegal. This rather large group people got used to the idea of being able to download whatever entertainment they wanted to whenever they wanted to. Thus these people got a taste of what it felt like to get something for free. On December 8th 1999 the Recording Industry Association of America (RIAA) announced it was suing Napster for violating copyright rules. This was the first peer-to-peer (P2P) technology case. This case set the example for future cases. The RIAA could not accuse Napster of direct infringement of copyright laws. This was because the program did not actually make copies of the entertainment files. Instead Napster was charged with contributory and mediated copyright infringement. On other words Napster was making it possible for others to violate copyright laws. This case marked the beginning of the end for Napster. The judge ruled in favor of the RIAA and Napster was ordered to shut down. However the damage had already been done. With Napster being shut down people already had a thirst and a taste for obtaining free entertainment. Thus they sought after different websites to quench their thirst. Currently internet piracy has reached an almost epidemic level. The New York Post reported that in 2009 only 37% of entertainment acquired by US consumers was actually paid for. According to the Information Technology Innovation Foundation (ITIF) the digital theft of music, movies and copyrighted content takes up huge amounts of Internet bandwidth. Overall Internet piracy accounts for 17.5 percent of the USA bandwidth and 27 percent of the global bandwidth.

2.7.10.1 Software Piracy:

Software piracy is the act of stealing software that is legally protected. This stealing includes copying, distributing, modifying or selling the software. When a user purchases software from a company, that user is considered to be a "Licensed User" and not the "owner" of that software. Many software creators provide buyers or users of their software with a number of licenses. The license can be for certain number of users or computers or specific period of time or limited number of transactions. The use of the software beyond the "License agreement" can also be referred as Software piracy. The buyer in such cases is supposed to renew the license or extend its capacity. As a licensed user, the buyer is permitted to make copies of his purchased software. But only as backups. This is to ensure that the buyer don't have to purchase it again in the event that buyer delete the software, or machine crashes. When buyer purchase a commercial software package, an end user license agreement (EULA) is included to protect that software program from copyright infringement.

Software piracy applies mainly to full-function commercial software. The time-limited or function-restricted versions of commercial software called shareware are less likely to be pirated since they are freely available. Similarly, freeware, a type of software that is copyrighted but freely distributed at no charge, also offers little incentive for piracy. The losses suffered as a result of software piracy directly affect the profitability of the software industry. Because of the money lost to software pirates, publishers have fewer resources to devote or research and development of new products, have less revenue to justify lowering software prices and are forced to pass these costs on to their customers.

Using pirated software is also risky for users. Aside from the legal consequences of using pirated software, users of pirated software forfeit some practical benefits as well. Those who use pirate software:

Increase the chances that the software will either not function correctly or will fail completely.

- Forfeit access to customer support, upgrades, technical documentation, training, and bug fixes.
- Have no warranty to protect them.
- Increase their risk of exposure to a debilitating virus that can destroy valuable data.
- May find that the software is actually an outdated version, a beta (test) version, or a non-functioning copy.
- Are subject to significant fines for copyright infringement; and Risk of potential negative publicity and public and private embarrassment.

Types of Software Piracy: There are five main types of software piracy. This variety of pirating techniques explains how some individuals purposely pirate software while others may unknowingly be an accomplice.

Soft-lifting: Softlifting is when someone purchases one version of the software and downloads it onto multiple computers, even though the software license states it should only be downloaded once. This often occurs in business or school environments and is usually done to save money. Softlifting is the most common type of software piracy.

Client-server overuse: Client-server overuse is when too many people on a network use one main copy of the program at the same time. This often happens when businesses are on a local area network and download the software for all employees to use. This becomes a type of software piracy if the license doesn't entitle users to use it multiple times.

Hard disk loading: Hard disk loading is a type of commercial software piracy in which someone buys a legal version of the software and then reproduces copies or installs it onto computer hard disks. The person then sells the product. This often happens at PC resale shops and buyers aren't always aware that the additional software they are buying is illegal.

Counterfeiting: Counterfeiting occurs when software programs are illegally duplicated and sold with the appearance of authenticity. Counterfeit software is usually sold at a discounted price in comparison to the legitimate software.

Online Piracy: Online piracy, also known as Internet piracy, is when illegal software is sold, shared or acquired by means of the Internet. This is usually done through a peer-to-peer (P2P) file sharing system, which is usually found in the form of online auction sites and blogs.

Music and Movie Piracy: Even before Internet became available publically; technological developments had allowed the Entertainment industry to discover and promote new formats. But it also enabled commercially-minded pirates and private citizens to pirate Entertainment on a larger scale. Piracy was a minor problem for the Entertainment industry until the arrival of the compact tape cassette in the late 1960s and the wide-spread availability of home cassette recorders in the 1970s. The advent of the CD in 1982 indicated a new era. Although this format boosted global Entertainment sales, the technology enabled high-quality copying in large quantities. Firstly, the development of encoding formats such as MP3, MOV, Mpeg, AVI etc. allowed users to easily transfer Entertainment to computers, transmit it via the Internet or decode the digitally recorded Entertainment for recording onto writable CDs. Secondly, when the switch was made from cassettes to CDs, most computers had limited storage capacity and were not always equipped with a sound card or external speakers. With the wide spread of computers however, personal computers have become much faster and more powerful and most of them nowadays came with CD-ripping software and CD-burners. Contemporary pirates were then able to create perfect, identical copies. The possibilities offered by the new technologies did not go unnoticed. Whereas the Entertainment industry always had some sort of monopoly over the distribution of entertainment to customers, they soon met with competition from entrepreneurs making the most of their chances to get a piece of the pie. Besides concerns about private citizens copying CDs onto CD-Rs, the Entertainment industry was – and still is – gravely concerned about full scale commercial Entertainment piracy.

Entertainment industry's monopoly position being shattered, consumers are now able to shop around. It is not, however, physical piracy that has received a lot of attention recently, but digital piracy due the rise of the Internet and the plummeted costs of personal computers. This is seen as one of the biggest threats to the Entertainment industry even today. Although Internet piracy can take many forms, one variant, file sharing through peer-to-peer (P2P) networks, is said to have a devastating impact on global Entertainment sales. With the global widespread of the personal computer, the increasing universality of the Internet and broadband connections, and the emergence of digital compression technologies, this type of piracy can indeed assume vast proportions.

Effects of Piracy: There are very clear laws about what people can and cannot do with purchased Entertainment content. Generally, purchasing content means users are allowed to listen, play, read, or use that content for self-consumption. It does not give users the right to copy it, share it, trade it, let others download it or make money off of it. Like buying a movie and then charging people to come see it. Piracy negatively affects every single person working in these industries and their supply chains. There is less money to invest in new software, developing music artists, and movies. There is less work for developers, testers, sound engineers, videographers, actors, scriptwriters, musicians, assistants, set designers, security guards, stores, salespeople, website developers and every other type of person who goes into creating, packaging, advertising, distributing, supporting, promoting or reviewing these products and services. Most of the people who lost work because of piracy and stolen profits will struggle for the means to support their business. When user download illegal content or share copyrighted content with others, they do not see their victims, but digital piracy steals the income from millions of hardworking people.

2.7.11 Malware

Malware is short for "malicious software." This is an umbrella term that describes any malicious program or code that is harmful to systems. Malware is typically delivered over a network, which infects, explores, steals or conducts virtually any behavior an attacker wants. Malware programs are designed to infiltrate and damage computers without the users consent. "Malware" is the general term covering all the different types of threats to user's computer safety such as viruses, spyware, worms, Trojans, rootkits and so on.

2.7.11.1 History of Malware

The first academic work on the theory of self-replicating computer programs was done in 1949 by John von Neumann. His essay "Theory of self-reproducing automata" he described how a computer program could be designed to reproduce itself. Von Neumann's design for a self-reproducing computer program is considered the world's first computer virus, and he is considered to be the theoretical "father" of computer virology. In 1972, Veith Risak directly building on von Neumann's work on self-replication published his article "Self-reproducing automata with minimal information exchange".

Creeper was an experimental computer program written by Bob Thomas at BBN in 1971. Creeper was actually designed as a security test to see if a self-replicating program was possible. With each new hard drive infected, Creeper would try to remove itself from the previous host. Creeper had no malicious intent and only displayed a simple message: "I'M THE CREEPER. CATCH ME IF YOU CAN!"

Virus creators, or "virus writers", started off writing viruses in the early 1980's. Until the late 1990's most of the viruses were just pranks made up in order to annoy users and to see how far a virus could spread. The writers were often young programmers, some still in their teens, who didn't always understand the vast consequences of their actions.

First PC virus: The first virus that attacked MS-DOC is called Brain and was written by two brothers, Basit Farooq Alvi and Amjad Farooq Alvi, from Lahore, Punjab, Pakistan in 1986. When the brothers created the virus, they were running a computer store in Lahore, Pakistan and noticed that their customers were circulating illegal copies of software they'd written. So, they thought of a unique way of teaching their customers a lesson, they created the Brain virus. Tired of customers making illegal copies of their software, they developed Brain, which replaced the boot sector of a floppy disk with a virus. The virus, which was also the first stealth virus, contained a hidden copyright message, but did not actually corrupt any data. It began infecting 5.2" floppy disks. The brothers stressed in interviews that they created the virus only for the illegal copies of the software, putting their names, phone numbers, and their shop's address in the virus code. Basit and Amjad never thought of the virus growing into a global-sized monster, with powers beyond their capacities to control it.

Screenshot of Brain Computer virus. On the right side the Name and address of its creator is also visible.

2.7.11.2 Types of Malwares

Malware is an inclusive term for all types of malicious software, such as:

Viruses – Programs that copy themselves throughout a computer or network. Viruses piggyback on existing programs and can only be activated when a user opens the program. At their worst, viruses can corrupt or delete data, use the user's email to spread, or erase everything on a hard disk.

Worms – Self-replicating viruses that exploit security vulnerabilities to automatically spread themselves across computers and networks. Unlike many viruses, worms do not attach to existing programs or alter files. They typically go unnoticed until replication reaches a scale that consumes significant system resources or network bandwidth.

Trojans – Malware disguised in what appears to be legitimate software. Once activated, Trojans will conduct whatever action they have been programmed to carry out. Unlike viruses and worms, Trojans do not replicate or reproduce through infection. "Trojan" alludes to the mythological story of Greek soldiers hidden inside a wooden horse that was given to the enemy city of Troy.

Rootkits – Programs that provide privileged (root-level) access to a computer. Rootkits hide themselves in the operating system.

Remote Administration Tools (RATs) – Software that allows a remote operator to control a system. These tools were originally built for legitimate use, but are now used by Cyber Criminals. RATs enable administrative control, allowing an attacker to do almost anything on an infected computer. They are difficult to detect, as they don't typically show up in lists of running programs or tasks, and their actions are often mistaken for the actions of legitimate programs.

Botnets – Short for "Robot Network," these are networks of infected computers under the control of single attacking party using command-and-control servers. Botnets are highly versatile and adaptable, able to maintain resilience through redundant servers and by using infected computers to relay traffic. Botnets are often the armies behind today's distributed denial-of-service (DDoS) attacks.

Spyware – Malware that collects information about the usage of the infected computer and communicates it back to the attacker. The term includes botnets, adware, backdoor behavior, key-loggers, data theft and net-worms.

Polymorphic Malware – Any of the above types of malware with the capacity to "morph" regularly, alters the appearance of the code while retaining the algorithm within. The alteration of the surface appearance of the software subverts detection via traditional virus signatures.

Ransomware – is a form of malware that locks users out of their device and/or encrypts users' files, then forces users to pay a ransom to get them back. Ransomware has been called the Cyber criminal's weapon of choice because it demands a quick, profitable payment in hard-to-trace crypto-currency. The code behind Ransomware is easy to obtain through online criminal marketplaces and defending against it is very difficult.

03 CYBER SECURITY COMPONENTS

Businesses of every size and industry are vulnerable to Cyber-attacks. Having a strong Cyber security strategy in place to defend organization against these attacks, and recover quickly to avoid downtime, is an absolute must when it comes to the success of any organization. Cyber security is important because government, military, corporate, financial, and medical organizations collect, process, and store unprecedented amounts of data on computers and other devices. A significant portion of that data can be sensitive information, whether that be intellectual property, financial data, personal information, or other types of data for which unauthorized access or exposure could have negative consequences. Organizations transmit sensitive data across networks and to other devices in the course of doing businesses. Cyber Security describes the discipline dedicated to protecting that information and the systems used to process or store it. As the volume and sophistication of Cyber-attacks grow, companies and organizations, especially those that are tasked with safeguarding information relating to national security, health, or financial records, needs to take steps to protect their sensitive business and personnel information.

The goal of implementing Cyber-security is to provide a good security posture for computers, servers, networks, mobile devices and the data stored on these devices from attackers with malicious intent. Cyber-security is a continuously changing field, with the development of technologies that open up new avenues for Cyber-attacks. One of the most problematic elements of Cyber-security is the continually evolving nature of security risks. As new technologies emerge, and technology is used in new or different ways, new avenues of attack are developed as well. Keeping up with these continual changes and advances in attacks can be challenging to organizations, as well as updating their practices to protect against them. This also includes ensuring that all the elements of Cyber-security are continually changed and updated to protect against potential vulnerabilities. This can be especially challenging for smaller organizations.

Before we discuss various components of the Cyber Security let look at the OSI layers.

3.1 OSI LAYER

The Open Systems Interconnection (OSI) model is a conceptual model created by the International Organization for Standardization which enables various communication systems to communicate using standard protocols. The OSI model can be seen as a universal language for computer networking. It's based on the concept of splitting up a communication system into seven abstract layers, each one stacked upon the last.

The 7 Layers of OSI

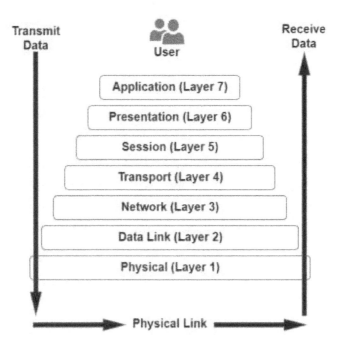

The seven layers of OSI and their description is as below.

1. The Application Layer: This is the only layer that directly interacts with data from the user. Software applications like web browsers and email clients rely on the application layer to initiate communications. Client software applications are not part of the application layer; rather the application layer is responsible for the protocols and data handling that the software relies on to present meaningful data to the user. Application layer protocols include HTTP as well as SMTP (Simple Mail Transfer Protocol is the protocols that enables email communications).

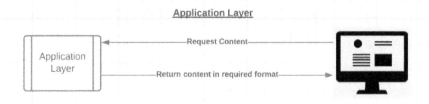

Handling of data in various ways is done in this layer which enables user or software to get access to the network. Some services provided by this layer includes: E-Mail, transferring files, distributing the results to user, directory services, network resources, etc. The Application Layer contains a variety of protocols that are commonly needed by users. One widely-used application protocol is HTTP (Hypertext Transfer Protocol), which is the basis for the World Wide Web. When a browser wants a web page, it sends the name of the page it wants to the server using HTTP. The server then sends the page back. Other Application protocols that are used are: File Transfer Protocol(FTP), Trivial File Transfer Protocol(TFTP), Simple Mail Transfer Protocol(SMTP), TELNET, Domain Name System(DNS) etc.

Functions of Application Layer

a) **Mail Services:** This layer provides the basis for E-mail forwarding and storage.

b) **Network Virtual Terminal:** It allows a user to log on to a remote host. The application creates software emulation of a terminal at the remote host. User's computer talks to the software terminal which in turn talks to the host and vice versa. Then the remote host believes it is communicating with one of its own terminals and allows user to log on.

c) **Directory Services:** This layer provides access for global information about various services.

d) **File Transfer, Access and Management (FTAM):** It is a standard mechanism to access files and manages it. Users can access files in a remote computer and manage it. They can also retrieve files from a remote computer.

2. The Presentation Layer: The primary goal of this layer is to take care of the syntax and semantics of the information exchanged between two communicating systems. Presentation layer ensures that the data is sent in such a way that the receiver will understand the data and will be able to use the data. Languages (syntax) can be different of the two communicating systems. Under this condition presentation layer plays a role of translator. In order to make it possible for computers with different data representations to communicate, the data structures to be exchanged can be defined in an abstract way. The presentation layer manages these abstract data structures and allows higher-level data structures (eg: accounting records), to be defined and exchanged.

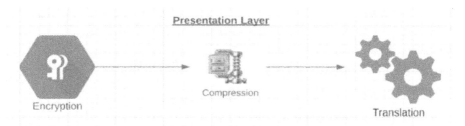

Functions of Presentation Layer

a) **Translation:** Before being transmitted, information in the form of characters and numbers should be changed to bit streams. The presentation layer is responsible for the ability of computer systems or software to exchange data and make use of information between encoding methods as different computers use different encoding methods. It translates data between the formats the network requires and the format of the computer.

b) **Encryption:** It carries out encryption at the transmitter end and decryption at the receiver end.

c) **Compression:** It carries out data compression of the data to be transmitted to reduce the bandwidth. The primary role of Data compression is to reduce the number of bits to be transmitted over network. It is important in transmitting multimedia such as audio, video, text etc. due to their higher sizes.

3. The Session Layer: This is the layer responsible for opening and closing communication between the two devices. The time between when the communication is opened and closed is known as the session. The session layer ensures that the session stays open long enough to transfer all the data being exchanged, and then promptly closes the session in order to avoid wasting resources. The session layer also synchronizes data transfer with checkpoints. For example, if a 100 megabyte file is being transferred, the session layer could set a checkpoint every 5 megabytes. In the case of a disconnect or a crash after 52 megabytes have been transferred, the session could be resumed from the last checkpoint, meaning only remaining 50 more megabytes of data need to be transferred. Without the checkpoints, the entire transfer would have to begin again from scratch.

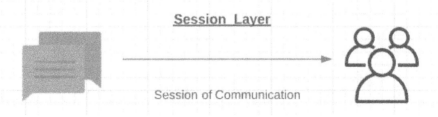

Session Layer

Session of Communication

The Session Layer allows users on different machines to establish active communication sessions between them. It's main aim is to establish, maintain and synchronize the interaction between communicating systems. Session layer manages and synchronize the conversation between two different applications. In Session layer, streams of data are marked and are resynchronized properly, so that the ends of the messages are not cut prematurely and data loss is avoided.

Functions of Session Layer

a) **Dialog Control:** This layer allows two systems to start communication with each other in either half-duplex or full-duplex mode.

b) **Token Management:** This layer prevents two parties from attempting the same critical operation at the same time.

c) **Synchronization:** This layer allows a process to add checkpoints which are considered as synchronization points into stream of data. Example: If a system is sending a file of 80 pages, adding checkpoints after every 5 pages is recommended. This ensures that 5 page unit is successfully received and acknowledged. This is beneficial at the time of crash as if a crash happens at page number 69; there is no need to retransmit 1 to 65 pages.

4. The Transport Layer: This layer is responsible for end-to-end communication between the two devices. This includes taking data from the session layer and breaking it up into chunks called segments before sending it to layer 3. The transport layer on the receiving device is responsible for re-assembling the segments into data so that the session layer can process it further. The transport layer is also responsible for flow control and error control. Flow control determines an optimal speed of transmission to ensure that a sender with a fast connection doesn't overwhelm a receiver with a slow connection. The transport layer performs error control on the receiving end by ensuring that the data received is complete, and requesting a retransmission if it isn't.

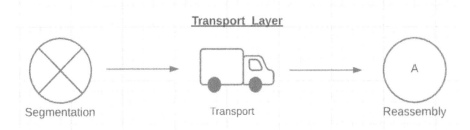

The basic function of the Transport layer is to accept data from the layer above, split it up into smaller units, pass these data units to the Network layer, and ensure that all the pieces arrive correctly at the other end. Furthermore, all this must be done efficiently and in a way that isolates the upper layers from the inevitable changes in the hardware technology. The Transport layer also determines what type of service to provide to the Session layer, and, ultimately, to the users of the network. The most popular type of transport connection is a point-to-point channel that delivers error free messages or bytes in the order in which they were sent. The Transport layer is a true end-to-end layer, all the way from the source to the destination. In other words, a program on the source machine carries on a conversation with a similar program on the destination machine, using the message headers and control messages.

Functions of Transport Layer

a) **Service Point Addressing:** Transport Layer header includes service point address which is port address. This layer gets the message to the correct process on the computer unlike Network Layer, which gets each packet to the correct computer.

b) **Segmentation and Reassembling:** A message is divided into segments; each segment contains sequence number, which enables this layer in reassembling the message. Message is reassembled correctly upon arrival at the destination and replaces packets which were lost in transmission.

c) **Connection Control:** It includes 2 types: *Connectionless Transport Layer:* Each segment is considered as an independent packet and delivered to the transport layer at the destination machine. *Connection Oriented Transport Layer:* Before delivering packets, connection is made with transport layer at the destination device.

d) **Flow Control:** In this layer, flow control is performed end to end.

e) **Error Control:** Error Control is performed end to end in this layer to ensure that the complete message arrives at the receiving transport layer without any error. Error Correction is done through retransmission.

5. The Network Layer: The network layer is responsible for facilitating data transfer between two different networks. The network layer breaks up segments from the transport layer into smaller units, called packets, on the sender's device, and reassembling these packets on the receiving device. The network layer also finds the best physical path for the data to reach its destination; this is known as routing.

The network Layer controls the operation of the subnet. The main aim of this layer is to deliver packets from source to destination across multiple links (networks). This layer routes the signal through different channels to the other end and acts as a network controller. It also divides the outgoing messages into packets and to assemble incoming packets into messages for higher layers. In broadcast networks, the routing problem is simple, so the network layer is often thin or even non-existent.

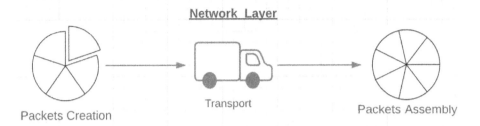

Functions of Network Layer

a) **Routing**: Responsible to finds the best physical path for the data to reach its destination. Routers and gateways operate in the layer. Mechanism is provided by Network Layer for routing the packets to on its way to destination.

b) **Logical Addressing**: This layer implements the logical addressing. It adds a header to the packet which includes the logical addresses of both the sender and the receiver.

c) **Internetworking**: This is the main role of the network layer that it provides the logical connection between different types of networks.

d) **Fragmentation**: The fragmentation is a process of breaking the packets into the smallest individual data units that travel through different networks.

6. The Data Link Layer: Data link layer performs the most reliable node to node delivery of data. It forms frames from the packets received from network layer and gives it to physical layer for transmission. It also synchronizes the information which is to be transmitted over the data. Error controlling is also done in this layer. Error detection bits are used by the data link layer. It also corrects the errors. The encoded data are then passed to physical layer. Outgoing messages are assembled into frames. Then the system waits for the acknowledgements to be received after the transmission. The main task of the data link layer is to transform a raw transmission facility into a line that appears free of undetected transmission errors to the network layer. It accomplishes this task by having the sender break up the input data into data frames (typically a few hundred or few thousand bytes) and transmits the frames sequentially. If the service is reliable, the receiver confirms correct receipt of each frame by sending back an acknowledgement frame.

The data link layer is very similar to the network layer, except the data link layer facilitates data transfer between two devices on the SAME network. The data link layer takes packets from the network layer and breaks them into smaller pieces called frames. Like the network layer, the data link layer is also responsible for flow control and error control in intra-network communication (The transport layer only does flow control and error control for inter-network communications).

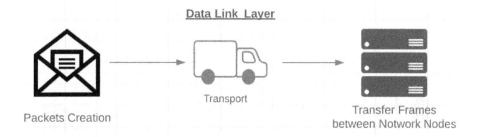

Data Link Layer

Packets Creation

Transport

Transfer Frames
between Notwork Nodes

Functions of Data Link Layer

a) **Framing:** Frames are the streams of bits received from the network layer into manageable data units. This division of stream of bits is done by Data Link Layer.

b) **Physical Addressing:** The Data Link layer adds a header to the frame in order to define physical address of the sender or receiver of the frame, if the frames are to be distributed to different systems on the network.

c) **Flow Control:** A flow control mechanism to avoid a fast transmitter from running a slow receiver by buffering the extra bit is provided by flow control. This prevents traffic jam at the receiver side.

d) **Error Control:** Error control is achieved by adding a trailer at the end of the frame. Duplication of frames is also prevented by using this mechanism.

e) **Access Control:** Protocols of this layer determine which of the devices has control over the link at any given time, when two or more devices are connected to the same link.

7. The Physical Layer: Physical layer is the lowest layer of the OSI reference model. It is responsible for sending bits from one computer to another. This layer is not concerned with the meaning of the bits and deals with the setup of physical connection to the network and with transmission and reception of signals.

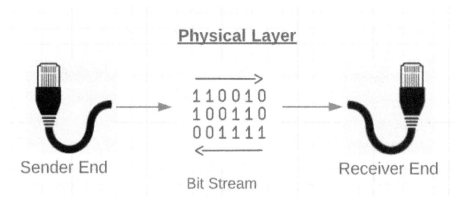

This layer includes the physical equipment involved in the data transfer, such as the cables and switches. This is also the layer where the data gets converted into a bit stream, which is a string of 1s and 0s. The physical layer of both devices must also agree on a signal convention so that the 1s can be distinguished from the 0s on both devices.

Functions of Physical Layer

a) **Representation of Bits:** Data in this layer consists of stream of bits. The bits must be encoded into signals for transmission. It defines the type of encoding i.e. how 0's and 1's are changed to signal.

b) **Data Rate:** This layer defines the rate of transmission which is the number of bits per second.

c) **Synchronization:** It deals with the synchronization of the transmitter and receiver. The sender and receiver are synchronized at bit level.

d) **Interface:** The physical layer defines the transmission interface between devices and transmission medium.

e) **Line Configuration:** This layer connects devices with the medium: Point to Point configuration and Multipoint configuration.

f) **Topologies:** Devices must be connected using the following topologies: Mesh, Star, Ring and Bus.

g) **Transmission Modes:** Physical Layer defines the direction of transmission between two devices: Simplex, Half Duplex, Full Duplex.

h) Deals with baseband and broadband transmission.

3.2 ZERO DAY ATTACKS

Organizations take great care to secure their network and infrastructure. But even with responsible and sustained investments in defenses Organizations are still at risk. Attackers can bypass Organizations robust security through an uncharted software vulnerability; a loophole revealed only by the persistent probing of a determined hacker. This is known as Zero Day. Zero Day is a software vulnerability that is previously unknown and unpatched and therefore can be exploited by cyber-criminals to gain entry to a target network. A hacker finds a Zero Day through hours. Weeks or even months of painstaking effort. The attacker scours through lines of code probing applications and operating systems to find some weakness, some flaw. He methodically investigates its target application with an array of reverse engineering tools and techniques forcing the software to reveal a small crack in the defenses that provides them a way to secretly execute a malicious code. With this vulnerability in hand the hacker has a choice help the software vendor by providing them information about the vulnerability or sell it to a broker in the hands of a black-market vendor of zero-day exploits.

A Zero-day vulnerability, at its core, is a flaw, a glitch or bugs. It is an unknown exploit in the wild that exposes vulnerability in software or hardware and can create complicated problems well before anyone realizes something is wrong. In fact, a zero-day exploit leaves NO opportunity for detection at first. Zero-day attacks exploit are usually programming errors or other vulnerabilities in hardware or software. It's called a zero-day because there are "Zero Days" for software developers or hardware vendors to patch the flaw. It's finding a way to open up or crack user data or communications that was previously unknown. Consider that user is putting all of their digital information into a safe and imagine that that safe has a combination at the front that only user know. So their information is very secure. A zero day flaw is like a cyber-criminal figuring out that he can take a hammer and hit one little screw on the back of users safe and the safe will pop open. So Cyber attacker is able to open users safe without the unlock code to get into users safe or get users communications and get users data without users permission. Zero Day vulnerabilities get their name from the fact that programmers have zero days to fix them before they are used in an attack. By the time a software developers or hardware vendor's finds out about them, everything is already exploding.

Who Uses Zero-Days: Glitches and bugs can show up in any new piece of software or software update. Lots of people spend their days searching for them. Some of those people are analysts and engineers who have positive intensions and focus on Cyber-Security. They look for bugs and problems so that they can fix software and protect computer systems. There is a legitimate part of the market, there are cyber security researchers and cyber security companies, technology companies who would discover zero-day vulnerabilities and those companies typically work with the software vendors to make sure that the vulnerability is patched in time. So that users are not left open and vulnerable to an attack by a Cyber-criminal.

But there's also a black market for Zero days and this is a place where Zero days are sold for large sums of money, including governments. Sometimes friendly; sometimes not. Those governments' will then stockpile the Zero days and use them at a later time for their own potentially nefarious purposes. Also on the lookout are Cyber-Criminals, also known as Black-Hat Hackers. They seek bugs that will let them weasel into computer systems, often to wreak havoc.

3.1.1 What are the risks of Zero Days?

Zero day vulnerabilities are weapons of Cyber Criminals. These digital weapons can weaken organizations Cyber security. If the organizations leave open a flaw and software that can be used to access data or communications that opening can be used by cyber criminals so it can be exploited for purposes of cyber identity theft and data theft. So patching systems does allow organizations to protect against whatever the known vulnerabilities are. But that is exactly the value of a zero-day it's that there is no patch. These types of vulnerabilities are known as Zero-Day because the original programmer has zero days after learning about it to patch. These flaws are usually the result of errors made during the writing of the software, giving an attacker wider access to the rest of the software. These attacks are rarely discovered right away. In fact, it often takes not just days but months and a sometimes year before a developer learns of the vulnerability that led to an attack.

Vulnerability timeline: A zero-day attack happens once that flaw, or software/hardware vulnerability is exploited and Cyber criminals release a malicious program to exploit the weakness / flaw, before a developer has an opportunity to create a patch to fix the vulnerability— hence "zero-day."

- A company's developers create software, but unbeknown to them this new software contains vulnerability.
- The Cyber-criminal spots that vulnerability either before the developer does or acts on it before the developer has a chance to fix it.
- The Cyber criminals' writes and implements exploit code while the vulnerability is still open and available for attack.
- After releasing the exploit, either the public recognizes it in the form of identity or information theft or the developer catches it and creates a patch to stop the cyber-bleeding.

3.1.2 Network Security

Network security consists of protecting the usability and reliability of network and data. A network penetration test is conducted to assess the vulnerabilities in a system and other security issues which occur in servers, hosts, devices and network services. Hubs, routers, switches and other network devices should be physically secured from unauthorized access. It is easy to forget that just because a device doesn't have a monitor on which user can see data; this does not mean the data can't be captured or destroyed at that access point.

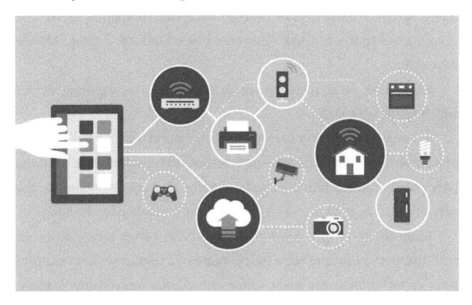

3.1.3 Basics of Networks

Broadly speaking a computer network is a set of communications channels that interconnects computing devices and enables them to exchange data electronically. In the simplest form of a network a single client is connected to a single server where a client is a computing device such as desktop PC, Laptop or a cell phone, which uses or consumes resources that are made available over a network. While a server is a computing device that provides resources or services to other devices over a network. The true power of computer networks emerges when many computing devices are able to communicate with each other. And for this reason networks are typically characterized by many different clients being connected to many different servers. When discussing computer security in the context of networks; several other terms besides client and server are commonly used to describe different parts of a network.

3.1.4 Network Terminology

Node: A node which refers to a single conceptual computing device that is connected to the network. This could be a Desktop, Laptop, Mobile device etc.

Host: This term refers to the actual physical computing device which resides at a node.

A node is therefore more of a logical concept while a host is more of a physical concept. It is important to note that computers are not the only possible hosts. Other physical devices that are connected to the network such as routers and so forth are also considered to be hosts.

Link: the term link refers to a connection between two hosts. As with the term node; the term link is more of a logical abstract concept since in reality there are many different methods and communications media through which two hosts might be interconnected. Such as physical cable, wireless or Bluetooth connection etc.

Network Advantages: Networks have become increasingly popular over the past several decades because they afford many advantages.

- Resource Sharing: allows common resources such as shared printers to be used efficiently.
- Distribution of workload: a computational workload to be distributed across multiple machines.
- Increased Reliability: a well-designed network can provide redundancy for many network resources.
- Expandability and Scalability: networks provide for easy expandability and scalability as its computational workload increases an organization can often simply add additional nodes to the

network in order to handle the increased demand for computational resources.

Network Vulnerabilities: Networks provide many different advantages. However networks also have several characteristics that make them vulnerable to attacks by Cyber Criminals.

- **Anonymity**: in a networked environment an attacker does not need to be in physical contact with an information system in order to attack. The attacker could be physically anywhere on the globe can still mount an attack on a network from outside the network.

- **Points of attack**: a networked environment can potentially expose many different points of attack. From a security perspective a network is only as strong as its weakest link and weak access controls on a single node can expose the entire network to risks.

- **Resource and Workload sharing**: Although networks allow computational resource and workload to be shared; this also means more users have access to computational assets thus exposing those assets to a greater risk.

- **System Complexity:** computer security expert and columnist Mikko Hyppönen once said complexity is enemy of security. In big organizations Network architecture is often complex. Since networks are intrinsically more complex than standalone systems there is a greater chance that security vulnerability will be overlooked in a networked environment

- **Unknown Boundary**: Networks often have unknown boundaries. Since the boundary of a network can change dynamically, it is often difficult to ensure that the entire network is secure. This is especially true in wireless networks where unknown nodes can join and leave the network on an ad-hoc basis.

3.3 TYPES OF NETWORK ATTACKS

A network attack is an attempt to gain unauthorized access to an organization's network, with the objective of stealing data or perform other malicious activity. There are two main types of network attacks:

- **Passive:** Attackers gain access to a network and can monitor or steal sensitive information, but without making any change to the data, leaving it intact.
- **Active:** Attackers not only gain unauthorized access but also modify data, deleting, encrypting or otherwise harming it.

3.3.1 Types of attacks

Endpoint attacks—gaining unauthorized access to user devices, servers or other endpoints, typically compromising them by infecting them with malware.

- Malware attacks—infecting IT resources with malware, allowing attackers to compromise systems, steal data and do damage. These also include Ransomware attacks.
- Vulnerabilities, exploits and attacks—exploiting vulnerabilities in software used in the organization, to gain unauthorized access, compromise or sabotage systems.
- Advanced persistent threats—these are complex multilayered threats, which include network attacks but also other attack types.

3.3.2 Common Types of Network Attacks

▲ Port Scanning

A computer hardware port is a connection point or interface between a computer and an external or internal physical device. Internal ports may connect such devices as hard drives and CD ROM or DVD drives; external ports may connect modems, printers, mice and other devices. These are physical in nature. E.g Serial Port, Parallel Port, SCSI Port, USB Port etc.

In computer networking, a port is a communication endpoint. At the software level, within an operating system, a port is a logical construct that identifies a specific process or a type of network service. A port is a virtual point where network connections start and end. Ports are software-based and managed by a computer's operating system. A port number is always associated with an IP address of a host and the type of transport protocol used for communication. Each port is associated with a specific process or service. Ports allow computers to easily differentiate between different kinds of traffic. E.g. emails go to a SMTP port 25, Webpages go t a HTTP Port 80 and HTTPS uses port 443. Etc

A port scanner is a software program that is designed to examine the hosts which reside at an IP addresses and record which ports are open on each host along with which known vulnerabilities are present. For network architecture or a Cyber security analyst port scanners can be extremely valuable. These port scanners can provide a useful way of identifying and evaluating the strengths and weaknesses of a network. As the same port scanner information that can be used by a network administrator or Cyber security analyst to evaluate the security of a network. It can also be used by Cyber criminals in order to identify network weaknesses or to assess how or at which point to attack a network. Now a day's high quality port scanner software are freely available online for Cyber Security engineers and to Cyber criminals. As with so many other tools that exists online; port scanners can be used with good intention or can be used to cause harm depending upon the goal of the user who is possess the tool.

A port scanner is a simple computer program that checks all of those ports – and responds with one of three possible responses: Open, Closed, or Filtered. There are two kinds of ports on each computer – TCP, and UDP – and 65,536 of each. The first 1024 TCP ports are the well-known ports like FTP(21), HTTP(80), or SSH(22). Anything above 1024 is available for use by services or applications.

Port scanning is quite simple: a port scanner sends a request to connect to a port on a computer and records the response. There are three possible responses:

a. **Open / Accepted:** The computer responds and asks if there is anything it can do in response.
b. **Closed / Not Listening:** The computer responds that "This port is currently in use and unavailable at this time."
c. **Filtered / Dropped / Blocked:** The computer doesn't even to respond to this requests.

Cybercriminals are looking for open ports that they can use as communication relays or penetration vectors into a network. Any open port they can find is a possible access point for further infiltration into the network.

3.3.2.1 Port Scanning Techniques

Ping Scan: The simplest port scans are ping scans. A ping is an Internet Control Message Protocol (ICMP) echo request – attackers are looking for any ICMP reply, which indicates that the target is alive. A ping scan is an automated blast of many ICMP echo requests to different targets to see who responds. Administrators usually disable ping either on the firewall or on the router. It's quick and easy to turn off this functionality and make it impossible to scout the network this way. However, ping is a good troubleshooting tool, and turning it off makes tracking down network problems a little more difficult.

TCP Half-Open: One of the more common and popular port scanning techniques is the TCP Half-Open port scan, sometimes referred to as SYN scan. It's a fast and sneaky scan that tries to find potential open ports on the target computer. This scan is fast because it never completes the full TCP 3 way-handshake. The scanner sends a SYN message and just notes the SYN-ACK responses. The scanner doesn't complete the connection by sending the final ACK: it leaves the target hanging. Any SYN-ACK responses are possible connections: an RST(reset) response means the port is closed, but there is a live computer here. No responses indicate SYN is filtered on the network. Any SYN-ACK replies are a quick way cybercriminals can find the next potential target.

TCP Connect: This port scanning technique is basically the same as the TCP Half-Open scan, but instead of leaving the target hanging, the port scanner completes the TCP connection. It's not as popular a technique as the TCP Half-Open. First, attacker has to send one more packet per scan, which increases the amount of traffic attacker are causing on the network. Second, since the attacker completes the connection with the target, it might trip an alarm that the Half-Open scan wouldn't.

UDP Connect: When attacker runs a UDP port scan, he sends either an empty packet or a packet that has a different payload per port, depending on attacker purpose. The trick with a UDP scan is that the attacker will only get a response if the port is closed, which means the attacker might know that there is a computer there. Depending on which port responded attacker might know that it has DNS or SNMP running, but that's pretty much it. No response means that either the port is open or it's filtered, and attacker might have to run the scan more than once before he figures anything out about the target. Attacker could be waiting a while to get a response that might never come. One more logical use of a UDP scan is to send a DNS request to UDP port 53 and see if he get a DNS reply. If attacker does get a reply, then he knows that there is a DNS server on that computer. A UDP scan can be useful to scout for active services that way, and the nmap port scanner is preconfigured to send requests for many standard services.

3.3.2.2 Difference between TCP and UDP

TCP and UDP are the two most common protocols in use for Internet Protocol (IP) networks. Transmission Control Protocol (TCP) is a nice orderly transaction protocol: TCP sends each packet in order, complete with error checking, verification, and a 3-way handshake to confirm each packet delivery is successful. UDP doesn't have any of the error checking, but gains on speed: live streaming and online video games often use UDP for this reason. Programs that use UDP just send the data – and it misses a packet, receiver will never get it again.

Stealth Scanning: Sometimes an attacker wants to run a port scan that is even quieter and less obvious than the other kinds of scans. Thankfully, TCP includes some flags that allow attackers to do just that. When attacker sends a port scan with a packet and the FIN flag, attacker are sending the packet and not expecting a response. If he does get an RST he can assume that the port is closed. If he get nothing back that indicates the port is open. Firewalls are looking for SYN packets, so FIN packets slip through undetected. The X-MAS scan sends a packet with the FIN, URG, and PUSH flags, and expects an RST or no response, just like the FIN scan. There isn't much practical use for this scan, but it does make the packet resemble a Christmas tree. Attacker can also send packets with no flags, called a NULL packet, and the response is either an RST or nothing. The good thing – for the hacker – about these scans is that they don't usually show up in logs. More recent Intrusion

Detection Software (IDS) and WireShark tool will catch these scans. If the target is a Microsoft OS, attacker will only see closed ports – but if attacker does find an open port he can assume that it's not a Windows machine. The biggest advantage of using these flags is that they can slip past the firewall, which makes the results more reliable. Port scanning and penetration testing are important parts of the cyber kill-chain that can lead to intrusion, exploitation, privilege escalation, and more. Port scanning is often just one part of the bigger picture in a cyber-attack.

3.3.4 Unauthorized Access

Although the category "unauthorized access" is not limited to specific attacks against networks, it does cover the most common type of attack that is executed now a day. When users, whether legitimate or not, connect to a service, they may be greeted with a message stating "Unauthorized Access Is Prohibited." If user continues to attempt to access the system, their actions are unauthorized. Unauthorized access is when someone gains access to a website, program, server, service, or other system using someone else's account or other methods. Unauthorized access refers to attackers accessing a network without receiving authorization. These attacks can occur both outside of and within a network. This attack category does not include an attacker who is connecting to see whether a service is active there; that typically falls into the "reconnaissance" category. Nor does the absence of any warning banner mean that access by anyone is authorized. This category includes any attempt by a user who knowingly tries to access a system to which that person does not have specific access permissions. Among the causes of unauthorized access attacks are weak passwords, lacking protection against social engineering, previously compromised accounts, and insider threats. From doors that are left open when they should be closed to easily forged credentials, there are a number of types of unauthorized access that can leave an organization at risk. There are 5 different ways an outsider can gain access to secure area. They are as follows:

Tailgating: One of the most common types of unauthorized access is tailgating, which occurs when one or more people follow an authorized user through a door. Often the user will hold the door for an unauthorized individual out of common courtesy, unwittingly exposing the secure area to unauthorized person. One way to decrease the likelihood of tailgating is by giving training to all credentialed users on security and awareness. An even more effective reduction technique is to implement turnstiles, mantraps or another solution that restricts entry to one individual at a time and generates an alarm if someone tries to circumvent the system.

Door Propping: Similar to tailgating, propping doors open, most often for convenience, is another common way unauthorized individuals gain access to a location. Some access control systems include the capability to detect when doors are propped and alert security personnel, who can respond and investigate the situation as needed.

Levering Doors: Many doors can be easily levered open using something as small as a screwdriver or as large as a crowbar. Advanced access control systems include forced-door monitoring and will generate alarms if a door is forced. The effectiveness of these systems varies, with many systems prone to a high rate of false positives, poor database configuration or lack of active intrusion monitoring. With proper tools and tactics in place, they are highly effective at detecting door levering.

Keys: Whether stolen, lost or loaned out, keys pose a major problem. They are often impossible to track when lost, forgotten, stolen or loaned to someone else, and if an individual tends to tailgate to enter the building, he or she may not notice missing keys for several days. During that time, there is huge risk, and the only way to ensure the continued security of a building is to re-core locks on multiple doors, which can be very expensive. Electronic key management solutions can be deployed to track keys, with the added benefit that many of these systems can be integrated with access control for an added layer of security.

Access Cards: With the added advantage of identifying authorized users who swipe in with an access control reader, electronic key cards are a more high-tech alternative to traditional keys. However, they are prone to the same risks associated with keys, namely the potential to be lost, stolen or shared with an authorized or unauthorized person. From a technology perspective, there are four main categories of access cards: Magnetic stripe, proximity smart cards and contact smart cards. Each has its pros and cons, with some more susceptible to risk than the others. Magnetic stripe cards are the easiest to duplicate and are susceptible to wear and tear or damage from magnetic fields. Proximity cards and smart cards are much less susceptible to duplication, and smart proximity cards can be programmed with much more information than access cards, allowing them to be used for a variety of interactive applications in addition to physical access, including network access. Some proximity smart cards, however, require a small battery, which can diminish their lifespan.

3.3.5 Man in the middle attacks (MitM)

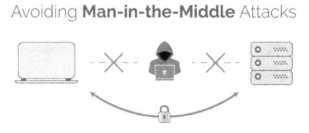

Avoiding **Man-in-the-Middle** Attacks

A man-in-the-middle (MitM) attack is when an attacker intercepts communications between two parties either to secretly eavesdrop or modify traffic traveling between the two. Attackers might use MitM attacks to steal login credentials or personal information, spy on the victim, or sabotage communications or corrupt data. A man-in-the-middle attack requires three players. There's the victim, the entity with which the victim is trying to communicate, and the "man in the middle," who's intercepting the victim's communications. Critical to the scenario is that the victim isn't aware of the man in the middle. The attack is a type of eavesdropping in which the entire conversation is controlled by the attacker. Sometimes referred to as a session hijacking attack, MiTM has a strong chance of success when the attacker can impersonate each party to the satisfaction of the other. MiTM attacks pose a serious threat to online security because they give the attacker the ability to capture and manipulate sensitive information in real-time.

A common method of executing a MiTM attack involves distributing malware that provides the attacker with access to a user's Web browser and the data it sends and receives during transactions and conversations. Most cryptographic protocols include some form of endpoint authentication specifically to prevent MITM attacks. For example, the Transport Layer Security (TLS) protocol can be required to authenticate one or both parties using a mutually trusted certification authority.

3.3.5.1 Types of MitM attacks.

Cybercriminals can use MitM attacks to gain control of devices in a variety of ways. There are 7 types of this attack.

1. **IP spoofing:** Every device capable of connecting to the internet has an internet protocol (IP) address, which is similar to the street address of home. By spoofing an IP address, an attacker can trick user into thinking they're interacting with a website or someone its

not, perhaps giving the attacker access to information user otherwise would not share.

2. **DNS spoofing:** Domain Name Server, or DNS, spoofing is a technique that forces a user to a fake website rather than the real one the user intends to visit. When a use becomes a victim of DNS spoofing, user may think he is visiting a safe, trusted website when in reality he is actually interacting with a fraudster. The attacker's goal is to divert traffic from the real site or capture user login credentials.

3. **HTTPS spoofing:** When doing business on the internet, seeing "HTTPS" in the URL, rather than "HTTP" is a sign that the website is secure and can be trusted. In fact, the "S" stands for "secure." An attacker can fool a web browser into believing it's visiting a trusted website when it's not. By redirecting the browser to an unsecure website, the attacker can monitor users' interactions with that website and possibly steal personal information user is sharing with the website.

4. **SSL hijacking:** When a device connects to an unsecure server — indicated by "HTTP" — the server can often automatically redirect user to the secure version of the server, indicated by "HTTPS." A connection to a secure server means standard security protocols are in place, protecting the data user share with that server. SSL stands for Secure Sockets Layer, a protocol that establishes encrypted links between web browser and the web server. In an SSL hijacking, the attacker uses another computer and secure server and intercepts the entire information passing between the server and the user's computer.

5. **Email hijacking:** Cyber criminals sometimes target email accounts of banks and other financial institutions. Once they gain access, they can monitor transactions between the institution and its customers. The attackers can then spoof the bank's email address and send

their own instructions to customers. This convinces the customer to follow the attackers' instructions rather than the banks. As a result, an unwitting customer may end up putting money in the attackers' hands.

6. **Wi-Fi eavesdropping:** Cyber criminals can set up Wi-Fi connections with very legitimate sounding names, similar to a nearby business. Once a user connects to the attackers Wi-Fi network, the attacker will be able to monitor the victims' online activity and be able to intercept login credentials, payment card information, and more. This is just one of several risks associated with using public or unprotected Wi-Fi networks.

7. **Stealing browser cookies:** A browser cookie is a small piece of information a website stores on user's computer. For example, an online retailer might store the personal information user enters and shopping cart items user have selected on a cookie so user don't have to re-enter that information when he return to the website. A Cyber-criminal can hijack these browser cookies. Since cookies store information from user's browsing session, attackers can gain access to user's passwords, address, and other sensitive information.

3.3.6 Code and SQL injection attacks

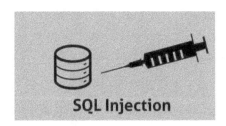

This is a common attack vector that uses malicious SQL code for backend database manipulation to access information that was not intended to be displayed. SQL Injection (SQLi) is a type of an injection attack that makes it possible to execute malicious SQL statements. These statements control a database server behind a web application. Attackers can use SQL Injection vulnerabilities to bypass application security measures. They can go around authentication and authorization of a web page or web application and retrieve the content of the entire backend SQL database. They can also use SQL Injection to add, modify, and delete records in the database. SQL Injection vulnerability may affect any website or web application that uses an SQL database such as MySQL, Oracle, SQL Server, or others. Criminals may use it to gain unauthorized access to users' sensitive data: customer information, personal data, trade secrets, intellectual property, and more. SQL Injection attacks are one of the oldest, most prevalent, and most dangerous web application vulnerabilities.

3.3.6.1 Types of SQL Injections:

SQL injections typically fall under three categories: In-band SQLi (Classic), Inferential SQLi (Blind) and Out-of-band SQLi.

In-band SQLi: The attacker uses the same channel of communication to launch their attacks and to gather their results. In-band SQLi's simplicity and efficiency make it one of the most common types of SQLi attack. There are two sub-variations of this method:

- **Error-based SQLi** — the attacker performs actions that cause the database to produce error messages. The attacker can potentially use the data provided by these error messages to gather information about the structure of the database.
- **Union-based SQLi** —this technique takes advantage of the UNION SQL operator, which fuses multiple select statements generated by the database to get a single HTTP response. This response may contain data that can be leveraged by the attacker.

3.3.6.2 Inferential (Blind) SQLi

The attacker sends data payloads to the server and observes the response and behavior of the server to learn more about its structure. This method is called blind SQLi because the data is not transferred from the website database to the attacker, thus the attacker cannot see information about the attack in-band. Blind SQL injections rely on the response and behavioral patterns of the server so they are typically slower to execute but may be just as harmful. Blind SQL injections can be classified as follows:

- **Boolean** — that attacker sends a SQL query to the database prompting the application to return a result. The result will vary depending on whether the query is true or false. Based on the result, the information within the HTTP response will modify or stay unchanged. The attacker can then work out if the message generated a true or false result.

- **Time-based** — attacker sends a SQL query to the database, which makes the database wait (for a period in seconds) before it can react. The attacker can see from the time the database takes to respond, whether a query is true or false. Based on the result, an HTTP response will be generated instantly or after a waiting period. The attacker can thus work out if the message they used returned true or false, without relying on data from the database.

Out-of-band SQLi: The attacker can only carry out this form of attack when certain features are enabled on the database server used by the web application. This form of attack is primarily used as an alternative to the in-band and inferential SQLi techniques. Out-of-band SQLi is performed when the attacker can't use the same channel to launch the attack and gather information, or when a server is too slow or unstable for these actions to be performed. These techniques count on the capacity of the server to create DNS or HTTP requests to transfer data to an attacker.

3.3.7 Privilege Escalation

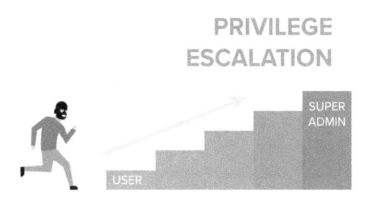

Privilege escalation is a type of Cyber-attack used to obtain unauthorized access to systems within the security perimeter, or sensitive systems, of an organization. Privilege escalation is the act of exploiting a bug, design flaw or configuration oversight in an operating system or software application to gain elevated access to resources that are normally protected from an application or user. Privilege escalation attacks exploit weaknesses and vulnerabilities with the goal of elevating access to a network, applications, and mission-critical systems. This attack takes advantage of programming errors or design flaws to grant the attacker elevated access to the network and its associated data and applications. Not every system hack will initially provide an unauthorized user with full access to the targeted system. In those circumstances privilege escalation is required. There are two types of privilege escalation attacks including vertical and horizontal. Vertical attacks are when an attacker gains access to an account with the intent to perform actions as that user. Horizontal attacks gain access to account(s) with limited permissions requiring an escalation of privileges, such as to an administrator role, to perform the desired actions.

Vertical Privilege Escalation: Vertical privilege escalation occurs when an attacker gains access directly to an account with the intent to perform actions as that person. This type of attack is easier to pull off since there is no desire to elevate permissions. The goal here is to access an account to further spread an attack or access data the user has permissions to.

Horizontal Privilege Escalation: Horizontal privilege escalation is a bit tricky to pull off as it requires the attacker to gain access to the account credentials as well as elevating the permissions. This type of attack tends to require a deep understanding of the vulnerabilities that affect certain operating systems or the use of hacking tools.

3.3.7.1 Windows Privilege Escalation Techniques:

Access Token Manipulation: Windows uses access tokens to determine the owners of running processes. When a process tries to perform a task that requires privileges, the system checks who owns the process and to see if they have sufficient permissions. Access token manipulation involves fooling the system into believing that the running process belongs to someone other than the user who started the process, granting the process the permissions of the other user.

3.3.7.2 Techniques:

- **Duplication:** Duplicating an access token using the Windows DuplicateToken(Ex) and then using *ImpersonateLoggedOnUserfunction* or *SetThreadToken* function to assign the impersonated token to a thread.

- **Impersonation:** Creating a new process with an impersonated token using the *DuplicateToken(Ex)* function together with the *CreateProcessWithTokenW* function.
- **Leveraging:** Leveraging username and password to create a token using the LogonUser function. The attacker possesses a username and password, and without logging on, they create a logon session, obtain the new token and use SetThreadToken to assign it to a thread. In this method, an adversary has a username and password, but the user is not logged.

Bypass User Account Control: The Windows User Account Control (UAC) mechanism creates a distinction between regular users and administrators. It limits all applications to standard user permissions unless specifically authorized by an administrator, to prevent malware from compromising the operating system. However, if UAC protection is not at the highest level, some Windows programs can escalate privileges, or execute COM objects with administrative privileges.

   DLL search order hijacking: Attackers can perform "DLL preloading". This involves planting a malicious DLL with the same name as a legitimate DLL, in a location which is searched by the system before the legitimate DLL is used by the system. Often this will be the current working directory, or in some cases attackers may remotely set the working directory to an external file volume. The system finds the DLL in the working folder, thinking it is the legitimate DLL, and executes it. There are several other ways to achieve DLL search order hijacking:

- Replacing an existing DLL or modifying a. manifest or. local redirection file, directory, or junction
- Performing search order DLL hijacking on a vulnerable program that has a higher privilege level, causing the attacker's DLL to run at the

same privilege level. This can be used to elevate privileges from user to administrator or from administrator to SYSTEM.

- Covering the attack by loading the legitimate DLLS together with the malicious DLLs, so that systems appear to run as usual.

3.3.7.3   Linux Privilege Escalation:

Enumeration: Attackers use automated tools to perform enumeration on Linux systems. In Linux systems, attackers use a process called "enumeration" to identify weaknesses that may allow privilege escalation. Enumeration involves:

- Using Google searches, port scanning and direct interaction with a system to learn more about it and see how it responds to inputs.
- Seeing if compilers, or high-level programming languages like Perl or Python, are available, this can allow an attacker to run exploit code.
- Identifying software components, such as web servers and their versions.
- Retrieving data from key system directories such as /etc, /proc, ipconfig, lsof, netstat and uname.

Kernel Exploit: From time to time, vulnerabilities are discovered in the Linux kernel. Attackers can exploit these vulnerabilities to gain root access to a Linux system, and once the system is infected with the exploit, there is no way to defend against it.

Attackers go through the following steps:

1) Learn about the vulnerabilities.
2) Develop or acquire exploit code.
3) Transfer the exploit onto the target.
4) Execute the exploit on the target.

Exploiting SUDO Rights: SUDO is a Linux program that lets users run programs with the security privileges of another user. Older versions would run as the super user (SU) by default. Attackers can try to compromise a user who has SUDO access to a system, and if successful, they can get gain root privileges.

A common scenario is administrators granting access to some users to perform supposedly harmless SUDO commands, such as 'find'. However, the 'find' command contains parameters that enable command execution, and so if attackers compromise that user's account, they can execute commands with root privileges.

3.3.8 Insider Threats

Insider threat is defined as an attack perpetrated by a user or malicious code that already inside the defended perimeter security of the organization. This type of attack is especially dangerous because often the attacker knows how the system is configured and also knows its weaknesses. An external attacker has to break the perimeter security such firewall, Proxy, DMZ etc. To get into the system to learn about the infrastructure. Whereas the inside attacker is already inside network. This kind of attacker can use his knowledge of the infrastructure to customize the attack to exploit the known system weakness and vulnerabilities. Often the inside attacker is a disgruntled employee; however along with malicious insider both clueless and careless insiders can bring external threat inside the network. The Insider threat can inflict intentional harm to the infrastructure and data such as theft, sabotage or espionage. Similarly the clueless and careless insiders expose the risks through social engineering, malwares, poor attention to security best practices or stealing or loss of the organization equipment's that result into loss of data. An insider threat is a security risk that originates within the targeted organization. This doesn't mean that the actor must be a current employee or officer in the organization. They could be a consultant, former employee, business partner, or board member. A network is especially vulnerable to malicious insiders, who already have privileged access to organizational systems. Insider threats can be difficult to detect and protect against, because insiders do not need to penetrate the network in order to do harm. New technologies like User and Even Behavioral Analytics (UEBA) can help identify suspicious or anomalous behavior by internal users, which can help identify insider attacks.

3.3.8.1 Types of Insider Threats:

In order to protect users' organization from insider threats, it's important to understand what insider threats look like.

A) **Negligent**: Negligent insiders may not intend to put the organization at risk, but do so non-maliciously by behaving in insecure ways. Clue-less and Care-less insiders both belong to this category. These insiders may be non-responsive to security awareness and training exercises or may make isolated errors by exercising bad judgment. In either case, negligence is often cited as the most expensive type of employee risk. Careless employees or vendors can become targets for attackers. Leaving a computer or terminal unlocked for a few minutes can be enough for one to gain access.

B) **Collusive:** Collusive insiders will collaborate with malicious external cyber-criminal to compromise the organization security. While it is risky and rare, this type of insider threat is becoming more common as professional Cyber criminals are increasingly using the dark web to recruit employees as allies. These cases often involve fraud, intellectual property theft or a combination of the two, which can make them very costly. This type of collusion may also take longer to detect as malicious external threat actors are typically well-versed in security technology and strategies for avoiding detection.

C) **Malicious:** Malicious insiders steal data or commit other negative acts against the organization with the goal of financial rewards or other personal gains. Malicious insiders looking for a second stream of income will typically steal data slowly to personal accounts to avoid detection. Another type of malicious insider, the disgruntled employee, will aim to deliberately sabotage a company or steal its intellectual property. They may be seen combing through sensitive company information or completing large data exports, especially around the time they resign from their position or give the customary a time bound notice before leaving a position.

D) **Third-party:** These insiders are contractors or vendors that a business has typically given some kind of access to its network. These insiders may have employees that fall under one of the categories above or may simply have flaws in their own systems and devices that open vulnerabilities to attackers.

3.4 APPLICATION SECURITY

Application security is the process of developing, adding, and testing security features within applications to prevent security vulnerabilities against threats such as unauthorized access and modification. Application security describes security measures at the application level that aim to prevent data or code within the app from being stolen or hijacked. It encompasses the security considerations that happen during application development and design, but it also involves systems and approaches to protect apps after they get deployed. Application security may include hardware, software, and procedures that identify or minimize security vulnerabilities. Application security is important because today's applications are often available over various networks and connected to the cloud, increasing vulnerabilities to security threats and breaches. There is increasing pressure and incentive to not only ensure security at the network level but also within applications themselves.

3.4.1 Types of application security

Different types of application security features include authentication, authorization, encryption, logging, and application security testing. Developers are always trying to code applications to reduce security vulnerabilities. They achieve this by releasing newer versions of the applications as they find and fix the bugs within the existing applications.

Authentication: When software developers build procedures into an application to ensure that only authorized users gain access to it. Authentication procedures ensure that a user is who they say they are. This can be accomplished by requiring the user to provide a user name and password when logging in to an application. Multi-factor authentication requires more than one form of authentication—the factors might include something user know (a password), something user have (a mobile device), and something user is (a thumb print or facial recognition).

Authorization: After a user has been authenticated, the user may be authorized to access and use the application. The system can validate that a user has permission to access the application by comparing the user's identity with a list of authorized users. Authentication must happen before authorization so that the application matches only validated user credentials to the authorized user list.

Encryption: After a user has been authenticated and is using the application, other security measures can protect sensitive data from being seen or even used by a cybercriminal. In cloud-based applications, where traffic containing sensitive data travels between the end user and the cloud, that traffic can be encrypted to keep the data safe.

Logging: If there is a security breach in an application, logging can help identify who got access to the data and how. Application log files provide a time-stamped record of which aspects of the application were accessed and by whom.

Application security testing: A necessary process to ensure that all of these security controls work properly.

Application security in the cloud: Application security in the cloud poses some extra challenges. Because cloud environments provide shared resources, special care must be taken to ensure that users only have access to the data they are authorized to view in their cloud-based applications. Sensitive data is also more vulnerable in cloud-based applications because that data is transmitted across the Internet from the user to the application and back.

Mobile application security: Mobile devices also transmit and receive information across the Internet, as opposed to a private network, making them vulnerable to attack. Enterprises can use virtual private networks (VPNs) to add a layer of mobile application security for employees who log in to applications remotely. IT departments may also decide to vet mobile apps and make sure they conform to company security policies before allowing employees to use them on mobile devices that connect to the corporate network.

Web application security: Web application security applies to web applications—apps or services that users access through a browser interface over the Internet. Because web applications live on remote servers, not locally on user machines, information must be transmitted to and from the user over the Internet. Web application security is of special concern to businesses that host web applications or provide web services. These businesses often choose to protect their network from intrusion with a web application firewall. A web application firewall works by inspecting and, if necessary, blocking data packets that are considered harmful.

3.5 ENDPOINT SECURITY

Endpoint security refers to securing endpoints, or end-user devices like desktops, laptops, and mobile devices which are connected to the corporate networks. Endpoints serve as points of access to an enterprise network and create points of entry that can be exploited by Cyber Criminals. Any device, such as a smartphone, tablet, or laptop, provides an entry point for attacker. Endpoint security aims to adequately secure every endpoint connecting to organization's network to block access attempts and other risky activity at these points of entry. As more enterprises adopt practices such as BYOD (Bring Your Own Device) and remote / mobile employees, the enterprise network security perimeter has essentially dissolved. With the proliferation of mobile devices like laptops, smartphones, tablets, notebooks etc., there has been a sharp increase in the number of devices being lost or stolen as well. These incidents potentially translate as huge loss of sensitive data for enterprises which allow their employees to bring in these mobile devices (enterprise-provided or otherwise) into their enterprise.

Endpoint security solutions often use a client-server model of protection, employing both a centrally managed security solution to protect the network as well as client software locally installed on each endpoint used to access that network. Some work on a SaaS (Software as a Service) model, by which both central and endpoint security solutions are maintained remotely. It also helps organizations successfully prevent any misuse of their data which they've made available on the employee's mobile devices. Example: a disgruntled employee trying to cause nuisance to the enterprise or someone who may be a friend of the employee trying to misuse the enterprise data available on the device. Every device which can connect to a network poses a considerable danger. And as these devices are placed outside of the corporate firewall, on the edge of the network using which individuals have to connect to the central network, they are called as endpoints. Meaning endpoints of that network. As already stated endpoint can be any mobile device ranging from laptops to the notebooks of today, which can be connected to a network. And the strategy organizations employ in security these endpoints are known as 'endpoint security'. Although the objective of endpoint security solutions is the same – secure devices – there is a considerable difference between endpoint security and antivirus. Antivirus is about protecting PC(s), – single or many depending upon the type of antivirus being deployed – whereas endpoint security covers the entire picture. It's about securing every aspect of the network.

Difference between Antivirus and Endpoint Security: Antivirus is one of the components of endpoint security. Whereas endpoint security is a much broader concept including not just antivirus but many security tools (like Firewall, HIPS system, White Listing tools, Patching and Logging/Monitoring tools etc.,) for safeguarding the various endpoints of the enterprise (and the enterprise itself against these endpoints) and from different types of security threats. More precisely, endpoints security employs a server/client model for protecting the various endpoints of the enterprise. The server would have a master instance of the security program and the clients (endpoints) would have agents installed within them. These agents would communicate with the server the respective devices' activities like the devices' health, user authentication/authorization etc., and thus keep the endpoints secure. Whereas antivirus is usually a single program responsible for scanning, detecting and removing viruses, malware, adware, spyware, Ransomware and other such malware. Simply put, antivirus is a one-stop shop for securing users home networks, and endpoint security is suitable for securing enterprises, which are larger and much more complex to handle.

Endpoint Security usually includes 'provisions for application whitelisting, network access control, endpoint detection and response', things which are usually not available in antivirus packages. It can also be said that antivirus packages are simpler forms of endpoint security. The major difference between the Consumer and Enterprise Endpoint Security is that there's no centralized management and administration for consumers, whereas, for enterprises, centralized management is necessary. This central administration (or server) streamlines the configuration or installation of endpoint security software on individual endpoint devices and performance logs and other alerts are sent to the central administration server for evaluation and analysis.

3.5.1 Types of Endpoint Security

1) Antivirus Solutions: Antivirus solutions can scan files present locally on the endpoint device for malicious threats via consulting against threat intelligence databases and can protect themselves against signature-based attacks and potential malware with unknown signatures by examining its behavior.

2) **Application Control:** As the name suggests Application control component controls applications' permissions, ensuring strict restrictions on what they can or cannot do. To accomplish this, it uses whitelisting, blacklisting, and gray-listing to prevent malicious

applications from running and compromised applications from running in malicious ways.

3) **Network Access Control:** NAC overlaps with identity and access management. The primary focus of NAC is on securing access to network nodes. This component what devices and users can access and do what on organizations network infrastructure.

4) **Endpoint Firewall:** Software Firewalls component of the Endpoint security software is responsible for filtering the traffic flowing into and going out of endpoint onto the network based on 'a set of security rules'. It provides granular management of inbound and outbound network activities, hides system ports from scans, and provides warnings when suspicious activities are detected.

5) **Host Intrusion Prevention:** Rules-based HIPS that monitors application activities and system processes, blocking those that are malicious by halting actions that could damage critical system components.

6) **URL Filtering:** This allows the organizations to restrict web traffic to trusted websites; in turn, this prevents users from accessing malicious websites with potentially harmful content. URL filtering can prevent surreptitious downloads on hosts, granting organizations more control over what gets downloaded.

7) **Browser Isolation:** Works to execute browsing sessions in isolated environments where it cannot reach valuable digital assets. Therefore, activity remains restricted to isolated environments. Additionally, the tool destroys web browser codes after the user browsing session is over.

8) **Cloud Perimeter Security:** Endpoint security can no longer merely concern itself with users' devices. In addition, it must form a protective perimeter around users cloud environments and databases. Cloud providers are not responsible for organizations enterprise's Cyber

security; hackers can target organizations cloud-stored assets too. Cloud perimeter security allows enterprise to harden their cloud infrastructure against incoming threats.

9) **Endpoint Encryption:** This component prevents issues such as data leaks (whether intentional or not) via data transfer by fully encrypting that data. Specifically, it encrypts data stored on endpoints.

10) **Sandboxing:** A "sandbox" serves as an isolated and secure digital environment which perfectly replicates typical end-user operating system. As such, it can contain potential threats for observation. This component helps contain zero-day threats and works well against zero-day attacks.

11) **Secure Email Gateways:** Secure email gateways monitor incoming and outgoing messages for suspicious behavior, preventing them from being delivered. They can be deployed according to organizations IT infrastructure to prevent phishing attacks.

12) **Internet of Things (IoT) Security:** This work to improve visibility in IoT devices on organization's network, and provide a consistent and easily upgradable layer of Cyber security, and close security vulnerabilities into the network introduced by the IoT devices.

3.6 IDENTITY AND ACCESS MANAGEMENT (IAM)

Identity Management and Access control is the discipline of managing access to enterprise resources to keep systems and data secure. IAM is about defining and managing the roles and access privileges of individual network users and the circumstances in which users are granted (or denied) those privileges. Those users might be customers (customer identity management) or employees (employee identity management. The core objective of IAM systems is one digital identity per individual. Once that digital identity has been established, it must be maintained, modified and monitored throughout each user's "access lifecycle."

IAM systems provide administrators with the tools and technologies to change a user's role, track user activities, create reports on those activities, and enforce policies on an ongoing basis. These systems are designed to provide a means of administering user access across an entire enterprise and to ensure compliance with corporate policies and government regulations. Identity management systems can allow a company to extend access to its information systems across a variety of on-premises applications, mobile apps, and SaaS tools without compromising security. By providing greater access to outsiders, organizations can drive collaboration throughout the organization, enhancing productivity, employee satisfaction, research and development, and, ultimately, revenue. Identity management can decrease the number of help-desk calls to IT support teams regarding password resets. Identity management systems allow administrators to automate these and other time-consuming, costly tasks. An identity management system can be a cornerstone of a secure network, because managing user identity is an essential piece of the access-control picture. An identity management system all but requires companies to define their access policies, specifically outlining who has access to which data resources and under which conditions they have access.

3.6.1 Identity Management Solutions Features & Capabilities

- Access (authorization or restriction of access to certain information to certain persons across locations and systems).
- Single sign-on (SSO, describes the ability to login to the system once and only once, gaining access to all systems without the need for logging in again via help from a server).
- Multi-factor authentication (using multiple, independent components to gain access, a simple step to increase security)
- Password management and self-help for password users.
- Identity federation related to SSO, access spanning system boundaries (e.g. cloud access).
- Directory / User Repository Management for tracking of users with access, and
- Security Analytics for auditing and compliance.

3.6.2 Identity and Access Management (IAM) Terms

- **Access management:** Access management refers to the processes and technologies used to control and monitor network access. Access management features, such as authentication, authorization, trust and security auditing, are part and parcel of the top ID management systems for both on-premises and cloud-based systems.
- **Biometric authentication:** A security process for authenticating users that relies upon the user's unique characteristics. Biometric authentication technologies include fingerprint sensors, iris and retina scanning, and facial recognition.
- **Credential:** An identifier employed by the user to gain access to a network such as the user's password, public key infrastructure (PKI) certificate, or biometric information (fingerprint, iris scan).
- **De-provisioning:** The process of removing an identity from an ID repository and terminating users access privileges.

- **Context-aware network access control:** Context-aware network access control is a policy-based method of granting access to network resources according to the current context of the user seeking access. For example, a user attempting to authenticate from an IP address that hasn't been whitelisted would be blocked.

- **Entitlement:** The set of attributes that specify the access rights and privileges of an authenticated security principal.

- **Digital identity:** The ID itself, including the description of the user and his/her/its access privileges. ("Its" because an endpoint, such as a laptop or smartphone, can have its own digital identity.)

- **Identity as a Service (IDaaS):** Cloud-based IDaaS offers identity and access management functionality to an organization's systems that reside on-premises and/or in the cloud.

- **Identity synchronization:** The process of ensuring that multiple identity stores—such as, the result of an acquisition—contain consistent data for a given digital ID.

- **Identity lifecycle management:** Similar to access lifecycle management, the term refers to the entire set of processes and technologies for maintaining and updating digital identities. Identity lifecycle management includes identity synchronization, provisioning, de-provisioning, and the ongoing management of user attributes, credentials and entitlements.

- **Multi-factor authentication (MFA):** MFA is when more than just a single factor, such as a user name and password, is required for authentication to a network or system. At least one additional step is also required, such as receiving a code sent via SMS to a smartphone, inserting a smart card or USB stick, or satisfying a biometric authentication requirement, such as a fingerprint scan.

- **Privileged account management:** This term refers to managing and auditing accounts and data access based on the privileges of the user.

In general terms, because of his or her job or function, a privileged user has been granted administrative access to systems. A privileged user, for example, would be able set up and delete user accounts and roles.

- **Provisioning:** The process of creating identities, defining their access privileges and adding them to an ID repository.
- **Single sign-on (SSO):** A type of access control for multiple related but separate systems. With a single username and password, a user can access a system or systems without using different credentials.
- **Risk-based authentication (RBA):** Risk-based authentication dynamically adjusts authentication requirements based on the user's situation at the moment authentication is attempted. For example, when users attempt to authenticate from a geographic location or IP address not previously associated with them, those users may face additional authentication requirements.

3.7 MOBILE SECURITY

Mobile Security

Involves protecting both personal and business information stored on and transmitted from smartphones, tablets, laptops and other mobile devices. The term mobile security is a broad one that covers everything from protecting mobile devices from malware threats to reducing risks and securing mobile devices and their data in the case of theft, unauthorized access or accidental loss of the mobile device. Since the outbreak of Covid-19 and subsequent government mandated lockdown; nearly all employees now routinely access corporate data from smartphones or mobile devices and that means keeping sensitive info out of the wrong hands is an increasingly complex puzzle.

Security threats on mobile devices come from a variety of places. Such as:

Device Loss or Theft: This is the top concern for organizations. If an employee leaves a tablet or smartphone in a taxi cab or at a restaurant, for example, sensitive data, such as customer information or corporate intellectual property stored on the device, can be at risk.

Application Security: Most of the mobile apps that request too many privileges. Most of the users don't hesitate to grant these permissions without giving a second thought. This allows these apps to access various data sources on the device. Many mobile apps — especially free ones — are built with ties to advertising networks, which makes contacts, browsing history and geo-location data extremely valuable marketing companies and Cyber criminals alike.

Data Leakage: Mobile apps are often the cause of unintentional data leakage. For example, "Riskware" apps pose a real problem for mobile users who grant them broad permissions, but don't always check security. These are typically free apps found in official app stores that perform as advertised, but also send personal—and potentially any corporate data present on the device —to a remote server, where it is mined by advertisers, and sometimes, by Cyber criminals. Data leakage can also happen through hostile enterprise-signed mobile apps. These mobile malware programs use distribution code native to popular mobile operating systems like iOS and Android to move valuable data across corporate networks without raising red flags.

Unsecured Wi-Fi: Many people don't want to use their Mobile / cellular data as it costs them. Also the mobile data do not provide the speed a compared to a Wi-Fi. Hence people usually prefer to connect to free Wi-Fi networks. Most of the free Wi-Fi networks are very unsecure. This creates an amazing opportunity for the hacker to get unrestricted access to unsecured devices on the same network.

Phishing scams: Since many of us use our phones to access office emails, it's highly likely user could click a malicious link and inadvertently cause a virus to spread through the device.

Malicious apps: Some phone manufacturers keep a pretty close eye on apps and their developers, but unprotected phones or apps downloaded from less reputable locations can be full of malicious content. Malicious software can infect all types of devices and, though rare, iPhones can be a target too.

Network spoofing: An attacker create a Wi-Fi network that mimics several legitimate Wi-Fi networks. Its a fake network designed to grab users personal information / data from their devices.

Spyware: Spyware allows hackers to break into users' phone and oversee everything users do, from where user is at any given time to users' credit card number to text messages user sends.

Bluetooth vulnerabilities: In late 2017, experts discovered that millions of devices had a vulnerability that made them susceptible to threats through Bluetooth technology that could pass from one device to another nearby relatively easily.

Mobile Device Management (MDM): Mobile device management (MDM) is a type of security software used by an organization to monitor, manage and secure employees' mobile devices that are deployed across multiple mobile service providers and across multiple mobile operating systems being used in the organization. Mobile device management software is often combined with additional security services and tools such as Mobile Application Management to create a complete mobile device and security Enterprise Mobility Management solution. Most mobile device management solutions provide organizations with end-to-end security — meaning the mobile apps, network and data used by the mobile device (in addition to the mobile device itself) are managed by an organization's Cyber Security team with a single mobile device software product. Mobile device management software to contain some or all of the following features: management and support of mobile applications, mobile policy management, inventory management, security management and telecom service management. Some of the Mobile Device Management suite offers following features.

Secure Browser: Every MDM solution comes with a built-in custom browser. The MDM suite usually disables any other browser on the device and force users to use the secure browser inside the MDM suite. This helps mitigate many potential security risks which may pose for mobile device using a unsecured and outdated browser. The MDM suite can also enforce some additional policies on the browser such as URL filtering, restricted download, running any script etc.

Secure Email: After browsing Email is the most commonly and frequently used tool on a mobile device. The users can also fall victim to many types of email attacks, such as phishing, spam, etc. To deal with this MDM products allow organizations to integrate their existing email setup with the email feature on the mobile device. MDM products support easy integration with Microsoft Exchange Server, Office 365 and others.

Secure Docs: Employees frequently share word documents, PDF and spreadsheets over email. Some user might misuse attachments downloaded from corporate email to their personal devices. MDM suite can restrict or disable device's clipboard to copy or move into or out the secure data, restrict the forwarding of attachments to other emails, or prevent saving attachments on the secondary storage location like removable memory card. This ensures corporate data is secured a remains restricted to the device itself.

Secure App Catalog: with the Bring Your Own Device (BYOD) culture proliferating in many organizations, it's difficult to keep track of the apps installed on the users' mobile devices. Organizations can use MDM suite to distribute, manage, and upgrade applications on an employee's device using an App Catalogue. This provides an option for the organization to deploy devices in Kiosk Mode or Lock-Down Mode.

3.8 DATA SECURITY

Organizations around the globe are investing heavily in information technology (IT) cyber security capabilities to protect their critical assets. The primary aim of data security is to protect the data that an organization collects, process, stores, creates, receives or transmits. Compliance is also a major consideration. It doesn't matter which device, technology or process is used to manage, store or collect data, it must be protected. Data breaches can result in lawsuit cases and huge fines, not to mention damage to an organization's reputation. The importance of shielding data from security threats is more important today than it has ever been. Data security is about protecting information form modification, use, destruction, and unauthorized access. And the slight difference from the cyber security lies in the fact that it covers both electronic and physical protection of the data. The data that an organization creates collects, stores, and exchanges is a valuable asset. Safeguarding it from corruption and unauthorized access by internal or external people protects organizations from financial loss, reputation damage, consumer confidence disintegration, and brand erosion. Furthermore, government and industry regulation around data security make it imperative that organizations achieve and maintain compliance with these rules wherever organizations do business.

3.8.1 Data Security Technologies

Data security technology comes in many shapes and forms to protect data from a growing number of threats. Many of these threats are from external sources, but organizations should also focus their efforts on safeguarding their data from the inside attacks, too. Ways of securing data include:

Data encryption: Data encryption applies a code to every individual piece of data and will not grant access to encrypted data without an authorized key being given. Data encryption software effectively enhances data security by using an algorithm (called a cipher) and an encryption key to turn normal text into encrypted cipher text. To an unauthorized person, the cipher data will be unreadable.

Data masking: Masking specific areas of data can protect it from disclosure to external malicious sources, and also internal personnel who could potentially use the data with malicious intent. For example, the first 12 digits of a credit card number may be masked within a database.

Data Erasure: There are times when data that is no longer active or used needs to be erased from all systems. For example, if a customer has requested for their name to be removed from a mailing list, the details should be deleted permanently.

Data Resilience: By creating backup copies of data, organizations can recover data should it be erased or corrupted accidentally or stolen during a data breach.

Authentication: Authentication and authorization happen through the process called access control. This ensures that the data access is given only to authorized persons and based on their Role they get the degree of control over data. An access control system includes:

Discretionary access control (the least restrictive), which allows access to resources based on the identity of users or groups.

- Role-based access control, which assigns access based on organizational role and allows users access only to specific information.
- Mandatory access control, which allows a system administrator to strictly control access to all information.

Data Security Standards (DSS): Many data breaches happened due to poor implementation or complete absence of security controls in private companies as well as in government organizations. Many countries work on improvement of security requirements and implementing them in their legislation. There are a number of compliance regulations that govern organizations dealing in personal data of any users. The regulations that affect any organization will depend on a selection of factors, such as any industry operating in and the type of data organizations store. Failure to comply with these regulations can incur hefty fines to the organizations.

Few of the Data Standards are as below:

1) **GDPR:** General Data Protection Regulation. It's the core of Europe's digital privacy legislation. GDPR is a set of rules designed to give European Union (EU) citizens more control over their

personal data. Any organization stores data relating to citizens in the European Union (EU) will need to comply with the latest GDPR regulations.

2) **PCI:** The Payment Card Industry Data Security Standard is an information security standard for organizations that store, process, and transmit Card holder data. The PCI Standard is mandated by the card brands but administered by the Payment Card Industry Security Standards Council.

3) **HIPAA:** The Health Insurance Portability and Accountability Act (HIPAA) set the standard for sensitive patient data protection. Companies that deal with Protected Health Information (PHI) must have physical, network, and process security measures in place and follow them to ensure HIPAA Compliance.

5) **ISO/IEC 27001:** ISO/IEC 27001 formally specifies an Information Security Management System, a governance arrangement comprising a structured suite of activities with which to manage information risks.

6) **FIPS:** FIPS standards are issued to establish requirements for various purposes such as ensuring computer security and inter-operability, and are intended for cases in which suitable industry standards do not already exist. Many FIPS specifications are modified versions of standards used in the technical communities, such as the American National Standards Institute (ANSI), the Institute of Electrical and Electronics Engineers (IEEE), and the International Organization for Standardization (ISO).

7) **NERC:** NERC Reliability Standards aim to regulate and ensure the quality of North American bulk power system. They set the minimum requirements regarding the reliability, efficiency, safety and risk management of operations that provide bulk power within the borders of the United States, Canada and Mexico.

8) **ANSI/ISA 62443:** is a series of standards, technical reports, and related information that define procedures for implementing secure Industrial Automation and Control Systems (IACS).

3.9 DRIVE-BY DOWNLOAD

Ever since the birth of Internet, people all over the world use it for almost everything. From food to fitness to fashion and Finance; the possibility of places to explore from comfort of home; are virtually endless. But at the same time there are Cyber criminals who are trying multiple ways to attack user computers for nefarious purposes. One of the most successful and common attack is Drive-By-Download. A drive-by download is when user is browsing a website and something is installed in the background or without users' knowledge or permission. These attacks can be pretty sophisticated. For example if user is running a vulnerable version of Flash in his browser. When this user visits a site that is looking to exploit that specific version of Flash and when user visit that site flash is activated to download something in the background. Such as Trojan, Ransomware and then automatically run it infecting users system. Another example is that sometimes advertisement networks might be compromised.

User may be browsing his favorite News site and an ad over on the right side of the screen exploits something in users browser and download something infecting users system. Because it's so easy to implement and users are so vulnerable; drive-by downloads are a significant risk. Drive-by downloads can load themselves onto computers without the user's knowledge. They are often the first step in multi-stage attacks, able to subtly bring other, more vicious malware onto a victim's computer. Ultimately, these attacks can end up wreaking havoc in a range of ways, from spying to intellectual property theft, to extortion via Ransomware. Even if the website is legitimate and users didn't make any clicks, drive-by downloads can set off a chain of events that lead to devastating attacks.

In the cases of drive-by download, the user doesn't realize that anything has been downloaded. These nonconsensual download typically take advantage of vulnerabilities in a user's operating system, apps, browser, plugins like Flash, or in the complexities of JavaScript. Sometimes attackers may take advantage of zero-day exploits. However, the bulk of these attacks are made possible because users have a tendency to operate outdated browsers and plugins that haven't been patched over with the latest security updates. This is the type of attack that most people think of when they hear the term drive-by download because victims can get infected without even stopping to click. It's as if they get hit even though they're just driving by the web page.

Even prestigious websites like the New York Times and the BBC have been known to host ads that infect visitors with drive-by downloads. Alternatively, malicious content can be served directly from the website itself. This strategy generally takes advantage of security vulnerabilities found in outdated software. Common culprits include:

Outdated browsers, such as old versions of Internet Explorer, Opera, Firefox or Chrome.

- Unpatched plugins like Adobe Flash or Microsoft Silverlight.
- Old versions of Windows or other operating systems.

Drive-by downloads also work their way on to computers and devices by tricking users. One technique involves attackers dressing up a file as something that it isn't. A user may accidentally install malware or a fake program under the assumption that they are downloading legitimate software. A good example of this is when attackers set up notifications that look like they come from legitimate antivirus programs. These scare users into thinking that they have a virus, prompting them to take action to remove it.

The real danger comes when users follow the directions. The virus notification is just a sneaky tactic, and the supposed remedy ends up downloading malware onto the victim's computer. While users may have actively chosen to install the file, they did so without any awareness of what it truly contained. This is what gets this tactic placed under the category of a drive-by download. A similar tactic involves exploiting a user's lack of technical knowledge to trick them into downloading something they don't need. While the user may have chosen to execute the download, they have done so without informed consent, which can often lead to unintended and harmful ramifications.

How Drive-By Download works: A common scenario involves a user coming across a malicious landing page, whether by clicking on it directly or by being redirected through malicious advertising. From this point, there is a wide range of variables as to how the attack can progress. It depends both on the objectives of the attacker and their sophistication.

Social engineering: Cyber Criminals may use social engineering to try and trick users into actively downloading a supposed antivirus program or a system update. Under this type of attack, victims are often deceived into directly downloading a Trojan or other malware. The initiation of the attack happens after a user installing software without their full understanding of the said software. This download may give the attacker backdoor access, allow them to steal sensitive data, or give them an avenue through which they can load other devastating software, such as Ransomware.

Exploit kit: An exploit kit is essentially a pre-packaged collection of exploits and tools that can attempt a range of different attacks to try and infect targets. Many exploit kits are already available on the dark web for purchase. Rudimentary exploit kits will cycle through every exploit in their package, in the hopes that one of them can penetrate the victim. This approach isn't sophisticated and can be detected relatively easily. However, it can still succeed against those who are using outdated software. In these cases, the security vulnerabilities allow the attack to be initiated, attacks that users are unaware of. More advanced exploit kits will begin by Finger-printing potential targets for suitability. This process involves scanning the user's configuration, which operating system they are using, their browser, plugins and which versions they have installed. Fingerprinting may also examine the user's IP address, allowing attackers to specifically target or exempt potential victims based on their geographic region. The fingerprinting process allows attackers to filter for appropriate targets. Sophisticated campaigns separate suitable victims according to which mode of attack their setup makes them vulnerable. Fingerprinting can also attempt to detect network tools and virtual machines – if these are spotted, the kit won't launch an attack against the target. When the fingerprinting process comes across candidates who are vulnerable to various exploits contained within the kits, they are then redirected – often multiple times – to a landing page containing malicious code that can take advantage of the appropriate security vulnerability. This is where the drive-by download occurs, often through JavaScript.

Drive-by downloads & Smartphones: It's not just computers that are vulnerable to drive-by downloads. As the user market has gone mobile, so have hackers, and they have been devising cunning campaigns to try to infect devices as well. By design, mobile setups are more secure than typical Windows configuration. Smartphone platforms are much more restrictive, limiting what users can do, as well as how easily they can screw up. If users keep their default security settings and make sure their operating system and apps are always updated to the latest version, they should be relatively safe from malware. Those who have jailbroken (iOS) or rooted (Android) their phones face significantly greater risks. Although the privilege escalation from jailbroken or rooted devices offers additional functionality, it also makes it easier for malware to infect devices. This is because mobile malware tends to need this level of access in order to take action. Also the jailbroken or rooted devices allow malwares to penetrate deeper into device OS than otherwise they can.

Preventing Drive-By downloads: In most cases where drive-by downloads infect targets without any user action; they accomplish it by exploiting security vulnerabilities in old versions of software like Internet Explorer and Flash. One of the security community's biggest battles is in convincing people to update their operating systems, browsers, add-ons, apps and every other piece of software as soon as patches are made available. Many users don't realize that updates aren't just a collection of annoying changes and the addition of new features that they probably don't need. Updates also act to plug up recently discovered security holes. To combat this huge threat, users need to be installing updates as soon as possible. They can do this manually, but it's easy to forget or ignore them, resulting in opportunities for attackers to strike. The best solution is to set software to update automatically wherever possible. The greater the numbers of programs and add-ons users have, the more users have to manage, which increases the chance of problems occurring. The best approach is to only install add-ons and other software that users really need and to thoroughly vet them beforehand. Users should periodically go through and get rid of any application that they no longer using because they simply add needless risk.

Avoiding Drive-By downloads: While drive-by downloads are occasionally found on reputable websites, they are far more common in the depths of the internet. Users should act cautiously whenever they are browsing online. It's best to stick to major sites that are more proactive about their security, and away from any dodgy websites that could do harm. Another protection measure is to run an ad blocker. This can be an effective strategy because malvertising is one of the core means that attackers use in their drive-by download campaigns. If ads are being blocked, then users can't be infected by malicious ads. People can also protect themselves by using a script blocker such as NoScript. When users browse without an extension like NoScript, JavaScript and Flash the malicious codes can run automatically. While these scripts make the online experience smoother and more functional, they are also the cause of many drive-by downloads. When users use NoScript, it disables them by default, removing these threats. The downside of this is that it also reduces the functionality on many websites, or can make them completely unusable.

3.10 INFRASTRUCTURE SECURITY

With the rise in Cyber terrorism and information spread across all possible infrastructures like private / public / hybrid cloud, there is a compelling need to manage architectures, algorithms, and controls to create a dependable IT infrastructure. As the client database and intellectual property increase its spread, so is the increase in vulnerability, opening the gate for newer ways of cyber-attacks. To avoid such situations, organizations must build a stronger and more strategic infrastructure, secured with advanced security platforms and cyber-attack detection techniques. An appropriate enterprise security platform with security orchestration is a way to maintain infrastructure security efficiently. Infrastructure security is at the root of organizations entire corporate security plan. Other individual security area plans may overlap with organizations Infrastructure security plan to some extent. For example, a wireless network is part of organizations infrastructure, but it's also a large enough area to be addressed in a separate project plan.

The Cyber security and Infrastructure Security Agency (CISA) was established on 16 November 2018 when President Donald Trump signed into law the Cyber security and Infrastructure Security Agency Act of 2018. The Infrastructure Security Division coordinates and collaborates across government and the private sector. The Division conducts and facilitates vulnerability and consequence assessments to help critical infrastructure owners and operators such as State, local, tribal, and territorial partners to understand and address risks to critical infrastructure. It also provides information on emerging threats and hazards so that appropriate actions can be taken, as well as tools and training to partners in government and industry manage the risks to their assets, systems, and networks.

Most of the organizations opt for a Layered Security model to achieve Infrastructure Security. The four key layers of the security modes are as below.

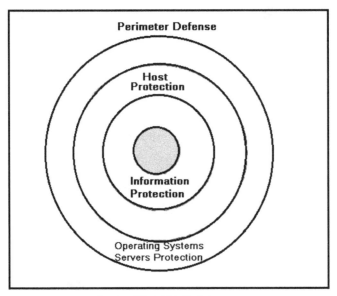

Layered Security Model

3.10.1 Security Layer-1: Perimeter Defense Security Systems

Physical and Logical security are both aspects to Perimeter security. These two must be utilized together in order to have high degree of Perimeter security. Logical security is the software or technological safeguards, often times this is a security that is not physically visible to human eyes. However it must be used in junction with physical security. Physical security is the security that is actually seen and it is the safeguard a person must face before accessing the logical safeguards. Examples are lock doors, fences, access cards, locked computers, security guards, and security cameras. Lock doors are the physical security and they can be self-locking or a user must lock it. However either way there must be a policy in place to keep the doors lock and keep unauthorized access out. A close circuit cameras are used to look at the actual physical people coming in and out of a building and will record logs. In an event of a breach the records can be utilized to evaluate traffic in and out and to see if any unauthorized users were accessing these physical devices.

When it comes to logical perimeter security; the most basic concept is the trusted versus untrusted zones. The trusted zone is everything inside of organizations network and the untrusted zone is anything outside of organizations network. Best practice demands that there should be only one point on the perimeter where data packets can pass in and out. A firewall is placed at this single point. This is also known as perimeter Firewall. The firewalls job is to stand at the border and regulate specifically what is allowed in and what is allowed out. Everything inside this perimeter firewall is trusted and everything outside perimeter firewall is untrusted. The two zones architecture is generally sufficient for small office/home office setups. Many organizations that have servers accessible to the public may add a third zone called the DMZ and place the public facing services servers in it. Because these servers may be vulnerable to attacks from the untrusted network, communication from the DMZ to the trusted zone is carefully controlled. Some organizations may also deploy another firewall between the DMZ and the internal network. The primary technology that underpins perimeter protection is a firewall, which filters out potentially dangerous or unknown traffic that may constitute a threat based on a set of rules about the types of traffic and permitted source/destination addresses on the network. Most organizations also deploy intrusion detection or intrusion prevention systems (IDS/IPS), which look for suspicious traffic once it has passed through the firewall.

The internet is filled with millions of users with bad intensions. Some users are not aware of vulnerabilities of their assets. Such assets are hacked and later used as a bot and used for various activities by hackers. One of the common attacks on Perimeter defense layer is DDoS (Distributed Denial of Service) attack, which involves flooding the point of connection to outside world with unproductive traffic. This brings communications with the Internet to a standstill. Some of the common DoS attacks on routers are Smurf, Ack and Rst attacks.

Some of the General Practices to Secure Server Hardware are:

- Organizations should Place servers and communication equipment in a secure room.
- Allow restricted access to server/communication room.
- Users should avoid using server consoles as much as possible.
- Match hardware compatibility while buying/installing the server.
- Disable CD-ROM and external disk boot on all the devices.

3.10.2 Security Layer-2: OS and Application Server Security Systems

This layer holds protection of operating system, the application servers, web servers, and mail servers. While traffic is regulated at the perimeter depending on the needs of the organization, the applications utilizing the traffic run on different application and web-servers which in turn run on operating systems. An abuse of operating system privileges can potentially compromise network security. Users with access to the underlying operating system can jeopardize the availability and integrity of the firewall and expose critical network resources to both internal and external security threats. Hardening this layer can protect the network from number of internal threats. Vulnerabilities exist in operating systems, web servers, proxy servers, mail servers and application servers that need patches / service packs / hotfixes to mitigate those weaknesses. An organization may have multiple operating systems in its network. It is the responsibility of the OS vendors to make their products secure. In addition the users in organization also have the responsibility of applying the available security patches and fixes. It is an important issue to make sure that the operating system and application servers are patched with updated releases and appropriate hot fixes.

While different operating systems have their own complexities, there are recommended hardening practices that apply universally. These practices are as below.

a) **Systems clean-up:** Every program is another potential entrance point for a hacker. Attackers look for backdoors and security holes when attempting to compromise systems. Removing unnecessary programs / applications is the best way to reduce the attack surface. Cleaning these out helps organizations limit the number of ways in for an attacker. If the program is not something the company has assessed and "locked down," it shouldn't be allowed within the environment.

b) **Patch Management:** Planning, testing, implementing and auditing patch management software should be part of a regular security regimen. Organizations should make sure the OS is patched regularly, as well as the individual programs on the client's computer. This helps mitigate the known vulnerabilities. Keeping up-to-date and installing the latest versions also helps reduce the attack surface.

c) **Security templates:** Groups of policies that can be loaded in one procedure; they are commonly used in corporate environments. It defines what groups can or can't access and maintain these rules. Organizations should also establish or update user policies and ensure all users are aware and comply with these procedures.

d) **Configuration baselines:** Base lining is the process of measuring changes in networking, hardware, software, etc. Organizations should establish a baselines and measure on a schedule that is acceptable to both organization standards for maintaining security and meeting clients' needs.

3.10.3   Security Layer-3: Host Protection

Along with Perimeter Defense and the OS and Application Security, organizations need to look at another threat from the internal workstations connected to the network. Organizations need to have workstation security for two reasons:

- To protect against someone trying to attack from within the network also known as Insider Threat..
- To protect the data stored on workstation from someone coming in through the firewall.

Some of the key characteristics related to workstation security are listed below.

- Formulate User Access Policy and implement the same.
- Update regularly the patches/hotfixes for the workstation operating system and applications.
- Limit the Network Resources Access from workstations. Assign only what is a "MUST REQUIRED".
- Install Endpoint Security software and update it regularly on all the workstations.
- Ensure Sensitive and critical data on workstation is included in daily nightly backups.
- Allow no modems or other means to connect to internet other than office network on workstations
- If nature of work permits (or if organizations can make it work) allow only one user to login in on each workstation.
- Have as much logging enabled for workstations, as possible.

3.10.4   Security Layer-4: Data/Information Protection

Data protection refers to the practices, safeguards, and binding rules put in place to protect users personal information and ensure that organizations remain in control of it. Data protection should be an integral part of organizations process to ensure compliance with the Data protection standards as well.

3.10.5 Data Protection Methods

Data security refers to the process of protecting data from unauthorized access and data corruption throughout its lifecycle. Data security includes data encryption, hashing, tokenization, and key management practices that protect data across all applications and platforms. The most commonly employed data protection methods are as follows:

1) Risk Assessments: The riskier the data, the more protection it has to be afforded. Sensitive data should be closely guarded, whereas low-risk data can be afforded less protection. The major reason for these assessments is the cost benefit, as better data security equals greater expense. However, it is a good test to determine what data needs to be guarded more closely and makes the whole data processing system more efficient. There are two factors upon which organizations risk assessment should be based: the potential severity in case of a data breach and the probability of a breach. The higher the risk on each of these factors, the more sensitive the data is. These assessments will often require the assistance of a data protection officer (privacy officer) who will help organizations establish valid ground rules. Mischaracterized data, if lost, could prove disastrous.

2) Backups: The purpose of the backup is to create a copy of data that can be recovered in the event of a primary data failure. Primary data failures can be the result of hardware or software failure, data corruption, or a human-caused event, such as a malicious attack (virus or malware), or accidental deletion of data. Backups should be regularly made and updated. Backups should be performed in accordance with the principle explained above – data of low-

importance does not have to be backed up as often, but sensitive data should be backed up regularly. Such backups should be stored in a safe place, and possibly encrypted.

There's also the threat of Ransomware. That's when a hacker puts a malware on organizations computer that encrypts important data, making it useless. Organization may have to pay a ransom in order for the hacker to unencrypt that data, with no guarantee of successful recovery. If current backup of data is available, this is less of a worry. Organizations can just wipe hard drive and restore it to from latest backup.

3) Encryption: Encryption is the act of encoding data to render it unintelligible to someone who doesn't have the authorization to access the data. Once data is encrypted, only authorized parties who have a "key" can read it or use it. That is, if the encryption method is effective, it should completely protect data from unauthorized access. High-risk data is the prime candidate for encryption every step on the way. This includes during acquisition (online cryptographic protocols), processing (full memory encryption) and subsequent storage (RSA or AES). Well-encrypted data is inherently safe; even in cases of a data breach, the data will be useless and irrecoverable to attackers. The key benefit of cloud encryption is that it keeps sensitive data in a read-only state that only authorized parties with access to the necessary keys can decrypt. When data is being stored in the cloud, encryption protects it in the event that a provider, account, or system is compromised.

4) Pseudonymisation: 'Pseudonymisation' means the processing of personal data in such a manner that the personal data can no longer be attributed to a specific data subject without the use of additional information, provided that such additional information is kept separately and is subject to technical and organizational measures

to ensure that the personal data are not attributed to an identified or identifiable natural person. Pseudonymisation is another method advocated in the GDPR that increases data security and privacy of the individuals. It works well with larger sets of data, and consists of stripping identifying information from snippets of data.

Cloud Security.

Traditional network security makes sense when organizations used to have applications that were hosted in the data center and users were all on the same network. But with apps moving to the cloud, and users increasingly becoming mobile, the stacks of appliances sitting in the data center are becoming increasingly irrelevant. The old model forces all traffic through the centralized data center for security and access controls—a complex configuration that could result into a terrible user experience. As organizations increase their use of cloud-based apps, like Salesforce, Box, and Office 365, and move to infrastructures services like Microsoft Azure and Amazon Web Services (AWS), it makes sense to have traffic secured in the cloud as well.

Cloud security, also known as cloud computing security, consists of a set of policies, controls, procedures and technologies that work together to protect cloud-based systems, data, and infrastructure. These security measures are configured to protect cloud data, support regulatory compliance and protect customers' privacy as well as setting authentication rules for individual users and devices. From authenticating access to filtering traffic; cloud security can be configured to the exact needs of the organizations. And because these rules can be configured and managed in one place, administration overheads are reduced and IT teams empowered to focus on other areas of the business. For businesses making the transition to the cloud, robust cloud security is imperative. Security threats are constantly evolving and becoming more sophisticated, and cloud computing is no less at risk than an on-premise environment. For this reason, it is essential to work with a cloud provider that offers best-in-class security that has been customized for organizations infrastructure. Cloud security and security management best practices designed to prevent unauthorized access are required to keep data and applications in the cloud secure from current and emerging Cyber-security threats.

3.10.6   Cloud Computing Categories

Cloud security differs based on the category of cloud computing being used. There are four main categories of cloud computing:

Public cloud services, operated by a public cloud provider — these include

- Software-as-a-Service (SaaS)
- Infrastructure-as-a-Service (IaaS)
- Platform-as-a-Service (PaaS).
- Private cloud services, operated by a public cloud provider — these services provide a computing environment dedicated to one customer, operated by a third party.
- Private cloud services, operated by internal staff — these services are an evolution of the traditional data center, where internal staff operates a virtual environment they control.

- Hybrid cloud services — Private and public cloud computing configurations can be combined, hosting workloads and data based on optimizing factors such as cost, security, operations and access. Operation will involve internal staff, and optionally the public cloud provider.

3.10.7 Cloud Security Threats

Every new technology bring with it new set of challenges. The same is true for cloud computing. Although the Cloud Computing reduces the need for physical security, it does not diminish the need or security completely. There are threats which are equally damaging to the Cloud infrastructure as to the physical or as it's called On Premise infrastructure. Let's look at some of the risks the Cloud Computing has to deal with.

Cloud security has three main vectors.

1) Outsider 2) Insider 3) End User

The Top 5 threats that cloud security needs address are

1) **Malicious Insiders:** This can be employees, former employees, contractors, vendors or business associates who have legitimate access to organizations systems and data, but use that access to destroy data, steal data or sabotage organizations systems. It does not include well-meaning staff that accidentally put users' cyber security at risk or spill data.

2) **Data Breach:** A data breach is an incident that exposes confidential or protected information. A data breach is a security incident in which information is accessed without authorization. Common data breach exposures include personal information, such as credit card numbers, Social Security numbers and healthcare histories, as well as corporate information, such as customer lists, manufacturing processes and software source code.

When it comes to Cloud Security the data breach can occur in two ways.

a.   Media Breach: This is when the physical device, such as hard drive, memory device is stolen, removed without permission.

b.   Man-in-the-Middle: When an attacker is able to intercept the communication in between the clouds service and user.

3) **Data Loss:** Data loss is an error condition in information systems in which information is destroyed by failures (like failed spindle motors or head crashes on hard drives) or neglect (like mishandling, careless handling or storage under unsuitable conditions) in storage, transmission, or processing.

4) **Insufficient Due Diligence:** Organizations migrating to the cloud often perform insufficient due diligence. They move data to the cloud without understanding the full scope of doing so, the security measures used by the Cloud Service Provider, and their own responsibility to provide security measures. They make decisions to use cloud services without fully understanding how those services must be secured.

5) **Account Hijacking:** Cloud account hijacking is a process in which an individual or organization's cloud account is stolen or hijacked by an attacker. Cloud account hijacking is a common tactic in identity theft schemes in which the attacker uses the stolen account information to conduct malicious or unauthorized activity.

Cloud Security Controls: Cloud security involves the procedures and technology that secure cloud computing environments against both external and insider Cyber security threats. Cloud security architecture is effective only if the correct defensive implementations are in place. Efficient cloud security architecture should recognize the issues that will arise with security management. These controls are put in place to safeguard any weaknesses in the system and reduce the effect of an attack. While there are many types of controls behind cloud security architecture, they can usually be found in one of the following categories:

Deterrent controls: These controls are intended to reduce attacks on a cloud system. Much like a warning sign on a fence or a property, deterrent controls typically reduce the threat level by informing potential attackers that there will be adverse consequences for them if they proceed. This is also considered as a subset of preventive controls.

Preventive controls: Preventive controls strengthen the system against incidents, generally by reducing if not actually eliminating vulnerabilities. Strong authentication of cloud users, for instance, makes it less likely that unauthorized users can access cloud systems, and more likely that cloud users are positively identified.

Detective controls: Detective controls are intended to detect and react appropriately to any incidents that occur. In the event of an attack, a detective control will signal the preventative or corrective controls to address the issue. System and network security monitoring, including intrusion detection and prevention arrangements, are typically employed to detect attacks on cloud systems and the supporting communications infrastructure.

Corrective controls: Corrective controls reduce the consequences of an incident, normally by limiting the damage. They come into effect during or after an incident. Restoring system backups in order to rebuild a compromised system is an example of a corrective control.

3.11   DISASTER RECOVERY (DR)

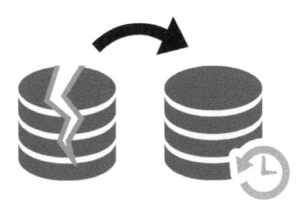

Disaster recovery is an organization's method of regaining access and functionality to its IT infrastructure after events like a natural disaster, cyber-attack, or even business disruptions related to the COVID-19 pandemic. This encompasses the procedures, policies or processes that prepare an organization's vital IT infrastructure to effectively recover from natural or human-induced disasters, and ensure business continuity from cyber-attacks and equipment failure, through natural disasters. A disaster recovery plan (DRP) defines how an organization will respond to any given disaster scenario, with the goal of supporting time-sensitive business processes and functions, and maintaining full business continuity. More specifically, a Disaster Recovery planning needs to anticipate and delineate a plan of action in response to the loss of such mission-critical IT components and services.

Importance of DR Plan: Organizations can't always avoid disasters. The organization may face Theft, Cyber Attack, Natural Disaster, Device failure, Sabotage, Arson etc. Regardless of industry type, when an unforeseen event takes place that brings day-to-day operations of that organization to a halt, organizations' needs to recover as quickly as possible. After all Time is money, the longer Organization takes to recover its normal operations, the higher the losses are going to be. Not having a disaster recovery plan in place can put the organization at risk of high financial costs, reputation loss and even greater risks for its clients and customers. Organization might even have to face regulatory fines due to absence of Disaster recovery Plan. The importance of a disaster recovery plan cannot be overstated.

Organizations that don't currently have a plan in place may recognize the importance of DR but struggle with getting started. Those who have not been affected by unforeseen events and costly unplanned downtime may even think that they are immune from disaster. However, it is better to be prepared since the cost of not having a plan in place can pose serious risks for an organization.

3.11.1   Disaster Recovery Plan Benefits

- Minimizes recovery time & possible delays
- Prevents potential legal liability
- Improves security
- Avoids potentially damaging last-second decision-making during a disaster

Disaster Recovery Measures: This can be classified mainly into three types:

- **Preventive measures:** Preventive measures aim at preventing an event from occurring The first step of any organization is to avoid Disaster by identifying the attack surface and points. Organizations needs to imply measured such as Anti-Virus, Anti-Spam Software. Organization should have a Robust Systems patching routine which should patch software vulnerabilities as they are identified. The network entry points should have Anti-Intrusion Systems. Local Hard drive mirroring (Raid) should also be used. In case of power failure a power backup or an Uninterrupted Power Supply must be kept ready.

- **Detective measures**: Detective measures focus on detecting and discovering negative events. No matter how many preventive measures organizations' may apply, all these measures should be checked for their proper functionality periodically. This is when detective measured comes in picture. This includes automated alarms which include Fire Detection systems, CCTV surveillance Systems, Monitoring software etc.

- **Corrective measures:** Corrective measures are for correcting a system in case of a negative event or disaster. Along with the two measures organizations' should also imply corrective measures such as Offsite Backups, Real-time or periodic offsite data replication and implementation of High availability systems. Organizations should also execute recovery systems to bring back normal functionality after the disaster by implementing following elements of Disaster recovery Plans.

Elements of Disaster Recovery Plan: Disaster recovery relies upon the replication of data and computer processing in an off-premises location not affected by the disaster. When servers go down because of a natural disaster, equipment failure or cyber-attack, a business needs to recover lost data from a second location where the data is backed up.

1) Disaster recovery team: This assigned group of specialists will be responsible for creating, implementing and managing the disaster recovery plan. This plan should define each team member's role and responsibilities. In the event of a disaster, the recovery team should

know how to communicate with each other, employees, vendors, and customers.

2) Risk evaluation: This involves assessing potential hazards that put organization at risk. Depending on the type of event, strategize the measures and resources will be needed to resume business. For example, in the event of a cyber-attack, data protection measures the recovery team have in place to respond.

3) Business-critical asset identification: A good disaster recovery plan includes documentation of which systems, applications, data, and other resources are most critical for business continuity, as well as the necessary steps to recover data.

4) Backups: Determine what needs backup (or to be relocated), who should perform backups, and how backups will be implemented. Include a recovery point objective (RPO) that states the frequency of backups and a recovery time objective (RTO) that defines the maximum amount of downtime allowable after a disaster. These metrics create limits to guide the choice of IT strategy, processes and procedures that make up an organization's disaster recovery plan. The amount of downtime an organization can handle and how frequently the organization backs up its data will inform the disaster recovery strategy.

5) Testing and optimization: The recovery team should continually test and update its strategy to address ever-evolving threats and business needs. By continually ensuring that a company is ready to face the worst-case scenarios in disaster situations, it can successfully navigate such challenges. In planning how to respond to a cyber-attack, for example, it's important that organizations continually test and optimize their security and data protection strategies and have protective measures in place to detect potential security breaches.

3.12 END-USER EDUCATION

For any organization an end-user is a person who ultimately uses or is intended to ultimately use a product or the services. The end user differs from the users who support or maintain the product, such as system administrators, database administrators, information technology experts, software professionals and computer technicians. End users typically do not possess the technical understanding or skill of the product designers. A fact that is easy for designers to forget or overlook leading to features with which the end user is dissatisfied. In information technology, End users are not customers in the usual sense. They are typically employees of the customer. For example if a large retail corporation buys a software package (e.g. Microsoft Office Suite) for its employees to use even though the large retail corporation was the customer who purchased the software, the end users are the employees of the company who will use the software at work.

Importance of End User Training: As technology advances and continues to change with each passing day, so too do the Cyber threats to organizations'. With every new update to software, new technological innovation, new environmental refresh, comes the need to ensure the staff are kept fully up-to-date with the goings-on. Changing technology and software updates not only cause an annoyance, but also create a pitfall for employees which they are unaware of.

What: In order to keep an organization as safe as possible, organizations' must train their employees on Cyber Security. By teaching employees what it is they need to be weary of, they will be able to recognize illegitimate from legitimate emails, phone calls, attachments, links, etc. This provides one extra layer of security on top of any firewalls or antivirus software organizations' may already have in place. And when it comes to protecting organizations' data and business, no security should be too much. Providing the training and raising awareness among staff members about the types of security threats that target them directly, should be at the top of every security investment.

Why: By teaching and training organizations' employees about the threats the organization faces and what those threats are, organization can teach employees why those things are a threat to the organization. Giving employees even a basic understanding about what these are, and how they affect organizations' is a good place to start teaching employees why data protection is important. The training helps turn the employees from a liability into an asset to fight against the Cyber-attacks. A company's IT security is more dependent on its end-users that most realize. With healthcare, finance, biotech, and other industries becoming more dependent on IT solutions, security training needs to be a priority for both managers and employees alike.

How: After teaching employees what to look out for and why, the last step is to teach them how to avoid these problems. This can involve lessons such as how to recognize a spam email, what to do if they find a malicious link or attachment in an email. This can also include reaction measures such as what to do if discover they been hacked, and who to report this issue to. The reality of the matter is that end-user security training will increase organizations' employees' ability to keep the organization secure, keep up with the changes in system updates, company policies, and new threats. By helping the staff members recognize these dangers and handle various security incidents, many cyber-attacks will be circumvented.

Benefits of End User Training: Every company faces financial challenges. As a result of limited budgets, training is typically under-resourced and under-valued. Restricting the educational resources needed to properly manage equipment can greatly harm an organization. The same applies to software. Without proper training, a company reduces their employees' efficiency and, in turn, the organization's return on investment. But when these challenges are compared with the benefits of the training, the choice is obvious. Let's look at the benefits of End user Training –

1) **Employee Efficiency:** As Cyber technology and tools are evolving day by day; the Employees feel frustrated and confused because they can't understand the new technology and frequently get stuck. Many users fall behind as they are not able to use the tools and equipment's effectively. The training helps bridge the gap. The end users are able to use the software more effectively and don't get stuck.

2) **Increased Productivity:** Training sessions elicit conversations that serve as forums for troubleshooting. During these sessions, employees are provided with the opportunity to speak with other professionals in the organization and share ideas on how to use the program more efficiently and solve common problems; increasing productivity. The time wasted understanding the product and its pitfalls, after training, are used productively.

3) **Increased Security:** A well trained end user is less likely to fall victim to the common fishing or social engineering attacks. A trained end user is well prepared to handle and avoid the common pitfalls which the Cyber attacker expects them to fall for. A trained end user is also able to handle security issues. Training turns an End user from a liability into an Asset against the Cyber-attacks.

4) **Empowered Employees:** Group training sessions encourage participation. When trained in groups, employees are more invested and empowered to learn the fundamental skills. Employees can undertake more complex and collaborative tasks. End-user training sessions do not only benefit each individual employee, but are valuable to the entire organization moving forward.

5) **Greater sense of value:** Training gives the user a greater sense of value in the company, which boosts employee morale. The trained employee becomes a respected source of information on the software and is able to help others when needed. Training helps offset work performance gaps by giving employees knowledge they can apply to their software instantaneously. Less valuable time is spent reviewing a manual to figure out how to use the software.

04 FIGHTING CYBER ATTACKS

In modern world Surfing the net has become a natural pastime for everyone who has access to the Internet. Smartphones has made going online easier than ever. Even people who usually do not use computers are using internet on smartphones. Now a day it's next to impossible to find a smartphone without internet access built into it. The amount of penetration smartphone has achieved is significantly higher than computer as people catch up on the latest news, check up on our stock portfolios, or just connect with our social media friends. Every one of us has our favorite places bookmark and the Internet can be a fun place to visit. The Internet is really nothing more than a virtual representation of the real world. The good and evil of the real world can be found online as well. While there are plenty of legitimate websites, blogs and social media sites that can provide users with lots of valuable information and tons of entertainment. There's also a seedy underbelly to the Internet. This is where websites are used for illegal or destructive activity like infecting users' computers with viruses or malware.

4.1 DEFENSE IN DEPTH

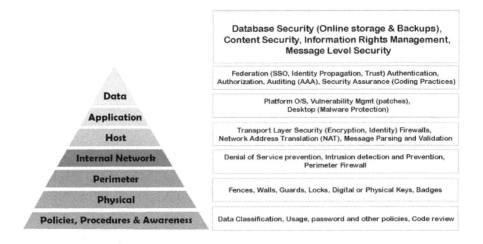

There are threats to every system and several ways an attacker may try to exploit them. In order to secure a system Cyber Security Professionals need to consider defense in depth. The defense in depth principle states that there is no one or even two things that will completely secure a system. The point of this is that if one part of the security solution would have fail then another part should be able to resist the attack. In practice this means applying security in layers. For example organization could have a firewall and maybe an IPS on the edge of the network. Behind the firewall there may a DMZ zone which houses an email scanning service. On the workstation there would be antivirus software. An attacker may try to send some malicious cover through email. The firewall and IPS may not pick this up as email is a valid application. For such threats organization rely on the email scanner. But if that fails to detect the malicious email some reason. In that case organizations' still have the antivirus software on the workstation to fall back on. This is an oversimplified example but it's evident that using the defense in depth strategy reduces the risk of a successful and possibly very expensive security breach. A common security mistake is to rely too heavily on the firewall. All too often people think organizations' have a firewall so it's secure. Unfortunately that's just not true. Firewalls are only a piece of the much larger Cyber security structure. Consider this a simple firewall uses IP addresses and ports to allow or deny traffic. Organizations may want to allow web browsing on the network but is all web browsing traffic secure? An advanced firewall will take it a step further. Organizations can implement things like state-full inspection where it determines if a packet is part of a valid flow of traffic or whether an attacker is trying to slip a packet into the middle of a conversation. An IPS can take this even further and look deeply into the traffic to see if it matches known patterns of attacks. Still this is just the edge of the network. Organizations may go for encrypting traffic with HTTPS, requiring authentication and authorization before accessing secure resources. New security flaws are found regularly. Is the organization patching these flaws in their systems? And of course Cyber Security Professionals need to consider organizations' endpoints, workstations, laptops, phones and any other device that connects to the network. This is where a Cyber Security Professionals think about antivirus host-based firewalls and VPN connections. But we can't consider something to be reasonably secured without considering all aspects of the system. Organizations often think about technical controls like firewalls and antivirus, but what about physical and administrative controls. Cyber Security Professionals need to consider things like the security of the building locking the door to the server room and putting equipment in locked racks or cabinets. Administrative controls these relate to policies and procedures things like background checks for staff identifying the proper way to handle data. So a big part of this is simply educating the users teach them to use strong passwords how to avoid social engineering. How to recognize the threats in general. This is by no means a comprehensive list of everything Cyber Security Professionals need to think about. The key point to take away from this is that security should be applied in layers and these layers are more than just technical controls. Cyber Security Professionals should think about what would happen if a particular layer were to fail and if it does other any other layers there to back it up? Defense in Depth principles help to design the Cyber security architecture in more effective way.

Using more than one of the following layers constitutes an example of defense in depth.

4.1.1 Physical Security

Physical Barriers
- Combination barriers
- Alarm systems and sensors
- Video surveillance
- Access control

4.1.1.1 System/application security:

Antivirus software
- Authentication and password security
- Encryption
- Hashing passwords
- Logging and auditing
- Multi-factor authentication
- Vulnerability scanners
- Timed access control
- Internet Security Awareness Training
- Sandboxing
- Intrusion detection systems (IDS)

4.1.1.2 Network security:

Firewalls (hardware or software)
- Demilitarized zones (DMZ)

- Virtual private network (VPN)
- Physical security

4.1.1.3 Biometrics:

Data-centric security
- Physical security (e.g. deadbolt locks)

The most important thing to understand about defense in depth is that a potential attack should be stopped by several independent methods. This means security solutions must address security vulnerabilities over the life cycle of the system, rather than at one point in time. The increasing sophistication of cyber-attacks means organizations can no longer rely on one security product to protect them. Here is no one layer of security that protects against all cyber threats. Cyber-criminals are becoming increasingly sophisticated in their attacks and organizations need to respond by improving their defense in depth.

Lets look at the these in more detail

Physical Security.

This kind of security refers to the practice of restricting entrance to a property, a building, a room or office Premise. This is the initial layer of security for a campus, building, office, or other physical space designed to deter physical threats. Physical access control can be achieved by a human such as a Security guard, bouncer, or receptionist. It can also be achieved by mechanical means such as locks and keys, turn style, magnetic access card etc. And finally by technological means such as access control systems like the mantrap. These means can also be combined in implement a hybrid Physical access control. Physical security systems for protected facilities are generally intended to deter potential intruders, monitor/record activities of intruders and trigger appropriate incident responses.

Physical barriers such as fences, walls, and vehicle barriers act as the outermost layer of physical security. Tall fencing, topped with barbed wire, razor wire or metal spikes are often emplaced on the perimeter of a property, generally with some type of signage that warns people not to attempt entry. Mechanical means such as locks and keys becomes a problem with large user populations and any user turnover. Keys quickly become unmanageable, often forcing the adoption of electronic access control. Electronic access control helps to manages large user populations, controlling for user life cycles times, dates, and individual access points. These access control systems are often interfaced with turnstiles for entry control in buildings to prevent unauthorized access. The use of turnstiles also reduces the need for additional security personnel to monitor each individual entering the building allowing faster throughput. Surveillance cameras such as CCTV cameras are placed in highly visible locations and are useful for incident assessment and historical analysis. Video monitoring does not necessarily guarantee a human response. A human must be monitoring the situation in real time in order to respond in a timely manner; otherwise, video monitoring is simply a means to gather evidence for later analysis.

Alarm systems can be implemented if any one of the physical means of security is breached. The alarm can be set to notify the security personals about the breach. The alarm system can also trigger siren or lights to deter the intruder in case any security is breached.

4.1.2 Access control Policy

Access control is a method of guaranteeing that users are who they say they are and that they have the appropriate access to company data. At a high level, access control is a selective restriction of access to data. It consists of two main components: authentication and authorization. Authentication is a technique used to verify that someone is who they claim to be. Authentication isn't sufficient by itself to protect data. Authorization provides an additional layer of security. Without authentication and authorization, there is no data security. The access control policy outlines the controls placed on both physical accesses to the computer system (that is, having locked access to where the system is physically present) and to the software in order to limit access to computer networks and data. Access control policies provide details on controlling access to information and systems. Most security professionals understand how critical access control is to their organization. A sophisticated access control policy can be adapted dynamically to respond to evolving risk factors, enabling an organization that's been breached to isolate the relevant employees and data resources to minimize the damage. Access control mechanisms can take many forms. Perimeter barrier devices are often first considered when securing a network. Firewalls in the form of packet filters, proxies, and state-full inspection devices are all helpful agents in permitting or denying specific traffic through the network.

Types of access control: Organizations must determine the appropriate access control model to adopt based on the type and sensitivity of data they're processing.

Discretionary access control (DAC): With DAC models, the data owners decide on access. DAC is a means of assigning access rights based on rules that are specified by the Data owners.

Mandatory access control (MAC): MAC was developed using a non-discretionary model, in which people are granted access based on an information clearance. MAC is a policy in which access rights are assigned based on regulations from a central authority. Data owners' suggestions and advice is taken into consideration, but the primary role of decision of access rights is up to central authority. Data owner can also be a part of this central authority.

Role Based Access Control (RBAC): RBAC grants access based on a user's role and implements key security principles, such as "least privilege" and "separation of privilege." Thus, someone attempting to access information can only access data that's deemed necessary for their role.

Attribute Based Access Control (ABAC): In ABAC, each resource and user are assigned a series of attributes. In this dynamic method, a comparative assessment of the user's attributes, including time of day, position and location, are used to make a decision on access to a resource.

4.2 AUTHENTICATION

Authentication is the process of recognizing a user's identity. It's the process of determining whether someone or something is, in fact, who or what it declares itself to be. It is the mechanism of associating an incoming request with a set of identifying credentials. Authentication technology provides access control for systems by checking to see if a user's credentials match the credentials in a database of authorized users or in a data authentication server. The credentials provided are compared to those on a file in a database of the authorized user's information on a local operating system or with an authentication server. Authentication is important because it enables organizations to keep their resources secure by permitting only authenticated users (or processes) to access its protected resources, which may include computer systems, networks, databases, websites and other network-based applications or services.

The authentication process always runs at the start of the application, before the permission and throttling checks occur, and before any other code is allowed to proceed. Different systems may require different types of credentials to ascertain a user's identity. The credential often takes the form of a password, which is a secret and known only to the individual and the system. Three categories in which someone may be authenticated are: something the user knows, something the user is, and something the user has.

Authentication process can be described in two distinct phases - identification and actual authentication. Identification phase provides a user identity to the security system. This identity is provided in the form of a user ID. The security system will search all the abstract objects that it knows and find the specific one of which the actual user is currently applying. Once this is done, the user has been identified. The fact that the user claims does not necessarily mean that this is true. An actual user can be mapped to other abstract user object in the system, and therefore be granted rights and permissions to the user and user must give evidence to prove his identity to the system. The process of determining claimed user identity by checking user-provided evidence is called authentication and the evidence which is provided by the user during process of authentication is called a credential.

Once authenticated, a user or process is usually subjected to an authorization process as well, to determine whether the authenticated entity should be permitted access to a protected resource or system. A user can be authenticated but fail to be given access to a resource if that user was not granted permission to access it.

How it is used: User authentication is performed in almost all human-to-computer interactions other than guest and automatically logged in accounts. Authentication authorizes human-to-machine interactions on both wired and wireless networks to enable access to network and Internet connected systems and resources. Users are usually identified with a user ID, and authentication is accomplished when the user provides a credential, for example a password, that matches with that user ID. Most users are most familiar with using a password, which, as a piece of information that should be known only to the user, is called a knowledge authentication factor. Other authentication factors and how they are used for two-factor or multifactor authentication (MFA).

How it works: User authentication is the verification of an active human-to-machine transfer of credentials required for confirmation of a user's authenticity. User authentication is a security process that covers all of the human-to-computer interactions that require the user to register and log in. Said more simply, authentication asks each user, "Who are you?" and verifies their response.

When a user registers for an account, they must create a unique ID and key that will allow them to access their account later on. Generally, a username and password are used as the ID and key, but the credentials can include other forms of keys as well. In order to gain access, users must prove to the Authenticator that they are who they say they are. The ID and key are enough to confirm the user's identity, which will allow the system to authorize the user.

Generally speaking authentication has three tasks:

Manage the connection between the human (user) and the physical server (computer).

- Verify users' identities.
- Approve (or decline) the authentication so the system can move to authorizing the user.

The process is fairly simple; users input their credentials. That information is then sent to the authentication server where the information is compared with all the user's credentials on file. When a match is found, the system will authenticate users and grant them access to their accounts. If a match isn't found, users will be prompted to re-enter their credentials and try again. After several unsuccessful attempts, the account may be flagged for suspicious activity or require alternative authentication methods such as a password reset or a one-time password.

However, the web's application protocols, HTTP and HTTPS, are stateless, meaning that strict authentication would require end users re-authenticate each time they access a resource using HTTPS. Rather than burden end users with that process for each interaction over the web, protected systems often rely on token-based authentication, in which authentication is performed once at the start of a session. The authenticating system issues a signed authentication token to the end-user application, and that token is appended to every request from the client.

Authentication Server: An authentication server is an application that facilitates authentication of an entity that attempts to access a network. Such an entity may be a human user or another server. An authentication server can reside in a dedicated computer, an Ethernet switch, an access point or a network access server. An authentication server is a database that stores user credentials—username and password—and typically group and attribute information. When a user signs in to the host, the user specifies an authentication realm, which is associated with an authentication server. The system forwards the user's credentials to this authentication server to verify the user's identity.

An authentication server supports the most common authentication servers, including Windows NT Domain, Active Directory, RADIUS, LDAP, NIS, RSA ACE/Server, SAML Server, and eTrust SiteMinder, and enables organizations' to create one or more local databases of users who are authenticated. The system is preconfigured with one local authentication server for users called "System Local." This predefined local authentication server is a system database that enables organizations' to quickly create user accounts for user authentication. This ability provides flexibility for testing purposes and for providing third-party access by eliminating the need to create user accounts in an external authentication server.

Authentication is the process of determining whether someone or something is actually who or what it declares itself to be. When a potential subscriber accesses an authentication server, a username and password may be the only identifying data required. In a more sophisticated system called Kerberos, the subscriber must request and receive an encrypted security token that can be used to access a particular service. RADIUS (Remote Authentication Dial-In User Service) is a commonly used authentication method. TACACS+ (Terminal Access Controller Access Control System Plus) is similar to RADIUS but is used with Unix networks. RADIUS employs UDP (User Datagram Protocol) and TACACS+ employs TCP (Transmission Control Protocol).

4.2.1 Authentication Factors

Knowledge: This factors include all things a user must know in order to log in, User names or ID password and pin numbers all fall under this category. To withdraw the money from ATM machines the card holder must know the Pin Number of the card.

Possession: This factor consist of anything a user must have in their possession in order to log in; this category includes access cards, one-time password tokens, or smartphone apps, employee ID cards and SIM card-based mobile phones etc.

Inherence: This include any inherent traits the user has that are confirmed to identity; this category includes the biometrics features of user such as: Retina scans, Iris scans, Fingerprint scans, facial recognition, voice recognition. Now days these features are also present in most modern Cell Phones.

Supplemental Authentication Factors: These three factors correspond to the knowledge factor, the possession factor and the inherence factor. Additional factors have been proposed and put into use in recent years. Adding more than one authentication factor to the login or transaction typically improves security. The above three factors can be and sometimes manipulated. In order to impose additional factors which a Cyber attacker cannot manipulate can be introduced to improve authentication security. These factors are called as Supplemental Authentication Factors. There are as below.

Location: User location is sometimes considered a fourth factor for authentication. Now days most smartphones are equipped with GPS, enabling reasonable surety confirmation of the login location.

Time: This factor consist of "When user is authenticating." Like the location factor, the time factor is not sufficient on its own, but it can be a supplemental mechanism for weeding out attackers who attempt to access a resource at a time when that resource is not available to the authorized user.

Device: In most organizations' users are given company assets, such as Laptops, desktops, Tablet PCs, Smart phones etc. The users are expected to use these devices only to access the organizations' resources. The Authentication mechanism can be designed to allow the users log in from these devices only. The MAC address / Physical address present on the assets can also be used as a Supplemental Authentication Factors. Any attempt to log into Organizations network from any other asset other than allotted asset can be blocked using the Device ID.

The reliability of authentication is affected not only by the number of factors involved but also the specific technologies and the manner in which they are implemented. Well-designed and appropriately enforced implementation rules can help ensure the security of user authentication.

Single Sign On (SSO): Although Authentication is important process but it is also important not to overburden users with difficult authentication routines, which can lead to non-compliance that undermines the purpose. Organizations also use authentication to control which users have access to corporate networks and resources, as well as to identify and control which machines and servers have access. Companies also use authentication to enable remote employees to securely access their applications and networks. But once logged in; the user may need to access various resources / services to do his work. Such as Email, Instant messaging, file servers, print servers, Intranet, file servers etc. Forcing user to authenticate at every step can overwhelm and frustrate the user. To avoid this in large organizations, authentication may be accomplished using a single sign-on (SSO) system, which grants access to multiple systems with a single set of login credentials.

Single-Factor Authentication (SFA): Single-factor authentication is the simplest form of authentication methods. With SFA, a person matches one credential to verify himself or herself online. The most popular example of this would be a password (credential) to a username. Most verification today uses this type of authentication method. The traditional user authentication process for accessing computer resources. With single-factor authentication, only one category of credentials is specified, for example, username and password.

While single factor authentication is commonly used in web-emails, this Cyber-security measure is also common as a perceived defensive measure in protecting endpoints – devices such as desktops and laptops that connect to a computer network and communicates with the network resources.

One-factor authentications typically consist of passwords and passphrases, yet in recent years have also come to include biometric authentication. Most work-related activities, including emails and building access, are only set up for single-factor authentication, which isn't ideal as this tends to be the least secure option.

Risks of Single-factor Authentication: The biggest challenge with the SFA is the password. Most of the users either don't understand how to make strong and memorable passwords or underestimate the need for security. There are two major mistakes users do which makes the Single-factor Authentication weaker than it inherently is. The first one being **Simple Password**. Passwords are inherently flawed, users rely on memory; therefor they will underestimate the need for higher security choosing simple passwords that can be easily guessed or social engineered. As computing power becomes increasingly available at affordable prices, attackers find it easier to break into accounts through brute-force methods, such as testing every possible combination in super-rapid succession to find the right password. To avoid being brute-forced, users must choose passwords that are longer and more complex, containing lower- and upper-case letters, digits and symbols. Users should also change their passwords regularly. This puts a lot of strain on users, especially when they must make the same considerations for dozens of online accounts. A lot of users avoid taking such measures. Year after year, studies find that such as "123456," "password" and other poor passwords remain extremely popular.

Second most common mistake users make is to reuse the same password across multiple accounts, which is also known as **Password Reuse.** One of the recommendations any Cyber security expert will give is to avoid reusing passwords across multiple accounts. However, when users must maintain long and complex passwords across several accounts, they tend to reuse their passwords with small or with no variations at all. When hackers find the password to an account, they can quickly gain access to other accounts that use a similar password. Password-based security may be adequate to protect systems that don't require high levels of security but even in those cases, constraints should be enforced to make them reasonably stringent. And for any system that needs high security, stronger authentication methods should be used.

Single-Factor Authentication isn't necessarily weak. Multiple challenge response questions can make for secure SFA authentication when properly implemented. Many biometric authentication methods, for example, are strong when properly implemented. Biometrics can often make for secure SFA so long as the right kinds and implementations are chosen. Retina scans, finger vein scans and voice recognition are good candidates. One must be doubly sure about the biometric scanner and its implementation when it is a standalone SFA solution rather than one component of MFA. Now a day's many cellphone devices incorporate biometric authentication such as Fingerprint scan or Facial recognition. However, biometric verification systems may require a significant outlay for enterprise deployment. Depending on the degree of security required, it may be preferable to implement multifactor authentication.

4.2.2   Two-Factor Authentication (TFA)

Sometimes called 2-step verification or dual factor authentication. Two-Factor Authentication is a security process to better protect users and resources by asking users to verify identity in two ways. This process is done to better protect both the user's credentials and the resources the user can access. There are several ways to do this. Most common is a knowledge factor or something the user knows like a password, pin.

Security question or some other shared secret. A possession factor is something the user has such as an ID card, security token or mobile device. An inherent factor or biometric factor is something physically inherent in the user like fingerprints or facial or voice recognition. Location factors and time factors are less common methods. Two-factor authentication requires two factors from two different categories. For example a locked email account might ask security questions or knowledge factors and then send a code to a mobile device or other email account on record; a possession factor. Similarly when facial-recognition a biometric factor fails on users' mobile device it typically asks for a pin code and not a fingerprint which would be another biometric factor. Two-Factor Authentication is much more secure than single factor authentication. Especially considering most single factor services are password based. Two-factor authentication provides a higher level of security than authentication methods that depend on single-factor authentication (SFA), in which the user provides only one factor - typically, a password or passcode.

Two-factor authentication adds an additional layer of security to the authentication process by making it harder for attackers to gain access to a person's devices or online accounts because knowing the victim's password alone is not enough to pass the authentication check. The vast majority of two-factor authentication methods rely on the three authentication factors. Knowledge, Possession and inherence, though systems requiring greater security may use them to implement multifactor authentication (MFA), which can rely on two or more independent credentials for more secure authentication.

Setting up Two-Factor Authentication: The user needs to sign up / provide the necessary details to the authenticator before the Two-Factor authentication system can be activated. When user signs up for two-factor authentication for a website or a service, user generally provide his mobile phone number, which is one of the most common two factor authentication mode used in general. If biometric systems are used in the two factor authentication mode then the user may be asked to scan his Retina, Iris, Fingerprint, Face scan. Etc. These details are then stored in the Authentication Server for later use.

Most forms of two-factor authentication ask users to sign in with username and password, and then enter a code that is sent to user's phone via SMS. This method is used by banking websites, shopping websites, such as Amazon, Flipcart and webmail services like Gmail. This method not only proves that user know something (the username and password), but also that user have something (the mobile phone), which user have "registered" as a device to receive these codes.

How does two-factor authentication work? Here's how the process breaks down step-by-step:

1. The user is prompted to log in by the website or application.
2. The user enters what they know. This is usually a traditional username and password combo. The site's server finds a match and recognizes the user. This step relies on the knowledge factor.
3. For processes that don't require passwords, the website generates a unique security key for the user. The authentication tool processes the key, and the authentication server validates it.
4. The site then prompts the user to initiate the second login step. Although this step can take a number of forms, users have to prove that they have something only they would have, such as a security token, ID card, smartphone or other mobile device. This step relies on the possession factor.
5. Then, the user enters a one-time code that was generated during step four. Some services use additional security measure such as time

factor where in the user has to enter the password within 30 seconds or a minute. Failing to do so will take the user back to first step.

6. After providing both factors, the user is authenticated and granted access to the application or website.

Two-Factor Authentication Products: Most two-factor authentication solutions have multiple options, such as using hardware tokens, software tokens or token-less authentication by utilizing SMS mobile phone technology. Two-factor authentication products can be divided into two categories: tokens that are given to users to use when logging in and infrastructure or software that recognizes and authenticates access for users who are using their tokens correctly. Authentication tokens may be A security token (or sometimes a hardware token, authentication token, USB token, cryptographic token, software token, virtual token, or key fob) may be a physical device that an authorized user of computer services is given to ease authentication. Examples are RSA Token, Symantec VIP Token.

Hard Tokens: A core feature of hard tokens is a screen for inputting and requesting access. This action can be done through an authentication code, biometric data, fingerprints, cryptographic keys or a secure PIN. The types of tokens used can include USB tokens, Bluetooth tokens, smart cards and more. In general, hard tokens are small and designed to be easily carried on a keychain or in a pocket or purse. Other types of hard tokens include connected tokens, which need a physical connection to automatically connect or transfer data and require host input services installed on the intended device. USB tokens and smart cards are common connected tokens that are still popular today. Disconnected tokens are the most common types of hard tokens. They require two-factor authentication, usually including a PIN, before allowing access. While disconnected tokens don't need to be plugged into their intended device, authentication is manually entered through a small screen on the token itself.

Soft Tokens: Soft tokens don't so much have "types" in the same sense as hard tokens, as they perform a variety of authentication options based on the program or app organizations' choose for their authentication method. This process usually incorporates two or more steps to ensure maximum security, and can include one-time passwords that last a limited time (often associated with RSA SecurID soft tokens, which allow for approximately one minute before generating a new one-time password to use). Authentication codes can also be sent to users' smartphone or other connected device, or even use biometric data. While the hardware-based systems are more secure, they are also costly and difficult to deploy on a large scale. A smartphone soft token app performs the same task as a hardware-based security token. Like a hardware token, a smartphone provides an easy-to-protect and easy-to-remember location for secure login information on the device itself. Unlike a hardware token, smartphones are connected devices, which make them inherently less secure. Examples of Software Token are: Microsoft Authenticator, Symantec Validation and ID Protection Service (VIP), CA Strong Authentication, Okta Verify etc.

Hard vs Soft Tokens: Hard tokens, while considered incredibly secure, do have their downsides. Carrying a small physical "key" for access can lead to problems if it gets lost, for example. Also, hardware token batteries have a limited life and cannot be recharged, with the typical lifespan being between three and five years. For small businesses, this expense can add up: after all, hard tokens, being a physical object, are a monetary investment in terms of their procurement. Soft tokens have some benefits and drawbacks worth considering as well. Soft tokens tend to rely on apps on devices such as smartphones to work, so users have to make sure to always have their phone with them when they want to use these devices. Smartphone batteries tend to die much faster than hard token batteries. Another consideration is the price. While hard tokens have come a long way in both convenience and security, they're an investment and may not be the most convenient for small businesses. However, that price gets organizations' high-quality security and reliability without the security concerns of hacked devices or compromised software. Soft tokens, on the other hand, are usually free to use and compensate for potential security issues through multi-factor authentication methods that are often time-based.

When choosing the "Type" of token one has several considerations to keep in mind: price, ease of use and confidentiality. For little to no cost, a simple SMS authentication or RSA soft token is the way to go, especially if there's not much need for securing private data. However, if the need for security of confidential information is high, contactless hard tokens are easily the best bet, as they do not store any of the user's data and are not subject to hacking. If organization are considering the use of biometric information in security tokens, then that is quite costly to implement, though worth it if the organization handles highly sensitive information. In many cases, two-factor authentication is a reliable solution for accessing software as needed. However, in case one or both authentication factors are compromised, a hard token backup is very secure and reliable.

4.2.3   Multi Factor Authentication

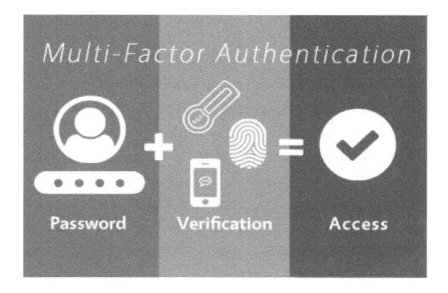

Multi -factor authentication is mainly used in businesses and government agencies that require high degrees of security. The use of at least one element from each category is required for a system to be considered multi-factor authentication. It is important to know that the reliability of authentication is affected not only the number of factors involved but also how they are implemented. The factors includes the following:

- Something user is – Finger Print, Retina or Iris Scan, Face recognition, voice recognition.
- Something user has – Hard Token, Access / Smart card, USB Authentication token.
- Something user know – Password, Pin number.
- Something user do – Signature, hand writing pattern, wipe stroke on cell phone,
- Somewhere user is – Location (GPS), Time-zone

Multi-Factor Authentication or MFA is an approach to protecting users login credentials that requires the presentation of two or more of the three independent authentication factors. A knowledge factor-something only the user knows. A possession factor- something only the user has. And an Inherence Factor-something only the user is. The most popular form of multi-factor authentication is two-factor authentication which is used by online services like Gmail, Steam, and Amazon. The three factors are pretty clearly defined. Knowledge factors include pin codes; personal questions like users' mother's maiden name, passwords and swipe tap or lock patterns like those on smartphone lock screens. Possession factors are physical items like an identification card that one would swipe to access secure areas of a building or a USB Drive with an encryption key on it that decrypts the protected folder on a computer. Though for the most part possession factors are being eliminated and replaced by smartphone features and apps. Making users smartphone users possession factor. Inherence factors are also known as biometric identifiers. There are relatively new form of authentication and include face recognition, fingerprint scans, voice prints and Iris and retinal scans.

Now there's no doubt that biometric authentication factors are very robust and quickly being pushed into the mainstream; they're also meeting a fair bit of resistance and for good reason. One issue is that biometric information can be easily repeated once compromised. Second reason is that many individuals object to having their biometric information tracked and stored in a database. This seems like a fairly valid concern, given the amount of secure data that gets compromised on a daily basis. Unlike a password user can't run around changing their fingerprints, retinas or other biometric features.

Logging in by combining a knowledge factor like password with a possession factor like a physical key or a code sent to smartphone makes account much more difficult to target for online attacks. Let's think Gmail's two-factor authentication as an example even. If a Cyber Criminal obtains users password with a key logger or a security question exploit, Google will require the entry of a six digit code that they send to user that must be entered within a couple of minutes. Something that hijacker can't get without users smartphone. On top of that if someone tries to log-in with the correct password that notification will go straight to user and user will immediately know that someone is trying to access his/her account without permission.

Authentication vs Authorization: Although both the terms sound similar, they refer to entirely different security processes. The scope of customer identity and access management (CIAM), authentication verifies a user's identity, while authorization validates if the user has access to perform a specific function. Authentication is identifying users by confirming who they say they are, while authorization is the process of establishing the rights and privileges of a user. Both processes play equally important roles in securing sensitive data assets from breaches and unauthorized access.

Authentication: Authentication is the process of identifying users and validating who they claim to be. One of the most common and obvious factors to authenticate identity is a password. If the user name matches the password credential, it means the identity is valid, and the system grants access to the user. To improve the security organizations' many use modern authentication techniques like One-Time Passcodes (OTP) via SMS, or Email, Single Sign-In (SSO), Multi-Factor Authentication (MFA) and biometrics, etc. to authenticate users and deploy security beyond what passwords usually provide.

Authorization: Authorization happens after a user's identity has been successfully authenticated. It is about offering full or partial access rights to resources like database, network resource, and other critical information to get the work done. In an organization, for example, after an employee is verified and confirmed via ID and password authentication, the next step would be defining what resources the employee would have access to.

4.2.4 Authentication Techniques

Password-based authentication: is a simple method of authentication that requires a password to verify the user's identity.

- **Password-less authentication**: is where a user is verified through OTP or Access/ Smart Card or Token.
- **2FA/MFA:** This requires more than one security level, like an additional PIN or security question, to identify a user and grant access to a system.
- **Biometric:** This requires users' physical characteristics such as Finger Print, Retina / Iris Scan, Voice recognition etc.
- **Single sign-on (SSO):** allows users to access multiple applications with a single set of credentials.
- **Role-based Access Controls (RBAC)** can be implemented for system-to-system and user-to-system privilege management.
- **JSON web token (JWT)** is an open standard for securely transmitting data between parties, and users are authorized using a public/private key pair.
- **SAML** (Security Assurance Markup Language) is a standard Single Sign-On format (SSO) where authentication information is exchanged through XML documents that are digitally signed.
- **OpenID Authorization** verifies user identity based on an authorization server's authentication.
- **OAuth** allows the API to authenticate and access the requested system or resource.

4.2.5 Biometric

Modern Cyber security is focused on reducing the risks for this powerful security solution: traditional passwords have long been a point of weakness for security systems. Biometrics is biological measurements or physical characteristics that can be used to identify individuals. Physical characteristics are relatively fixed and individualized even in the case of twins. Each person's unique biometric identity can be used to replace or at least supplement password systems. Once biometric data is obtained and mapped, it is then saved to be matched with future attempts at access. Most of the time, this data is encrypted and stored within the device or in a remote server. Biometrics scanners are hardware used to capture the biometric for verification of identity. These scans match against the saved database to approve or deny access to the system. In other words, biometric security means users' body becomes the "key" to unlock users' access.

Biometrics aims to answer this issue by linking proof-of-identity to users' bodies and behavior patterns. Biometrics is physical or behavioral human characteristics to that can be used to digitally identify a person to grant access to systems, devices or data. Examples of these biometric identifiers are fingerprints, facial patterns, Retina or iris, voice or typing rhythm. Each of these identifiers is considered unique to the individual, and they may be used in combination to ensure greater accuracy of identification.

Types of biometrics: The two main types of biometric identifiers are either Physiological Characteristics or Behavioral Characteristics.

4.2.5.1 Physiological Characteristics:

- Fingerprints: Every human being is born with a unique set of finger prints. These are used to identify a user.
- Iris: The Iris is a thin, annular structure in the eye, responsible for controlling the diameter and size of the pupil.
- Blood Veins: Vein matching, also called vascular technology, is a technique of biometric identification through the analysis of the patterns of blood vessels visible from the surface of the skin.
- Retina: The blood vessels within the retina absorb light more readily than the surrounding tissue and are easily identified with appropriate lighting.
- Face: facial recognition system uses biometrics to map facial features such as shape and distance between eyes, nose and lips, ears, eyebrows etc. and save them digitally for later reference.
- Finger Geometry: Hand geometry readers measure a user's hand along many dimension, size and shape of gingers, nails etc.
- Ear Shape: Users Ear Shape, its curve segments and other ear morphology.
- DNA (Deoxyribo Nucleic Acid): Within human cells, DNA found in the nucleus of the cell. DNA is variable repetitive coding unique to an individual.

4.2.5.2 Behavioral Characteristics:

Hand writing: Similar to finger prints, every user's hand writing is unique and can be used to identify the user.

- Signature: This is the most common type of Hand writing technique used almost all the banks.
- Voice: The sophisticated statistical algorithm after recording and analyzing the voice of many distinctive characteristics creates a voiceprint or biometric model.
- Keystroke Dynamic: This uses the manner and rhythm in which an individual types characters on a keyboard or keypad
- Gait: This is based on the notion that each person has a distinctive and idiosyncratic way of walking, which can easily be discerned from a biomechanics viewpoint.
- Gesture: Utilizing sensors that detect body motion, gesture recognition makes it possible to control devices such as televisions, computers and video games, primarily with hand or finger movement

4.2.5.3 Pros of using Biometrics:

1. Biometrics is extremely hard to fake. A biometric property such as a fingerprint or an eye scanner is unique by definition for each individual.
2. Biometrics are stable and enduring, which means it changes very little over the course of one's life and can identify a person in spite of little variation over time.
3. The biometric servers usually require very less database memory, as the templates use small storage.
4. Biometric credentials are non-transferable like passwords and cannot be separated from the user.
5. Biometrics provides strong authentication and accountability, which someone cannot later renounce or reprobate having taken an action.

4.2.5.4 Cons of using Biometrics:

1. Major drawback is the high cost which is involved in getting the systems up and running and also storing and maintaining the biometrics.

2. Integration of Biometric Authentication into the security program is relatively complex when compared to the deployment of password-based solutions.

3. The process by which the biometric is captured and mapped to an identity. Lack of accuracy in capturing, partial capture of data and binding can lead to failure of the system.

4. Biometric systems are not yet standardized as compared to other authentication systems. Errors in biometric devices i.e. false rejects and false accept. The false accept is a scenario in which the device accepts an unauthorized person, and the false reject is the scenario in which the device falsely rejects an authorized person.

5. User acceptance is a significant challenge, especially if individuals are uncomfortable with the idea of biometrics and see the technology as privacy invasive.

Biometrics - Identity & Privacy Concerns: Biometric authentication is convenient, but privacy advocates fear that biometric security erodes personal privacy. The concern is that personal data could be collected easily and without consent. When someone steals users' password, user may be notified to change it. This can be done repeatedly until user have strong enough password that won't be hacked. Unfortunately, with biometrics, if a hacker steals users' information, it cannot be altered. This means, cyber criminals will have it forever and user remain vulnerable indefinitely. User cannot change his fingerprint or eye scan like he can with his email password.

4.2.6 Passwords

A password, sometimes also called a passcode. Passwords have been used since ancient times. Sentries would challenge those wishing to enter an area to supply a password or watchword, and would only allow a person or group to pass if they knew the password. Passwords in military use evolved to include not just a password, but a password and a counter-password.

Passwords have been used with computers since the earliest days of computing. Password may be the first thing a user gets to know then they start using a computer. Although there are currently many forms of authentication methods, such as biometric and smartcard, still the most common method for authentication is the combination of user ID (identification) and password (authentication). The Compatible Time-Sharing System (CTSS), an operating system introduced at MIT in 1961, was the first computer system to implement password login. In modern times, usernames and passwords are commonly used by people for almost everything from banking to watching television to even on coffee maker of IoT devices.

4.2.6.1 Password Security Attacks and Remedy:

- **Brute Force:** Using a program to generate likely passwords or even random character sets. These attacks start with commonly used, weak passwords like Password123 and move on from there. The programs running these attacks usually try variations on upper and lowercase characters, as well.

> ➢ **Remedy:** To block or to avoid this kind of attacks most Authentication system limit the attempts a user enter incorrect password. Usually after three attempts the account gets locked and needs to be locked using backup method of authentication. Some systems block the account for limited period of time.

- **Key Logger:** A cyber-criminal manages to install software that tracks the user's keystrokes, enabling the criminal to gather not only the username and password for an account but exactly which website or app the user was logging into with the credentials.

  > ➢ **Remedy:** Now a day banking websites offer a Virtual Keyboard. The user can enter his Username and passwords without using the physical keyboard.

- **Dictionary Attack:** People tend to use common words and short passwords because its easy to remember. The hacker uses a list of common words, the dictionary, and tries them, often with numbers before and/or after the words, against accounts in a company for each username.

  > ➢ **Remedy:** The easy way to avoid this kind of attack is not to use common words for passwords. The password can be a combination of letters, numbers and Special characters.

- **Traffic Interception:** In this attack, the cyber-criminal uses software such as packet sniffers to monitor network traffic and capture passwords as they're passed from users to authentication server or system. Similar to eavesdropping or tapping a phone line, the sniffer software monitors and captures critical information.

  > ➢ **Remedy:** This attack works only when the username and password are sent over the network unencrypted. An encrypted username and password are difficult to decipher.

- **Man In the Middle:** In this attack, the hacker's program doesn't just monitor information being passed but actively inserts itself in the middle of the interaction, usually by impersonating a website or app. This allows the program to capture the user's credentials and other sensitive information, such as account numbers, social security numbers, etc. Man in the middle (MITM) attacks is often facilitated by social engineering attacks which lure the user to a fake site.
  - ➢ **Remedy:** Only way to avoid this kind of attack is by being careful. A user must ensure that he is providing his credentials to the valid portal / website.
- **Social Engineering Attacks:** A social engineering attack refers to a broad range of methods to obtain information from users.
  - ➢ **Phishing**—Emails, texts, etc. sent to fool users into providing their credentials, clicking a link that installs malicious software, or going to a fake website.
  - ➢ **Spear phishing**—Similar to phishing but with better crafted, tailored emails/texts which rely on information already gathered about the users. For example, the hacker may know that the user has a particular type of insurance account and reference it in the email or use the company's logo and layout to make the email seem more legitimate.
  - ➢ **Baiting**—Attackers leave infected USBs or other devices in public or employer locations in the hopes they will be picked up and used by employees.
  - ➢ **Quid quo pro**—The cyber-criminal impersonates someone, like a helpdesk employee, and interacts with a user in a way that requires getting information from them.

4.2.7 Password Manager

The problems with a password are obvious: the login system was first designed for time-sharing computers in the 1960s, working on mainframes that took up an entire lab. To use the computer, users tapped in their login name and password, which told the computer who was sitting at the terminal and which files to make available. Stealing someone's password was good for a practical joke, but not much else: there was only one computer where users could use it, and not much personal information on display once someone broke into these computers.

Passwords are almost universally used as the primary means of authenticating the identity of a person for computer systems or applications. Security issues are particularly difficult to deal with because they are an annoyance to the user. Users just want to get at the tools and data they want to get the job done, but instead organizations' have to build barriers between the user and the application. Users must prove their identities. Systems can't trust any data they provide unless it's been thoroughly sanitized. Too short, too complex, too frequently used, too many to remember: There are many numbers of problems with passwords. In older days the user used to have only few passwords. Mostly Email, Banking and one or two social media platforms. Now days; one reason passwords are awful is that there are so many of them. Now day's users have to use password for almost every piece of technology. A password manager company, found in a survey that a user have an average of 130 accounts with passwords. Another big issue with the passwords is finding the perfect password is difficult, as it requires a unique balance of "easy to remember" and "hard to hack." And then the user have to find that sweet spot over and over again. A user on average has to enter the password 20 to 25 passwords or different portals on daily basis. A user is expected to use complicated passwords, combination of Uppercase, lower case special characters and numbers too. It is humanly very difficult if not impossible to remember all the passwords. As a result of this complexity because people to reuse their complex passwords or refuse to change them once they've committed them to memory. Many users tend to write down their passwords on either piece of paper or on a file in computer. In both the cases the chances of these passwords getting stolen are significantly high. The real purpose of a password security system is to try and make the user's life easy whilst making the attacker's life difficult. Password security systems that ignore the user are going to fail with the very community they are supposed to serve.

Password Fatigue: This is the stress that users experience due to stringent requirements to create, re-enters, remember and change a large number of passwords. Sometime, organizations' implement highly specific password requirements that force users to go through laborious process to create a complex password. Users find it particularly difficult to use mixed case passwords. Disturbing a user's during his work flow to ask them to change their password due to password expiry, results in user frustration and leads to weak or forgotten passwords. Same goes with Session expiry. A user's session times out while user is working and then they need to log back in to continue their work. The stress and fatigue caused by all this is referred as a Password Fatigue. This is one of the major reasons for users choosing to use simple, easy to guess / break password or users' forgetting password. This also leads to user reusing same password again and again.

4.2.7.1 What is a password manager?

A Password Manager like a book of users passwords, locked by a master key that only the user knows. It's an application specifically designed to store users login details. The Password Managers not only saves the passwords it also encrypt them. A password manager is a software application that is used to store and manage the passwords that a user has for various online accounts and security features. Password managers store the passwords in an encrypted format and provide secure access to all the password information with the help of a master password.

Password managers are applications that serve as the solution for maintaining a large number of passwords and account information. They store the login information of the various accounts and automatically enter them into the forms. This helps in the prevention of hacker attacks like keystroke logging and it prevents the need to remember multiple passwords. Password managers enable the use of strong and unique passwords for each online account and provide an efficient way to manage all the passwords. The login information is encrypted and stored in either the local memory of the user's system or in cloud storage. Portable password manager applications installed in mobile devices can also be used as a way to manage and remember passwords anywhere and use them on shared systems.

A password manager usually comes with additional features like automatic form filling and password generation. The automatic form filling feature fills in the login information for a particular URL whenever it loads, and thus reduces manual errors and protects systems from hacker attacks such as key-logging. As password managers can identify the right URL for a particular login ID and password pair automatically, they are capable of protecting credentials from phishing sites. The automatic password generation feature available in certain password managers helps to create strong, unique and random passwords for each account. A user can choose from a variety of password managers. The basic types, their Pros and cons are as below.

1. **Desktop-Based:** This is one of the oldest and most popular types of password manager category. Usernames and passwords are encrypted and stored on the user's machine locally.

   Pros: User data, usernames and passwords gets encrypted and stored directly on user machine where no one else can access it.

   Cons: Passwords cannot be accessed from other machines and devices. Also not suitable for users who share their computer with family, friends or colleagues.

2. **Cloud-Based:** User data such as usernames and passwords are stored on clouds service provider's servers. Data gets transmitted from the user's web-browser over the Internet using highly secure communication channel.

   Pros: Users can access their passwords from any device which has access to internet. This type of password manager can also sync across multiple devices where it's installed.

   Cons: Security of the user data is directly in the hands of their service provider.

3. **Browser-Based:** Browsers like Chrome, Firefox, and Internet Explorer have a built-in option to store and manage users' login credentials.

   Pros: Easy-to-use, integrates with almost all types of browsers and free service providers are also available.

   Cons: This kind of password manager lacks many advance features. No sync option across multiple devices. This is also less secure than other type of password managers.

4. **Portable:** This category of password managers store usernames and passwords on the user's mobile device or other portable storage devices, such as a USB stick or HDD.

   Pros: More secure and reliable than the desktop-based password manager category.

   Cons: Loss of confidential data if the portable device is lost or stolen.

5. **Token-Based:** In this password manager the usernames and passwords are protected with an additional layer of security. Users must provide their login credentials and a security token delivered to their device.

   Pros: A higher level of security is ensured by using multiple levels of authentication

   Cons: More expensive than other types of password managers Also Is use is highly complex and less likely to be recommended for non-technical users.

6. **Stateless:** In this password manager the passwords are generated randomly using the user's master passphrase and a tag using a key derivation function.

   Pros: Passwords are not stored in a database, thereby ensuring enhanced security. Passwords are usually generated using a combination of username, the site that the password is for, and a master password

Cons: Typically sync option is not available in this type of password managers. Also more vulnerable to brute-force attacks than many other types of password managers

Password Generators: To effectively protect user's accounts from being hacked, it's important that users have a strong password with each account that they create. However, it can be difficult to create a perfect password that will keep users account safe from any hacker. As a result most of the modern password managers come with a built in feature called as Password Generators. There are many ways to create strong passwords, the primary of which is through a password generator feature in password manager. A random password generator is a software program, hardware device, or online tool that automatically generates a password using parameters that a user sets, including mixed-case letters, numbers, symbols, pronounce-ability, length, and strength. Password Generators help users to create unique, strong passwords for each of their accounts. This feature of password managers helps reduce the password fatigue from the user.

4.3 CRYPTOGRAPHY

The internet is an open and public system. We all send and receive information over shared wires and connections. Even though it's an open system, we still exchange a lot of private data, things like credit card numbers, bank information, passwords, and emails. So how all this private stuff is kept secret? Cryptography is a method of protecting information and communications through the use of codes, so that only those for whom the information is intended can read and process it. Data of any kind can be kept secret through a process known as Encryption. Scrambling or changing of the message to hide the original text before sending it over network. Once received the data is then decrypted, the process of unscrambling that message to make it readable. The prefix "crypt-" means "hidden" or "vault" — and the suffix "-graphy" stands for "writing."

4.3.1 History of Cryptography

The first known evidence of cryptography can be traced to the use of 'hieroglyph'. Some 4000 years ago, the Egyptians used to communicate by messages written in hieroglyph. This code was the secret known only to the scribes who used to transmit messages on behalf of the kings.

Later, the scholars moved on to using simple mono-alphabetic substitution ciphers during 500 to 600 BC. This involved replacing alphabets of message with other alphabets with some secret rule. This rule became a key to retrieve the message back from the garbled message.

One of the first well-known methods of encryption was Caesar's cipher, named after Julius Caesar, a Roman general who encrypted his military commands to make sure that if a message was intercepted by enemies, they wouldn't be able to read it.. This method of cryptography, relies on shifting the letters of a message by an agreed number (three was a common choice), the recipient of this message would then shift the letters back by the same number and obtain the original message. If the number is something only the sender and receiver know, then it's called the key. It allows the reader to unlock the secret message. For example, if the original message is, "Hello", then, using the Caesar's cipher algorithm with a key of five, the encrypted message would be "Mjqqt".

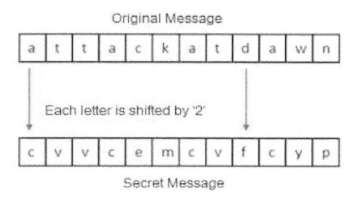

It is during and after the European Renaissance, various Italian and Papal states led the rapid proliferation of cryptographic techniques. Various analysis and attack techniques were researched in this era to break the secret codes. Improved coding techniques such as Vigenere Coding came into existence in the 15th century, which offered moving letters in the message with a number of variable places instead of moving them the same number of places.

Vigenere Cipher: Improved coding techniques such as Vigenere Coding came into existence in the 15th century, which offered moving letters in the message with a number of variable places instead of moving them the same number of places. One of the earliest polyalphabetic ciphers was the VIGENERE cipher developed in the 16th century. It was pretty simple because the key was just a word. So let's say user want to encrypt "Today is Monday". Using a Vigenere cipher well the first thing user need to do is write out a Vigenere square. (Figure Below).

✕	A	B	C	D	E	F	G	H	I	J	K	L	M	N	O	P	Q	R	S	T	U	V	W	X	Y	Z
A	A	B	C	D	E	F	G	H	I	J	K	L	M	N	O	P	Q	R	S	T	U	V	W	X	Y	Z
B	B	C	D	E	F	G	H	I	J	K	L	M	N	O	P	Q	R	S	T	U	V	W	X	Y	Z	A
C	C	D	E	F	G	H	I	J	K	L	M	N	O	P	Q	R	S	T	U	V	W	X	Y	Z	A	B
D	D	E	F	G	H	I	J	K	L	M	N	O	P	Q	R	S	T	U	V	W	X	Y	Z	A	B	C
E	E	F	G	H	I	J	K	L	M	N	O	P	Q	R	S	T	U	V	W	X	Y	Z	A	B	C	D
F	F	G	H	I	J	K	L	M	N	O	P	Q	R	S	T	U	V	W	X	Y	Z	A	B	C	D	E
G	G	H	I	J	K	L	M	N	O	P	Q	R	S	T	U	V	W	X	Y	Z	A	B	C	D	E	F
H	H	I	J	K	L	M	N	O	P	Q	R	S	T	U	V	W	X	Y	Z	A	B	C	D	E	F	G
I	I	J	K	L	M	N	O	P	Q	R	S	T	U	V	W	X	Y	Z	A	B	C	D	E	F	G	H
J	J	K	L	M	N	O	P	Q	R	S	T	U	V	W	X	Y	Z	A	B	C	D	E	F	G	H	I
K	K	L	M	N	O	P	Q	R	S	T	U	V	W	X	Y	Z	A	B	C	D	E	F	G	H	I	J
L	L	M	N	O	P	Q	R	S	T	U	V	W	X	Y	Z	A	B	C	D	E	F	G	H	I	J	K
M	M	N	O	P	Q	R	S	T	U	V	W	X	Y	Z	A	B	C	D	E	F	G	H	I	J	K	L
N	N	O	P	Q	R	S	T	U	V	W	X	Y	Z	A	B	C	D	E	F	G	H	I	J	K	L	M
O	O	P	Q	R	S	T	U	V	W	X	Y	Z	A	B	C	D	E	F	G	H	I	J	K	L	M	N
P	P	Q	R	S	T	U	V	W	X	Y	Z	A	B	C	D	E	F	G	H	I	J	K	L	M	N	O
Q	Q	R	S	T	U	V	W	X	Y	Z	A	B	C	D	E	F	G	H	I	J	K	L	M	N	O	P
R	R	S	T	U	V	W	X	Y	Z	A	B	C	D	E	F	G	H	I	J	K	L	M	N	O	P	Q
S	S	T	U	V	W	X	Y	Z	A	B	C	D	E	F	G	H	I	J	K	L	M	N	O	P	Q	R
T	T	U	V	W	X	Y	Z	A	B	C	D	E	F	G	H	I	J	K	L	M	N	O	P	Q	R	S
U	U	V	W	X	Y	Z	A	B	C	D	E	F	G	H	I	J	K	L	M	N	O	P	Q	R	S	T
V	V	W	X	Y	Z	A	B	C	D	E	F	G	H	I	J	K	L	M	N	O	P	Q	R	S	T	U
W	W	X	Y	Z	A	B	C	D	E	F	G	H	I	J	K	L	M	N	O	P	Q	R	S	T	U	V
X	X	Y	Z	A	B	C	D	E	F	G	H	I	J	K	L	M	N	O	P	Q	R	S	T	U	V	W
Y	Y	Z	A	B	C	D	E	F	G	H	I	J	K	L	M	N	O	P	Q	R	S	T	U	V	W	X
Z	Z	A	B	C	D	E	F	G	H	I	J	K	L	M	N	O	P	Q	R	S	T	U	V	W	X	Y

The alphabet goes across the top and along the left side and each row contains the letters A to Z shifted over by one. So the first line starts with A and ends with Z. But the second line starts with B and goes all through the letters until Z and then ends with A and so on. User end up with 26 differently scrambled alphabets and now user is ready to encode the message. User just have to pick a key. Then to encrypt it, users take each letter of the message and move along its row in the VIGENERE square until user get to the column of the corresponding letter in Vigenere square. So the text "Today is Monday becomes "Vfbpr qa Oflstg". The recipient of this message can convert the message back using the Vigenere square.

Only after the 19th century, cryptography evolved from the ad hoc approaches to encryption to the more sophisticated art and science of information security. In the early 20th century, the invention of mechanical and electromechanical machines, such as the **Enigma Rotor Machine**, provided more advanced and efficient means of coding the information.

Modern cryptography is a remarkable discipline. It is a cornerstone of computer and communications security, with end products that are imminently practical. Modern cryptography addresses a wide range of problems. But the most basic problem remains the classical one of ensuring security of communication across an insecure medium. Data Confidentiality, Data Integrity, Authentication and Non-repudiation are core principles of modern-day cryptography.

Objectives of Modern Cryptography:

1. **Confidentiality:** refers to certain rules and guidelines usually executed under confidentiality agreements which ensure that the information is restricted to certain people or places.

2. **Data integrity:** refers to maintaining and making sure that the data stays accurate and consistent over its entire life cycle.

3. **Authentication:** is the process of making sure that the piece of data being claimed by the user belongs to it.

4. **Non-repudiation:** refers to ability to make sure that a person or a party associated with a contract or a communication cannot deny the authenticity of their signature over their document or the sending of a message.

Encryption: To encrypt a message, users need two main parts - the Cipher and the key. The cipher is the set of rules that are used to encode the information for example shifting the alphabet by certain number of letters. The key tells users how to arrange those rules otherwise they'd be the same every time and it would be easy to decode the message. In Caesar's cipher case the key would be one because we shifted the alphabet by one letter. To decrypt the information user need to know what kind of cipher was used and also have the key or user can just crack the code either by trying all possible combinations. Users can think of or by analyzing the code and working backward from it, known as deciphering.

Decryption: To decrypt the message, the recipient would simply use the key to reverse the process. But there's a big problem with Caesar's cipher. Anybody can easily break or crack the encrypted message by trying every possible key. In the English alphabet, there are only 26 letters, which means hackers only need to try, at most, 26 keys to decrypt the message. Now, trying 26 possible keys isn't very hard. It would take, at most, an hour to do. So let's make it harder. Instead of shifting every letter by the same amount, let's shift each letter by a different amount. Using 10 digit encryption, there could be 10 billion possible key solutions. Obviously, that's more than any human could ever solve. It would take many centuries, but an average computer today would take just a few seconds to try all 10 billion possibilities.

But is it possible to come up with a combination of a cipher and key that could never be determined? Is there such a thing as an unbreakable code? So in a modern world, where the bad guys are armed with computers instead of pencils, how can users encrypt messages so securely that they're too hard to crack? A Caesar cipher is one simple type of mono-alphabetic ciphers. A class of ciphers for the whole code is based on one letter of the alphabet standing in for another letter, consistently throughout the whole message. Basically just scramble the alphabet. In that case the key would just be a list of which letters correspond to which letter.

Cipher: The cipher is the set of rules that are using to encode the information. Cipher, a method of transforming a message to conceal its meaning. The term is also used synonymously with cipher text or cryptogram in reference to the encrypted form of the message. In modern terms a cipher is an algorithm for encrypting and decrypting data. Symmetric key encryption, also called secret key encryption, depends on the use of ciphers, which operate symmetrically. With symmetric algorithms, the same cipher and encryption key are applied to data in the same way, whether the objective is to convert plaintext to cipher text or cipher text to plaintext. A cipher transforms data by processing the original, plaintext characters (or other data) into cipher text, which should appear to be random data. The most widely used types of ciphers fall into two categories: symmetric and asymmetric.

Symmetrical Ciphers: This is the simplest kind of encryption that involves only one secret key to cipher and decipher information. Symmetrical encryption is an old and best-known technique. It uses a secret key that can either be a number, a word or a string of random letters. It is a blended with the plain text of a message to change the content in a particular way. The sender and the recipient should know the secret key that is used to encrypt and decrypt all the messages. This form of encryption uses a secret key, called the shared secret, to scramble the data into unintelligible gibberish. The person on the other end needs the shared secret (key) to unlock the data—the encryption algorithm. User can change the key and change the results of the encryption. It is called symmetric cryptography because the same key is used on both ends for both encryption and decryption. Blowfish, AES, RC4, DES, RC5, and RC6 are examples of symmetric encryption. The most widely used symmetric algorithm is AES-128, AES-192, and AES-256

Symmetric Encryption

Secret Key · Same Key · Secret Key

A4$h*L@9.
T6=#/>B#1
R06/J2.>1L
1PRL39P20

Plain Text · Cipher Text · Plain Text

The problem with this method is that users have to communicate the secret key securely to the intended recipient. If hackers intercept the key, they can decipher the message. All kinds of systems were invented to try to get around this basic weakness, but the fact remained: users still had to communicate the secret key in some way to the intended recipient before user could commence subsequent secure communications.

Asymmetrical Ciphers: Also known as Public Key Encryption (PKE), use two different; but logically linked keys. Asymmetric cryptography uses encryption that splits the key into two smaller keys. One of the keys is made public and one is kept private. Users encrypt a message with the recipient's public key. The recipient can then decrypt it with their private key. And recipient can do the same for users, encrypting a message with user's public key so user can decrypt it with their private key. The difference here is that users don't need someone's private key to send him or her secure message. Users use his or her public key, which doesn't have to be kept secure (in fact, it can be published like a phone number). By using users' recipient's public key, everyone knows that only that person can encrypt it using his or her private key. This system allows two entities to communicate securely without any prior exchange of keys.

Asymmetric Encryption

Asymmetric encryption uses two keys to encrypt a plain text. Secret keys are exchanged over the Internet or a large network. It ensures that malicious persons do not misuse the keys. It is important to note that anyone with a secret key can decrypt the message and this is why asymmetrical encryption uses two related keys to boosting security. A public key is made freely available to anyone who might want to send user a message. The second private key is kept a secret so that users can only know. A message that is encrypted using a public key can only be decrypted using a private key, while also, a message encrypted using a private key can be decrypted using a public key. Security of the public key is not required because it is publicly available and can be passed over the internet. Asymmetric key has a far better power in ensuring the security of information transmitted during communication.

Asymmetric cryptography is usually implemented by the use of one-way functions. In mathematic terms, these are functions that are easy to compute in one direction but very difficult to compute in reverse. This is what allows people to publish users public key, which is derived from their private key. It is very difficult to work backwards and determine the private key. A common one-way function used today is factoring large prime numbers. It is easy to multiply two prime numbers together and get a product. However, to determine which of the many possibilities are the two factors of the product is one of the great mathematical problems. If anyone were to invent a method for easily deducing factors of large prime numbers, it could make obsolete much of the public key encryption used today. Public key encryption is now behind every Web server that offers users a secure purchase. Users' transaction is encrypted without giving or taking a secret key, and it all happens in the background. All we know as users is that the little SSL lock symbol displays in our browser and we feel safer. Imagine the effects on Internet commerce if every time users wanted to buy something online users had to think of a secret key, encrypt the message, and then somehow communicate that key to the other party. Obviously, e-commerce could not exist as it does today without public key cryptography. There are many different encryption algorithms, protocols, and applications based on these two main types of encryption.

Encryption Algorithms: Today, strength of encryption is usually measured by key size. No matter how strong the algorithm, the encrypted data can be subject to brute force attacks in which all possible combinations of keys are tried. Eventually the encryption can be cracked. For most modern ciphers with decent key lengths, the time to crack them with brute force them is measured in millennia. However, an undisclosed flaw in an algorithm or an advance in computer technology or mathematical methods could sharply decrease these times.

Generally, the thinking is that the key length should be suitable for keeping the data secure for a reasonable amount of time. If the item is very topical, such as battlefield communications or daily stock information, then a cipher that protects it for a matter of weeks or months is just fine. However, something like users credit card number or national security secrets need to be kept secure for a longer period, effectively forever. So using weaker encryption algorithms or shorter key lengths for some things is okay, as long as the information usefulness to an outsider expires in a short amount of time.

Data Encryption Standard (DES): DES is the original standard that the U.S. government began promoting for both government and business use. Originally thought to be practically unbreakable in the 1970s, the increase in power and decrease in cost of computing has made its 56-bit key functionally obsolete for highly sensitive information. However, it is still used in many commercial products and is considered acceptable for lower security applications. It also is used in products that have slower processors, such as smart cards and appliance devices that can't process a larger key size.

TripleDES: TripleDES, or 3DES as it is sometimes written, is the newer, improved version of DES, and its name implies what it does. It runs DES three times on the data in three phases: encrypt, decrypt, and then encrypt again. It actually doesn't give a threefold increase in the strength of the cipher (because the first encryption key is used twice to encrypt the data and then a second key is used to encrypt the results of that process), but it still gives an effective key length of 168 bits, which is plenty strong for almost all uses.

RC4, RC5, and RC6: This is an encryption algorithm developed by Ronald Rivest, one of the developers of RSA, the first commercial application of public key cryptography. Improvements have been made over time to make it stronger and fix minor issues. The current version, RC6, allows up to a 2,040-bit key size and variable block size up to 128 bits.

Advanced Encryption Standard (AES): When the U.S. government realized that DES would eventually reach the end of its useful life, it began a search for a replacement. The Advanced Encryption Standard, also known by its original name Rijndael, is a specification for the encryption of electronic data established by the U.S. National Institute of Standards and Technology in 2001. AES is rapidly becoming the new standard for encryption. It offers up to a 256-bit cipher key, which is more than enough power for the foreseeable future. Typically, AES is implemented in either 128- or 192-bit mode for performance considerations.

4.3.2 RSA

Rivest–Shamir–Adleman (RSA) encryption is an asymmetric cipher that functions on two keys: a public key for encryption and a private key for decryption. Considered as the best encryption algorithm, it functions on 1024-bit and can extend up to 2048-bit key length. This means that the larger the key size, the slower the encryption process becomes. Due to a larger key size, it is known to be as one of the strongest encryption types. It is also considered as an encryption standard for data shared over the internet because it is the most secure encryption algorithm up till now. As compared to other types of encryption, RSA gives hackers quite a tough time because of the length of the keys it works with.

4.3.3 Encryption Applications

Hashes: Hashes are a special use of one-way functions to provide authentication and verification using encryption. A hash function takes a file and puts it through a function so that it produces a much smaller file of a set size. By hashing a file, programs produce a unique fingerprint of it. This give user a way to make sure that the file has not been altered in any way. By hashing a suspect file and comparing the hash to the known good hash, users can tell if any changes have been made. It is unlikely that a file with a different structure would produce an identical hash. Even changing one character changes the hash significantly. The chances of two different files producing the same hash are infinitesimal. Hashes are often provided on downloaded versions of software to make sure users are getting the real thing. This is important, especially with open source software, where it may have been passed around quite a bit or downloaded from another site. The official Web site will usually post the correct hash of the latest version. If the two don't match, then users know some changes have been made, possibly without the permission or knowledge of the software developers. The most popular hashing algorithm is called MD5.

Digital Certificates: Digital certificates are the "signature" of the Internet commerce world. These use a combination of encryption types to provide authentication. They prove that who users are connecting to is really who they say they are. Simply put, a certificate is a "certification" of where the information is coming from. A certificate contains the public key of the organization encrypted with either its private key or the private key of a signing authority. Using a signing or certificate authority is considered the more secure method of the two. If users can decrypt the certificate with their public key, then users can reasonably assume the Web site belongs to that organization.

Certificates are usually tied to a particular domain. They can be issued by a central entity, called a Certificate Authority (CA), or created and signed locally as described above. There are several of these organizations, the biggest of which is VeriSign, the company that also runs the domain names system. They have sanctioned many other companies to offer certificates under their authority. Getting a certificate from VeriSign or one of the companies it authorizes is like having someone vouch for the authenticity of the certificate holder. Generally, they will not issue user or organization a certificate until they verify the information they are putting in the certificate, either by phone or via some kind of paper documentation, such as a corporate charter. Once they "certify" receiver, they will take this information, including the URLs users are going to use the certificate for, and digitally "sign" it by encrypting it with their private key. Then a Web server or other program can use this certificate. When outside users receive some data, such as a Web page from the server, and it has a certificate attached, they can use public key cryptography to decrypt the certificate and verify holders' identity. Certificates are used most often at e-commerce Web sites, but they can also be used for any form of communications. SSH and Nessus both can use certificates for authentication. VPNs also can use certificates for authentication instead of passwords.

4.3.4   Encryption Protocols

IPsec: It's a well-known fact that the IP protocol as designed originally was not very secure. IP version 4 (IPv4), which is what most of the world uses for IP communications, doesn't provide any kind of authentication or confidentiality. Packet payloads are sent in the clear, and packet headers can easily be modified since they are not verified at the destination. Many Internet attacks rely on this basic insecurity in the Internet infrastructure. A new IP standard, called IPv6, was developed to provide authentication and confidentiality via encryption. It also expanded the IP address space by using a 128-bit address rather than the 32-bit currently used and improved on a number of other things as well.

Fully implementing the IPv6 standard would require wide-scale hardware upgrades, so IPv6 deployment has been pretty slow. However, an implementation of security for IP, called IPsec, was developed that wouldn't require major changes in the addressing scheme. Hardware vendors have jumped on this, and IPsec has gradually become a de facto standard for creating Internet VPNs. IPsec is not a specific encryption algorithm, but rather a framework for encrypting and verifying packets within the IP protocol. IPsec can use different algorithms and can be implemented in whole or just partially. A combination of public key and private key cryptography is used to encrypt the packet contents, and hashes add authentication as well. This function is called Authentication Header (AH). With AH, a hash is made of the IP header and passed along. When the packet arrives at the destination, a new hash is made of each header. If it doesn't compare to the one sent, then users know the header has been altered somehow in transit. This provides a high level of assurance that the packet came from where it says it does. Users may choose to do encryption of the packet payload but not do AH, as this can slow down the throughput. AH can also get fouled up in some environments with NAT or firewalls. There are also different two operation modes user can run IPsec in: tunnel mode or transport mode.

Tunnel mode: In this mode the entire packet—header and all—is encapsulated and encrypted, placed in another packet, and forwarded to a central VPN processor. The endpoints decrypt the packets and then forward them to the correct IP. A benefit of this method is that outsiders can't even tell what the final destination is for the encrypted packet. Another advantage is that the VPN can be controlled and administered from a few central points. The downside is that this requires dedicated hardware at both ends to do the tunneling.

Transport Mode: In this mode only the packet payloads are encrypted; the headers are sent intact. This makes deployment a little easier and requires fewer infrastructures. Users can still do AH when using transport mode and verify the source address of the packets

Point-to-Point Tunneling Protocol (PPTP): PPTP is a standard that was developed by Microsoft, 3Com, and other large companies to provide encryption. Microsoft has added it to Windows 98 and later releases. This made it seem a likely candidate to be the major standard for widespread encryption technology. However, some major flaws were discovered in PPTP, which limited its acceptance. When Microsoft bundled IPsec with Windows 2000, it seemed a tacit admission that IPsec had won as the new encryption standard. However, PPTP is still a useful and inexpensive protocol for setting up VPNs between older Windows PCs.

Layer Two Tunneling Protocol (L2TP): This is another industry-developed protocol, and is endorsed by Microsoft and Cisco. Although used frequently in hardware-based encryption devices, its use in software is relatively limited.

SSTP: Secure Socket Tunneling Protocol secures the connection between the VPN client and the VPN server. Hence, all the data and Point-to-Point Protocol (PPP) traffic through the SSL channel, which passes in between, is encrypted. Therefore, it is highly secured as compared to PPTP.

Secure Socket Layer (SSL): This protocol was designed specifically for use on the Web, although it can be used for almost any type of TCP communications. Netscape originally developed it for their browser to help stimulate e-commerce. SSL provides data encryption, authentication on both ends, and message integrity using certificates. Most of the time, SSL is used when connecting to a Web server so that we know the information we send it is being protected along the way. Most people don't even realize that SSL is running in the background. Usually it only authenticates one end, the server side, since most end users don't have certificates.

HTTPS: Hypertext Transfer Protocol Secure (HTTPS) is HTTP combined with SSL. It is a secure version of HTTP, which we see in every website's URL. HTTPS makes sure that users sensitive data from a web browser to a website is highly secured and encrypted to avoid online theft of information. It works on asymmetric key encryption that is through private key, which is with the owner of the website, and a public key, which is available to everyone. So, the next time user use a website, check for an 's' after HTTP, to make users online browsing and data sharing secured.

4.4 FIREWALL

Internet is a Public Network. Being a public network used by people with good intensions and bad intensions. To protect computer from people with bad intensions a firewall is used. When surfing the internet there are many dangers in the form of malware that are trying to harm computers. Hackers all trying to gain access to every computer connected to Internet. Just like a security fence around a building protects home from burglars and intruders; a firewall keeps Cyber criminals and hackers from penetrating computers. A firewall's purpose is to create a safety barrier between a private network and the public internet. A firewall acts as a defense system for a network against viruses, worms, Trojans, brute force attacks and other network attacks or attacks that attempts to compromise a network. Firewall can take the form of software such as a security program or hardware such as a physical router. Both perform the same function which is scanning incoming network traffic to make sure it doesn't contain blacklisted data. Firewall scan each packet of data which are small chunks of the larger hole reduced in size for easy transmission and make sure these packets don't contain anything malicious. Internet security software companies often bundle firewall solutions built into their antivirus programs.

Example is Symantec and McAfee Endpoint Softwares. In many cases these firewalls are more sophisticated than those provided as part of a basic operating system. Common features of firewalls include the logging and reporting of attacks, successful or not along with alarm notifications in the event of a breach. Just as with any network system potential drawbacks of a firewall include a slowdown in traffic, especially if packets are being entirely analyzed by a user's local computer. In addition some firewalls accidentally block legitimate sites which can be corrected by making exceptions in the settings and specifying / white-listing the traffic and or ports are allowed past. Many computers lack even basic firewall protection which is why it's important to make sure every computer is protected by a Firewall.

4.4.1 History of Firewall

The idea of a wall to keep out intruders dates back thousands of years. For example, over two thousand years ago, the Chinese built the Great Wall as protection from neighboring northern tribes. A second example is that of European kings who built castles with high walls and moats to protect themselves and their subjects, both from invading armies and from marauding bands intent on pillaging and looting.

In the early years, the Internet supported a relatively small community of compatible users who valued openness for sharing and collaboration. This view was challenged by the Morris Worm in 1988. It was developed by a graduate student at Cornell University, Robert Morris. But he released the worm inside MIT in the hope of suggesting that its creator studied there. It is usually reported that around 6,000 major UNIX machines were infected by the Morris worm within first 12 hours. Back then there were only 60,000 computers on Internet. The Internet was partitioned for several days, as regional networks disconnected from the NSFNet backbone and from each other to prevent recontamination, as they cleaned their own networks. This forced the engineers to come up with a technology to keep the unwanted traffic from getting into the network. The first paper published on firewall technology was in 1987 when engineers from Digital Equipment Corporation (DEC) developed filter systems known as packet filter firewalls.

4.4.2 Generations of Firewall

First Generation: In 1988, engineers from Digital Equipment Corporation developed the first and simple generation of firewalls known as packet filter firewalls. This firewall used to inspect packets transferred between computers. The firewall maintained an access control list which dictates what packets will be looked at and what action should be applied. The default action set to silently discard the packet. Three basic actions regarding the packet consist of a silent discard; discard with Internet Control Message Protocol or TCP reset response to the sender, and forward to the next hop. Packets were filtered by source and destination IP addresses protocol, source and destination ports. The bulk of Internet communication in 20th and early 21st century used either Transmission Control Protocol (TCP) or User Datagram Protocol (UDP) in conjunction with well-known ports, enabling firewalls of that era to distinguish between specific types of traffic such as web browsing, remote printing, email transmission, file transfer.

Second Generation: The second generation firewall they introduced the concept of a connection state. From the perspective if a firewall, when users are on a network there are two zones. Trusted zone and an Un-trusted zone. So the trusted zone is permitted to go to the untrusted zone but the untrusted zone is not permitted to go to the trusted zone unless specified in the configuration. When a user on a LAN is browsing the web, user go out to a web server over the Internet and then the user have to open a connection to allow that return traffic to come back. When that connection is no longer needed the firewall breaks the connection down. This generation of firewalls attempted to increase the level of security between trusted and untrusted networks. Known as application proxy or gateway firewalls, this approach to protection is significantly different from packet filters and Stateful packet inspection. An application gateway firewall uses software to intercept connections for each Internet protocol and to perform security inspection. It involves what is commonly known as proxy services. These circuit level firewalls are simply an upgraded version of the first generation. They were required to keep up with advancing computer to computer linking technology through the internet.

Third generation: This generation firewall introduced application visibility, an application level filter. It was a state-of-the-art perimeter security integrated within major network components. These systems alert administrators in real time about suspicious activity that may be occurring on their systems. This generation of firewall had evolved to meet the major requirements demanded by corporate networks of increased security while minimizing the impact on network performance. The requirements of the third generation of firewalls were more demanding due to the growing support for VPNs, wireless communication, and enhanced virus protection. These new firewalls understood how many protocols normally works. It knew how FTP worked, it knew how email, SMTP worked and if some rogue application tries to hijack one of those ports and protocols and make it behave in a way that it's not supposed to, the application filter used to shut down the connection. The most difficult element of this evolution was maintaining the firewall's simplicity without compromising flexibility and Security.

Next Generation: A next generation firewall (NGFW) is, as Gartner defines it, a "deep-packet inspection firewall that moves beyond port/ protocol inspection and blocking to add application-level inspection, intrusion prevention, and bringing intelligence from outside the firewall." Next generation firewalls are a more advanced version of the traditional firewall, and they offer the same benefits. Like regular firewalls, NGFW use both static and dynamic packet filtering and VPN support to ensure that all connections between the network, internet, and firewall are valid and secure. These firewalls have extensive control and visibility of applications that it is able to identify malicious traffic / packet using analysis and signature matching. They can use whitelists or a signature-based IPS to distinguish between safe applications and unwanted ones, which are then identified using SSL decryption. Unlike most traditional firewalls, NGFWs also include a path through which future updates will be received.

4.4.3 Hardware vs Software Firewalls

Hardware Firewalls: A hardware firewall sits between organizations' local network of computers and the Internet. The firewall usually inspects all the data that comes in from the Internet, passing along the safe data packets while blocking the potentially dangerous packets. In order to properly protect a network without hindering performance, hardware firewalls require expert setup, and so Hardware Firewall may not be a feasible solution for companies without a dedicated IT department. For businesses with many computers, however, being able to control network security from one single device simplifies the job.

Software Firewalls: Software firewalls are installed on individual computers on a network. Unlike hardware firewalls, software firewalls can easily distinguish between programs on a computer. This lets them allow data to one program while blocking another. Software firewalls can also filter outgoing data, as well as remote responses to outgoing requests. The major downside to software firewalls for a business is their upkeep: they require installation, updating and administration on each individual computer.

Hybrid Firewall: In order to share an Internet connection between multiple computers, routers must distinguish which pieces of data need to go to which computer. The process of separating the data acts as a kind of firewall: if unwanted data comes in, the router will not identify it as belonging to any computer, and thus will discard it. This level of protection serves adequately for home use; along with a software firewall. It's also enough for many business networks that don't require high security. However, routers generally lack the options and advanced features that dedicated hardware firewalls offer. Using a single software firewall along with a router or hardware firewall will strengthen network security without posing any compatibility issues. Using multiple software firewalls, however, can cause conflicts, hampering proper operation. Businesses highly concerned with network security can put together multiple hardware firewalls, minimizing any weaknesses in each, but this requires careful expert setup to avoid incompatibilities and blocking of legitimate data traffic.

Firewalls, both hardware and software, protect computers from hackers and other online threats by blocking dangerous pieces of data from reaching the system. While hardware firewalls offer network-wide protection from external threats, software firewalls installed on individual computers can more closely inspect data, and can block specific programs from even sending data to the Internet. On networks with high security concerns, combining both kinds of firewalls provides a more complete safety net.

4.4.4 Types of Firewalls

Packet Filters: A packet-filtering firewall examines each packet that crosses the firewall and tests the packet according to a set of rules set up during initial configuration. If the packet passes the test, it's allowed to enter the network. If the packet doesn't pass, it's rejected or discarded. Packet filters are the least expensive type of firewall. As a result, packet-filtering firewalls are very common. However, packet filtering has a number of flaws that knowledgeable hackers can exploit. As a result, packet filtering by itself doesn't make for a fully effective firewall. Packet filters work by inspecting the source and destination IP and port addresses contained in each Transmission Control Protocol/Internet Protocol (TCP/IP) packet. TCP/IP ports are numbers that are assigned to specific services that help to identify for which service each packet is intended. For example, the port number for the HTTP protocol is 80. As a result, any incoming packets headed for an HTTP server will specify port 80 as the destination port.

Port numbers are often specified with a colon following an IP address. For example, the HTTP service on a server whose IP address is 192.168.10.133 would be 192.168.10.133:80. The rules that administrators set up for the packet filter either permit or deny packets that specify certain IP addresses or ports. For example, administrators may permit packets that are intended for mail server or web server and deny all other packets.

Circuit-Level Gateways / Firewalls: A circuit-level gateway monitors TCP handshaking between packets from trusted clients or servers to untrusted hosts and vice versa to determine whether a requested session is legitimate. To filter packets in this way, a circuit-level gateway relies on data contained in the packet headers for the Internet's TCP session-layer protocol. Because a circuit-level gateway filters packets at the session layer of the OSI model, this gateway operates two layers higher than a packet-filtering firewall does. Monitoring Handshaking—Circuitously. To determine whether a requested session is legitimate, a circuit-level gateway uses a process similar to the following: A trusted client requests a service, and the gateway accepts this request, assuming that the client meets basic filtering criteria (such as whether DNS can locate the client's IP address and associated name). Acting on behalf of the client, the gateway opens a connection to the requested untrusted host and then closely monitors the TCP handshaking that follows. This handshaking involves an exchange of TCP packets that are flagged SYN (synchronize) or ACK (acknowledge). These packet types are legitimate only at certain points during the session. A circuit-level gateway determines that a requested session is legitimate only if the SYN flags, ACK flags, and sequence numbers involved in the TCP handshaking between the trusted client and the untrusted host are logical. After a circuit-level gateway determines that the trusted client and the untrusted host are authorized to participate in a TCP session and verifies the legitimacy of this session, the gateway establishes a connection. From this point on, the circuit-level gateway simply copies and forwards packets back and forth without further filtering them. The gateway maintains a table of established connections, allowing data to pass when session information matches an entry in the table. When the session is completed, the gateway removes the associated entry in the table and closes the circuit this session used.

Stateful Inspection Firewalls: Stateful firewall is nothing but a combination of the Packet Filters and Circuit-level gateway. This type of Firewall inspects both the packets and handshake. Any traffic that does not fit the pre-configured criteria, it will drop the connection. This firewall monitors the full state of active network connections. This means that stateful firewalls are constantly analyzing the complete context of traffic and data packets, seeking entry to a network rather than discrete traffic and data packets in isolation. Once a certain kind of traffic has been approved by a stateful firewall, it is added to a state table and can travel more freely into the protected network. Traffic and data packets that don't successfully complete the required handshake will be blocked. By taking multiple factors into consideration before adding a type of connection to an approved list, such as TCP stages, stateful firewalls are able to observe traffic streams in their entirety.

Applications Level Gateways / Firewalls: Commonly known as the proxy firewall, this firewall operates at the Application layer by combining the attributes of both packet filtering firewalls and circuit-level gateways. This firewall first establishes a connection to the source of the traffic and scans all the way through the application layer when inspecting the incoming data packet. The verification is much more thorough on this firewall as it verifies the TCP handshake protocol as well as the contents of the packets. Another advantage of this firewall is that it has its own IP address, hence can prevent direct contact to any other networks. Firewalls working at the application level provide additional anonymity & data security and have advanced logging & inspection abilities, but they adversely affect the network performance due to the extra steps in the data packet verification process.

Application-specific proxies accept only packets generated by services they are designed to copy, forward, and filter. For example, only a Telnet proxy can copy, forward, and filter Telnet traffic. If a network relies only on an application-level gateway, incoming and outgoing packets cannot access services for which there is not a proxy. Unlike a circuit-level gateway, an application-level gateway runs proxies that examine and filter individual packets, rather than simply copying them and blindly forwarding them across the gateway. Application-specific proxies check each packet that passes through the gateway, verifying the contents of the packet up through the application layer (which is the highest layer) of the OSI model. These proxies can filter particular kinds of commands or information in the application protocols the proxies are designed to copy, forward, and filter.

Next Generation Firewall: The reality is that the firewall is rapidly evolving, not only in what it can do, but also in its business value to the enterprise. It is becoming the cornerstone of hybrid cloud network security, offering integration enablement, consistent controls and comprehensive monitoring and alerting across multiple cloud and on-premises environments. Simultaneously, the firewall's feature set is expanding beyond the realm of traditional network security to include a fascinating variety of features not necessarily limited to security. Looking forward, key technological developments, including encryption, artificial intelligence/machine learning (AI/ML) and the internet of things (IoT), will arguably make the enterprise firewall more important than it has ever been. A next generation firewall seeks to improve network security by inspecting more layers of the OSI model and looking at the contents of the data packets in order to make filtering decisions. In essence, a next generation firewall consolidates various established security mechanisms into a single device with the aim of making the security easier to manager and so makes it more effective.

The next generation firewall is expected to include following technologies.

- TLS/SSL decryption to spot data exfiltration
- Web content filtering
- Monitor or block use of cloud sharing platforms and redirect users to approved solutions
- Intrusion Detection and Intrusion Prevention
- Malware scanning and detection

DMZ (De-Militarized Zone): The term demilitarized zone or DMZ might conjure visions of the military buffer zone, the strip of land between two rival countries. While a military term, it's also analogous to computer security. Also known as a perimeter network, a networking DMZ can refer to a physical or logical subnet designed to add a layer of security to an organization's local area network. Just like a geographic DMZ, a networking DMZ acts as a buffer sitting between an enterprise's internal network and the internet. The goal of a DMZ is to add an extra layer of security to an organization's local area network. A protected and monitored network node that faces outside the internal network can access what is exposed in the DMZ, while the rest of the organization's network is safe behind a firewall. DMZ enables users and an organization to access necessary internet services in a secure way. DMZs not only isolate and keep potential target system separate from internal networks, but also reduce and control access to those systems. A DMZ contains external facing services like email, web and Domain Name System and exposes them to an untrusted network, like the public Internet without worrying about hackers directly accessing internal servers and data. Though there's various ways to implement the DMZ, most modern designs use two firewalls: one to allow external traffic flow to the DMZ, and one to allow traffic flow from the DMZ to the internal network. DMZs have been around as long as firewalls, but many enterprises have moved to virtual machines or containers to isolate networks or applications.

Any service provided to users on the public internet should be placed in the DMZ network. Some of the most common of these services include web servers and proxy servers, as well as servers for email, domain name system (DNS), File Transfer Protocol (FTP) and voice over IP (VoIP). Cyber criminals around the world can reach the systems running these services on DMZ servers, which need to be hardened to withstand constant attack.

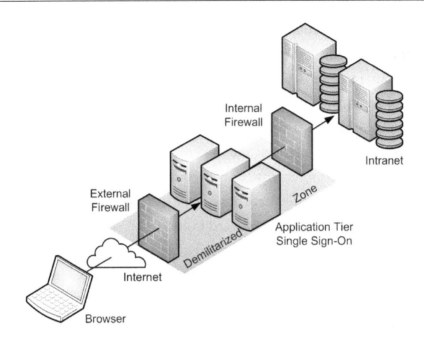

DMZ Architecture: In a computer network, the hosts most vulnerable to attack are those that provide services to users outside of the local area network, such as e-mail, web and Domain Name System (DNS) servers. Because of the increased potential of these hosts being compromised, they are placed into their own sub-network in order to protect the rest of the network if an intruder were to succeed in attacking any of them. Hosts in the DMZ have limited connectivity to specific hosts in the internal network, although communication with other hosts in the DMZ and to the external network is allowed. This allows hosts in the DMZ to provide services to both the internal and external network, while an intervening firewall controls the traffic between the DMZ servers and the internal network clients.

There are many different ways to design a network with a DMZ. Two of the most basic methods are with a single firewall, also known as the three legged model, and with dual firewalls, also known as back to back.

Single firewall: A modest approach to network architecture involves using a single firewall, with a minimum of 3 network interfaces. The DMZ will be placed Inside of this firewall. The tier of operations is as follows: the external network device makes the connection from the ISP, the internal network is connected by the second device, and connections within the DMZ are handled by the third network device.

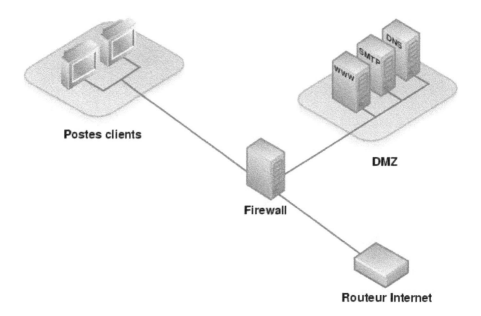

Dual firewall: The more secure approach is to use two firewalls to create a DMZ. The first firewall (referred to as the "frontend" firewall) is configured to only allow traffic destined for the DMZ. The second firewall (referred to as the "backend" firewall) is only responsible for the traffic that travels from the DMZ to the internal network. An effective way of further increasing protection is to use firewalls built by separate vendors, because they are less likely to have the same security vulnerabilities. While more effective, this scheme can be more costly to implement across a large network.

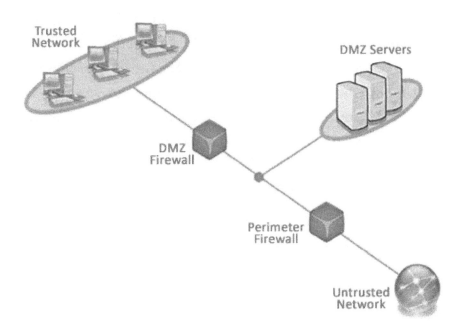

4.5 DATA LOSS PREVENTION

Also known as DLP; is a set of tools and processes used to ensure that confidential data is not lost, misused, or accessed by unauthorized users. A DLP software role include classifying regulated, confidential and business critical data and identifies violations of policies defined by organizations in the predefined policies pack. This is driven by regulatory compliance such as HIPAA, PCI-DSS, or GDPR. If those violations are identified, DLP feature enforces remediation with alerts, encryption, and other protective actions to prevent end users from accidentally or maliciously sharing data that could put the organization at risk. Data loss prevention software and tools monitor and control endpoint activities, filter data streams on corporate networks, and monitor data in the cloud to protect data at rest, in motion, and in use. DLP also provides reporting to meet compliance and auditing requirements and identify areas of weakness and anomalies for forensics and incident response. Adoption of DLP is being driven by insider threats and by more rigorous state privacy laws, many of which have stringent data protection or access components. In addition to being able to monitor and control endpoint activities, some DLP tools can also be used to filter data streams on the corporate network and protect data in motion.

There are several ways the data leaks can happen. The first common cause is a malicious insider, or an attacker who has compromised a privileged user account, abuses their permissions and attempts to move data outside the organization. Second is Extrusion by attackers. Many Cyber-attacks have sensitive data as their primary target. Attackers penetrate the security perimeter using techniques like phishing, malware or code injection, and gain access to sensitive data. The third common cause is Unintentional or negligent data exposure. Many data leaks occur as a result of employees who lose sensitive data in public, provide open Internet access to data, or fail to restrict access as per organizational policies.

4.5.1 Types of DLP technologies

Data In Use: One class of DLP technologies secures data in use, defined as data that is being actively processed by an application or an endpoint. These safeguards usually involve authenticating users and controlling their access to resources.

Data In Motion: When confidential data is in transit across a network, DLP technologies are needed to make sure it is not routed outside the organization or to insecure storage areas. Encryption plays a large role in this step. Email security is also critical since so much business communication goes through this channel.

Data At Rest: Even data that is not moving or in use needs safeguards. DLP technologies protect data residing in a variety of storage mediums, including the cloud. DLP can place controls to make sure that only authorized users are accessing the data and to track their access in case it is leaked or stolen.

Data Identification: it is crucial to determine if data needs to be protected or not. Data can be defined as sensitive either manually by applying rules and metadata, or automatically via techniques like machine learning.

Data Leak Detection: DLP solutions and other security systems like IDS, IPS, and SIEM, identify data transfers that are anomalous or suspicious. These solutions also alert security staff of a possible data leak.

DLP Solutions: The two major DLP Solutions are Network based DLP or Endpoint based DLP.

Endpoint DLP: The Endpoint DLP is installed on the Endpoints such as Desktops, Laptops, and mobile Devices. It gives organizations' visibility into the data as it is created. For example when a Excel file with Social Security Numbers is created or updated. This file can then be tagged to an alert that it contains sensitive data. The agent also sees processes such as copy/paste, print, etc and can protect sensitive data from being burned to a CD or DVD drive, or being copied to removable drives such as a USB device. The agent, being on the endpoint itself, is always protecting the data, even if the device is off the organizations' network and in some unprotected network using a public wireless network. The core downside of an agent is the management that's required. Each machine requires the agent be deployed, or added to the core load, then updated or patched like any other piece of software. The complexity comes from the volume and geographic spread of the laptops, desktops, and servers in any network.

Network DLP: The other DLP Solution is the Network DLP. As the name suggests this lives on the network, typically as a box or virtual machine that traffic passes through. Network DLP is also referred to as data in motion protection. Network DLP can be inserted into a network with little to no overhead. Network DLP sees data as it moves throughout the network and enforces the policies at that time, meaning when a user attempts to email a sensitive file, the nDLP device inspects the traffic and can, through pre-defined policies, block, quarantine, audit, forward, notify, or encrypt - all automatically. Network DLP also has visibility into web traffic such as social media sites. The core downside of the Network DLP is if the endpoint device is off the network, and not on a corporate VPN, organizations' don't have visibility into what's happening with that data.

4.6 ANTIVIRUS SOFTWARE

Antivirus software, also referred as AV Softwares, is a class of program designed to protect, prevent, detect and remove malware infections on computing devices, networks and IT systems. Antivirus software, originally designed to detect and remove malwares from computers, can also protect against a wide variety of threats, including other types of malicious software, such as key-loggers, browser hijackers, Trojan horses, worms, rootkits, spyware, adware, botnets and Ransomware etc. The early versions of Anti-virus programs were just signature based identification mechanism. As the nature of the malware changed over time, similarly the Antivirus programs evolved and included various component to deal with the ever-growing and evolving threats and malwares. Let's have a look at the history and evolution of Anti-Virus Softwares.

History of Malwares: Viruses have been around since the early 1970's. Even though they never had an internet connection back in the 70's viruses still infected computers and spread through removable media, A floppy disk. Back in those days computers were not connected with each other. Hence users used to copy data from one computer to another computer using floppy disks. Back then old 5 14″ disks were very popular. The first recorded virus was in 1971 and it was called the Creeper Virus, which was written by Bob Thomas. What the Creeper virus did was it infected a remote computer by the ARPNET and copied itself displaying the message "I'M THE CREEPER: CATCH ME IF YOU CAN!". The first computer virus the Creeper infected and spread to PDP-10 mainframe, computers manufactured by Digital Equipment Corporation (DEC). American computer programmer Ray Tomlinson developed the **Reaper**. Ray Tomlinson is the same guy who invented email. It was a program designed to delete the single Creeper virus. So in that sense it was the first Antivirus Program. Ironically the "Reaper" was created to delete the Creeper. The Reaper program was not like the anti-virus programs we know today, but in fact was a virus itself in that it was self-replicating and spread through a network.

First PC Virus: 34 years ago in January 1986 the first virus that attacked MS-DOC is called Brain and was written by two brothers, Basit Farooq Alvi and Amjad Farooq Alvi, from Lahore, Punjab province of Pakistan. When the brothers created the virus, they were running a computer store in Lahore city, Pakistan. They noticed that their customers were circulating illegal copies of software they'd written. So, they thought of a unique way of teaching their customers a lesson, they created the Brain virus. Tired of customers making illegal copies of their software, they developed Brain, which replaced the boot sector of a floppy disk with a virus. The virus, which was also the first stealth virus, contained a hidden copyright message, but did not actually corrupt any data. It began infecting 5.2" floppy disks. Both the brothers stressed in interviews that they created the virus only for the illegal copies of the software, putting their names, phone numbers, and their shop's address in the virus code. Basit and Amjad never thought of the virus growing into a global-sized monster, with powers beyond their capacities to control it.

▲ Amjad Farooq Alvi (Left) and Basit Farooq Alvi (Right)

The most interesting thing about the early generation of virus is the motive of the virus writers. They didn't really have a motive. The early viruses such as Brain, Stoned, Cascade, and Form were only written because the programmers wanted to write them. They were created for the purpose of bragging rights to show other programmers. They were basically jokes. Then in 1991 the first devastating virus was discovered. The Michelangelo computer virus, first discovered on 4 February 1991 in Australia, was a hidden virus that only attacked computers on March 6th, Michelangelo's birthday. On March 6th it would wipe the user's hard-drive. Most of the viruses in the early days were still just jokes, designed to play games with the user or simply annoy them. These viruses became things that would alert the users that their computer was infected with little animations or logos. For example, the Happy Birthday Joshi virus would infect the user's computer, then every January 5th the computer would halt during start up and would only continue when the user entered "Happy birthday Joshi".

Then the game changed in 1995, when the first virus was made that didn't infect users hard drive or floppy disk, instead it infected document files. Instead of having to load an executable to infect users' machine, now any document can be infected, and opening the compromised document infects the machine. Now while the Concept virus didn't do much of anything besides that, macro viruses became the common type of viruses. With the change from MSDOS to Windows 95, there came a graphical change in the way viruses were seen. The Boza virus in 1996 would infect Windows programs and show a message to the user.

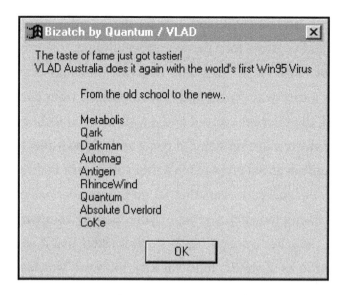

Happy 99 was the first e-mail virus in history, which came around celebrating the new year on a user's computer, then spread itself through e-mail contact list to other users. With the creation of the e-mail virus a new hybrid came out. **Melissa** virus was an e-mail virus and a macro virus. Users would see a document file sent from someone they knew and would open it, where the virus would infect documents and spread again through e-mail contact. This is where they became more complex, as viruses changed from a simple 1 step virus to a multi-step virus. One of the fastest growing viruses for it's time was the Code Red virus which utilized buffer overflow to spread. This virus cost billions of dollars in damage, and only affected a certain type of Microsoft web server application.

MyDoom: On January 26, 2004 the world witnesses a massive outbreak of a e-mail worm called as MyDoom. It was the fastest spreading worm till date. The record set by this mail worm is yet to surpassed even after 16 years. The worm contains the text message *"andy; I'm just doing my job, nothing personal, sorry,"* leading many to believe that the worm's creator was paid. It is believed that the worm originated from

Russia. Within an hour of its appearae it infected millions of computers worldwide and caused a total damage of $38 Billion.

Birth of Anti-Virus Software: Antivirus software was originally designed as a means to detect and remove viruses from computers. As time passed, the internet evolved and a wide array of technologies were invented. However, this growth did come with a downside: the creation of other, more advanced types of malicious software or malware. The late '80s were to be landmark years that set up the foundations of the entire antivirus software industry. German Cyber security company Avira was founded in 1986, but it wasn't until two years later that it would launch its first version of **AntiVir**. John McAfee founded McAfee Associates in 1987. McAfee Associates achieved early success as the creator of McAfee's first commercial antivirus software, The growth of the antivirus industry continued in 1988 and well into the '90s. Symantec—known for its Norton line of computer security products—released the first ever Norton Anti-Virus in 1991. Dutch cyber security company AVG Technologies was founded the same year, and its first AVG Anti-Virus product came out the year after. The mid to late '90s also saw the birth of several Cyber security companies. Bitdefender was founded in Romania in 1996, and Kaspersky Lab was started in 1997 by Eugene and Natalya Kaspersky (his wife at the time).

How Anti-Viru works: When an antivirus program is installed, it will start monitoring the activity of the system by searching files that are being created, Accessed, modified, Transferred, and stored to or from the hard disks and external/removable drives. Files that are being downloaded from the Internet are also scanned. If a suspicious activity is detected, the antivirus program will automatically quarantine the file or stop the processes that are posing risk to the operating system, contacts, or other computers or devices in on the network, unless user trusts the file and allows it to continue its work.

Traditional detection-based antivirus products have had a strong hold on the security market for years. However, recently, due to an exponential rise in Cyber-crime and malware, these traditional antiviruses have been rendered ineffective against many emerging threats. All the executable programs that pass through the system go through an antivirus scan. They then undergo a comparison test with the blacklisted signatures. If they appear to be the same as a blacklisted one, then they are considered to be a malware file. The other program files are then processed through Defense + HIPS (Host Intrusion Prevention System) – this permits only the known files while the unknown files that look suspicious are moved into a restricted virtual environment. The identified good files are documented in the Whitelist, while the suspicious files will be quarantined in the Sandboxed environment.

Scan Engines: Scan Engine is the core of the Anti-Virus Program. Two types of scanner engines are used by antivirus applications –on-demand scanners that are activated only by user in order to scan a part or all of computer and on-access (otherwise called real-time, background guard, resident shield, auto protect) scanners that monitor data real-time i.e. while data is coming into computer, files are being opened and during similar actions.

Almost all Anti-virus programs offer various scans. The most common types are.

Full Scan: As the name suggests this scan check everything that is present on the system. This scan usually will take a few hours to complete if the system happens to have a lot of data stored on it. The Antivirus system usually scans the following when it is running a full scan of the system: a) All network drives, hard drives, and removable storage. b) System memory (RAM) c) System Backups d) Startup folders e) Registry items. Most AV vendors recommend a full system scan every two weeks.

Quick Scan: A quick scan (or its equivalent) targets the entire system but it does not take as much time as a full scan, the files that they scan are the following: a) Commonly infected files and folders b) Running processes and threads c) System memory (RAM) d) Startup folders e) Registry items. This may seem quite similar to the files that are scanned during a full scan, but what sets it apart is that this system analyzes the most likely folders instead of every single one. And they focus only on the files that have been modified since the last scan.

Real Time / On-Access Scan: This is a persistent and ongoing scan. Each time a file is received, opened, downloaded, copied, or modified, Real-time Scan scans the file for security risks. If real time scan detects no security risk, the file remains in its location and users can proceed to access the file. If real time scan detects a security risk, it takes action set in the policy (e.g. quarantine/ block / delete etc) and displays a notification message, showing the name of the infected file, the specific security risk and action taken on the threat. This Scans actively monitors the system memory and all the common virus and security risk locations on the computer quickly. The scan includes all processes that run in memory, important registry files, and files such as config.sys and windows.ini. It also includes some critical operating system folders.

Multi Role Antivirus: Traditional Anti-Virus software only had signature based scan. As the nature of the malwares and cyber attacks has changed over the time, the Anti-virus software also have evolved to mitigate these ever changing nature of these attacks. There are several new features that have been added to the Anti-virus software. Lets have a look at them.

a) **Application Firewall:** The AV also contains an application based Firewall. This component monitors all active network connections on the endpoint and monitors all the incoming and outgoing traffic for suspicious activity. This also includes Intrusion Prevention component.

b) **Application and Device Control:** This feature allows the Cyber security engineer to control which applications are allowed to install and to be used on the machine. The applications can be blocked based on signature or class of applications. The same is true for devices. Specific devices can be allowed while rest (such as removable drives) can be blocked.

c) **Reputation Based Protection:** Signature based scan has its own limitations. The AV practically cannot hold signature of all the applications. This is when the Anti-virus can connect to the central cloud based database to check the reputation of a file or program. Based on the reputation the application is either allowed or blocked.

d) **Behaious Based Protection:** Heuristic scanning is a technique used to catch malicious applications. While traditional signature-based systems rely on predefined virus signatures to catch viruses, heuristics looks at the construction of files for characteristics commonly found in viruses. As a file is examined, the virus-like attributes are totaled. If a threshold in the number of virus-like attributes is passed the file is marked as 'suspicious.'

e) **Browser Protection:** This feature monitors the activity of the Browsers installed on the computer. This helps protect computer from drive-by-infection, scans files being downloaded using browser. Also warns and protects from malicious websites. This feature may also block BHO (Browser Helper Objects) from installing or monitoring user activity.

f) **Email Protection:** This features monitors mailboxes of outlook or other similar mail client programs. Every incoming and outgoing email is scanned and malicious emails are deleted or quarantined.

This feature is especially useful for protection against email sent to target user PC with Ransomware.

g) **Tamper Protection:** A retrovirus is also referred to as an anti-anti-virus virus. This type of malware tries to attack and disable any anti-virus or protective software on the system and is trying to infect to avoid detection. These viruses try to disable / deactivate the Antivirus software by stopping changing or lowering security settings, Registry changes, or group policies. The Tamper protection feature monitors all these features to ensure that malware is not able to disable or lower the security of the computer.

4.7   VIRTUAL PRIVATE NETWORK (VPN)

Normally; when a user connects to a website, user request emerging from users computer is routed directly to the host server of the website user is visiting. This user data is routed over Internet. The internet is an open and public system. We all send and receive information over shared wires and connections. Even though it's an open system, we still exchange a lot of private data, things like credit card numbers, bank information, passwords, and emails. One the data leaves the secure private network; it's out there in the open for anyone to take a peek, at any point in the process. Even the ISPs are in a position to see a lot of user's activity online.

This is where VPN comes in handy. A Virtual Private Network, popularly known as 'VPN' is programming that creates a safe, encrypted connection using tunneling protocols to encrypt data at the sending end, and decrypt it at the receiving end to ensure users online privacy and protect sensitive data. The originating and receiving network addresses are also encrypted to provide better security and anonymity for online activities. When VPN is enabled it creates an encrypted tunnel between user and a remote server operated by a VPN service. A user's internet traffic is routed through this tunnel, so user data remains secure from prying eyes along the way. Because user's traffic is exiting the VPN server, users' computer appears to have the IP address of said server, masking users' identity and location.

The first step of the security process for a VPN involves creating a tunnel protocol, which acts as well a tunnel or conduit for user data going to its destination for the information packets being transferred to pass through. It creates a security layer which instantly terminates the connection whenever it detects an intrusion. Then it reconnects the user back to the server using a different route avoiding the compromised point, points or the entire previous route altogether for the next re-connection. Some services even utilize highly specified routes which they consider being "Lower Risk" than other ones; usually based on some sort of internally established metrics or a working partnership with the operator. Inside this protective tunnel is where the data can be found. Data is also encrypted as one might expect but on top of this further efforts are made to ensure that the contents of users' data don't become public. Beyond standard encryption non-linear transfer methods such as utilizing multiple routes for the traffic or the introduction of dummy code into the information; packet prevents prying eyes from seeing anything but a small garbled slice of the overall data. Data transfers happen in basically the same way that all other internet traffic does while offering a tremendously higher level of personal protection and the ability to access secure networks from any geographical location. Some pages and services might not work correctly over a VPN. Also content loading performance can be affected as well. Since encryption efforts coupled with what can be considered less direct routes can lead to a slower overall experience. In many cases though this can be solved quite easily by installing another web browser on computer for non-critical work. It's also worth noting that many VPN users actually report faster speeds on certain popular sites such as content Streaming or Online Games at peak times presumably because their traffic is avoiding some of the congestion seen along the other traditional routes.

VPN Protocols: VPN protocols ensure an appropriate level of security to connected systems, when the underlying network infrastructure alone cannot provide it. There are several different protocols used to secure and encrypt users and corporate data. Popular VPN Protocols are as below.

a) **PPTP - Point-to-Point Tunneling Protocol:** PPTP is one of the oldest protocols by Microsoft, and it is the fastest of all VPN protocols. Due to its basic encryption and low security, PPTP offers a much faster connection. It supports most platforms and is easy to setup. PPTP has many well-known security issues. PPTP uses a TCP control channel and a Generic Routing Encapsulation tunnel to encapsulate PPP packets.

b) **L2TP - Layer 2 Tunneling Protocol:** Layer Two Tunneling Protocol (L2TP) is an extension of the Point-to-Point Tunneling Protocol (PPTP). An L2TP connection comprises two components: a tunnel and a session. The tunnel provides a reliable transport between two L2TP Control Connection Endpoints (LCCEs) and carries only control packets. The session is logically contained within the tunnel and carries user data. A single tunnel may contain multiple sessions, with user data kept separate by session identifier numbers in the L2TP data encapsulation headers. It is typical to deploy L2TP alongside other technologies, for example IPSec, to provide security features. This gives L2TP the flexibility to interoperate with various different security mechanisms within a network.

c) **SSTP - Secure Socket Tunneling Protocol:** SSTP, or Secure Socket Tunneling Protocol, is designed to safeguard PPP traffic using the SSL/TLS channel. It's a much better and safer for Windows users as opposed to L2TP/IPSec or PPTP. SSTP is a VPN tunnel that utilizes an SSL 3.0 channel to send PPP or L2TP traffic. SSL allows for transmission and data encryption, and traffic integrity checking. Due to this, SSTP can pass through most firewalls and proxy servers by using the SSL channel over TCP port 443. As with other IP-over-TCP tunneling protocols, SSTP only performs well if there is sufficient bandwidth on the network link that is not tunneled. If enough bandwidth is not available, the tunneled TCP timers will possibly expire, causing a large decrease in SSTP performance.

d) **IPSec - Internet Protocol Security:** This is a standardized framework for securing IP communications by encrypting and/or authenticating each IP packet in a data stream. The IPsec standard is commonly used for establishing an IPsec VPN over the Internet between fixed end-points, as well as for creating an encrypted VPN client-server connection between remote devices and a fixed network. IPsec VPNs have largely been supplanted by SSL VPNs, such as the F5 FirePass SSL VPN, because they enforce end-point security, require no configuration on the remote machine, and apply security at the application layer instead of at the network layer.

Security in the application layer alleviates typical configuration and implementation failures IPsec, which by design enforces security in the network layer and is functionally limited to usage on known and controlled networks.

e) **OpenVPN - Open-Source Protocol:** Unlike other IPSec-based tunneling protocols, OpenVPN relies on SSL/TLS for authentication and encryption. It is the standard security technology to create secure, remote site-to-site or point-to-point connections. SSL is widely used for protecting financial transactions, data transfers, email, and more. OpenVPN is compatible with most major and lesser-known operating systems in use today. It provides powerful encryption standards and is excellent when it comes to circumventing restrictive firewalls and prohibitive geo-blocking. The open-source VPN protocol can be configured to use either TCP or UDP and supports up to 256-bit encryption. Since it is open-source, security vulnerabilities are usually fixed by the open-source community as soon as they are found. OpenVPN is often used due to the various benefits it brings to the table. For starters, unlike other protocols, it is compatible with Android and iOS. It also can bypass any blockade that it encounters. Also, it can access many ports for communication.

f) **IKEv2 - Internet Key Exchange Version-2:** This Protocol dynamically establishes and maintains a shared state between the end-points of an IP datagram. IKEv2 performs mutual authentication between two parties and establishes the IKEv2 Security Association (SA). IKE typically uses X.509 PKI certificates for authentication and the Diffie–Hellman key exchange protocol to set up a shared session secret. IKE is part of the Internet Security Protocol (IPSec) which is responsible for negotiating security associations (SAs), which are a set of mutually agreed-upon keys and algorithms to be used by both parties trying to establish a VPN connection/tunnel. IKE is comprised of two phases. In phase 1, IKE creates an authenticated, secure channel between the two IKE peers. This is done using the Diffie-Hellman key agreement protocol. IKE supports multiple authentication methods as part of the phase 1 exchange. In phase 2, IKE negotiates the IPSec security associations and generates the required key material for IPSec.

g) **SSL/TLS** - Secure Socket Layer: SSL and its successor TLS are the most commonly used cryptographic protocols today. Every time users visit an HTTPS website, SSL or TLS secures users connection with the server. It is used in VPN protocols like OpenVPN for encryption, but is not a VPN protocol by itself.

h) **WireGuard:** WireGuard is the newest VPN protocol. This is protocol meant to be a replacement of IPSec, it is lighter and faster. Furthermore, it is open source, which means a reduced likelihood of security vulnerabilities. However, the protocol is still under development and lags behind in terms of cross-platform compatibility.

VPN Kill Switch: When VPN is used, user's data traffic is encrypted and it hides users' physical location and IP address. But when the VPN connection to the VPN server drops user sensitive data could be intercepted, and users' security can be compromised. In many cases, the VPN connection may drop because of issues on the user's end. For example, interruptions in users internet connection may cause interruptions in users connection to the VPN server. Or users firewall might block the VPN software. If users device has auto-updates turned on and its advised under best practices that it should — it may reboot the device itself and connect to the web without the protection of the VPN tunnel. Apart from that there are many other cases no one can foresee. This is when The Kill Switch comes to the rescue. Most of the modern VPN services and Softwares have a built in feature that monitors users connection to the VPN server all the time, and if the connection accidentally drops, the Kill Switch blocks users device from accessing the web. When the VPN tunnel is reestablished, the Kill Switch restores internet access. In a way, A VPN kill switch is the last line of users Cyber Security defense.

Benefits of VPN: A VPN can help user achieve more online privacy by masking users browsing activity from eavesdroppers, users ISP, and others. Let's look at the major benefits of the VPN service.

1) **Security:** One of the biggest and major benefits of VPN is the Cyber security it provides. If configured correctly a VPN can Protect user connection from spammers and hackers, which is arguably more common on insecure public networks. The entire data communication happens inside a secure tunnel.

2) **Privacy:** VPN users get to enjoy higher degree of Privacy than the non-VPN users. When a VPN is in place, ISP's will not be able to access a user's online activity. Instead, ISP can see encrypted statistics by the VPN server. Many VPN service providers also have no logs policy. As a result any trace of user activity does not remain behind for later review.

3) **Anonymity:** Using a VPN, one can easily browse the internet entirely without being traced, compared to other software, one of the benefits of using a VPN connection service is to allow users access to any websites and web applications anonymously. The websites can only see the IP address of the VPN server from where the traffic exited, keeping user identity hidden.

4) **Bypass Restriction:** Accessing blocked websites is achieved using VPN and for going through established Internet filters. For this reasons, there are a greater number of VPN services available in a country where Internet censorship are used. Netflix, Hulu and other streaming content service providers do not serve users outside

certain geographical area. Many VPN users are simply able to bypass this restriction by switching to a different VPN server located in a geographical location which is served by these services.

5) **Speed:** Depending on where user is based and the laws around Net-Neutrality, some internet service providers have been found to intentionally decrease the amount of content they allow users to watch giving them a higher level of profits. Having a VPN can thwart an ISP from identifying users activity and slowing down users speed.

4.8 WEB BROWSERS

Web browser is a program on a computer or a smart phone or a mobile device that allows users to view websites. Common web browsers are Internet Explorer, Google Chrome, Mozilla Firefox, and Safari on apple devices etc. Web browsers are often developed by the same companies that provide operating system or Search Engines. Operating systems like Microsoft's Windows, Ios (MAC OS from Apple), Linux or Android; these are the operating systems build into the device to operate the device and also to communicate with other hardware devices such as Printer, Scanner, Monitor screen etc. But Search engine like Google search or Bing is a website that helps users finds the information they need on World Wide Web. It's important to know that a web browser is also not the Internet or the World Wide Web itself; but just a program users use to view the web pages on the World Wide Web, first designed by Tim Berners-Lee. A Web browser is like a librarian and translator, finding a webpage user has requested and then converting codes into a user friendly and intelligible form. User can request a webpage either by clicking on a Hyperlink or typing a URL (Universal Resource Locator) into the address bar. The browser sends this request to a DNS (Domain Name System) serve which in turn sends user request to the server where the web page that user has requested resides referred as Host server. This host server then sends the source code for the webpage back to the user's browser. This source code could be written in variety of languages that instructs the browser how to show the webpage to the user. Example, HTML (Hypertext Markup Language) labels the content by Type. So the browser knows what it the title, what the paragraph is and what an image is. CSS (Cascading Style Sheets) tells the browser how these different types of content to be displayed indicating the size, shape, position and color of the text. Many complicated elements including interactive elements like Chat window are often developed using Java scripts. In addition to finding and displaying the web pages; most browsers includes the features that improves the Internet surfing experience. For example most browsers now a day include a history feature that shows date, time and URL of the web pages visited by user. Bookmark feature allows saving the URL for later use. Browsers sometime temporarily save the source code of some of the websites in cache memory so that the website can load faster in future. The browsers also allow some websites to save a small piece of data in something called as cookies, that is often used to save progress on the web games or to save user login session so that the user don't have to log in again and again. New features of the browser include extensions. These browser extensions offer additional feature such as appearance customization, popup blocking, password management and so on.

4.8.1 History of Web Browsers

Tim Berners-Lee, a British scientist, invented the World Wide Web (WWW) in 1989, while working at CERN. The Web was originally conceived and developed to meet the demand for automated information-sharing between scientists in universities and institutes around the world. By the end of 1990, Tim Berners-Lee had the first Web server and browser up and running at CERN, demonstrating his ideas. He developed the code for his Web server on a NeXT computer. To prevent it being accidentally switched off, the computer had a hand-written label in red ink: "This machine is a server. DO NOT POWER IT DOWN!!" 'info.cern.ch' was the address of the world's first website and Web server, running on a NeXT computer at CERN. The first Web page address was http://info.cern.ch/hypertext/WWW/TheProject.html This page contained links to information about the WWW project itself, including a description of hypertext, technical details for creating a Web server, and links to other Web servers as they became available. Berners-Lee's original Web browser running on NeXT computers showed his vision and had many of the features of current Web browsers. In addition, it included the ability to modify pages from directly inside the browser – the first Web editing capability. This screenshot shows the browser running on a NeXT computer in 1993.

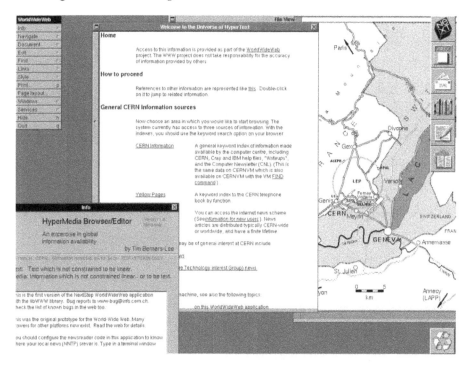

▲ A screenshot showing the NeXT World Wide Web browser created by Tim Berners-Lee (Image: CERN)

Growth of Web Browsers: Only a few users had access to a NeXT computer platform on which the first browser ran, but development soon started on a simpler, 'line-mode' browser, which could run on any system. It was written by Nicola Pellow during her student work placement at CERN. In 1991, Berners-Lee released his WWW software. It included the 'line-mode' browser, Web server software and a library for developers. In March 1991, the software became available to colleagues using CERN computers. A few months later, in August 1991, he announced the WWW software on Internet newsgroups and interest in the project spread around the world.

The first Web server in the US came online in December 1991, once again in a particle physics laboratory: the Stanford Linear Accelerator Center (SLAC) in California. At this stage, there were essentially only two kinds of browser. One was the original development version, which was sophisticated but available only on NeXT machines. The other was the 'line-mode' browser, which was easy to install and run on any platform but limited in power and user-friendliness. It was clear that the small team at CERN could not do all the work needed to develop the system further, so Berners-Lee launched a plea via the internet for other developers to join in. Several individuals wrote programs for browsers, mostly for the X-Window System. Notable among these were MIDAS by Tony Johnson from SLAC, Viola by Pei Wei from technical publisher O'Reilly Books, and Erwise by Finnish students from Helsinki University of Technology.

The software giant Microsoft Corporation became interested in supporting Internet applications on personal computers and developed its own Web browser (based initially on Mosaic), Internet Explorer (IE), in 1995 as an add-on to the Windows 95 operating system. IE was integrated into the Windows operating system in 1996. Apple's Safari was released in 2003 as the default browser on Macintosh personal computers and later on iPhones (2007) and iPads (2010). Safari 2.0 (2005) was the first browser with a privacy mode, Private Browsing, in which the application would not save Web sites in its history, downloaded files in its cache, or personal information entered on Web pages. The first serious challenger to IE's dominance was Mozilla's Firefox, released in 2004 and designed to address issues with speed and security that had plagued IE. In 2008 Google launched Chrome, the first browser with isolated tabs, which meant that when one tab crashed, other tabs and the whole browser would still function. By 2013 Chrome had become the dominant browser, surpassing IE and Firefox in popularity. Microsoft discontinued IE and replaced it with Edge in 2015. In the early 21st century, smartphones became more computer-like, and more-advanced services, such as Internet access, became possible. Web usage on smartphones steadily increased, and in 2016 it accounted for more than half of Web browsing.

Battle of the Browsers: On the internet today there are billions of websites. But before even visiting one of these websites a program must be consulted that of course being the web browser. The internet existed long before the world's first web browser having its roots as ARPANET in the mid-60s. What makes the World Wide Web a special entity within the internet though is that it makes up just about every webpage that we visit. The job of a web browser is pretty simple; ask website host computer for a document, get the document and then following instructions encoded within the document called HTML display the page to the user. The first program to do this unsurprisingly was called World Wide Web created by Sir Tim Berners-lee at CERN and released on Christmas Day 1990. Within a year another browser Viola-www had been released for Unix. The World Wide Web wasn't accessible to very many outside of universities since the only two browsers which could use it were written for next step in UNIX. Both of which were exotic higher end computing platforms and mostly unknown to home and business computer users who inclined towards Windows and Macintosh. This divide quickly changed though with the introduction of the browser Mosaic in 1993. The University of Illinois had recently received funding for the National Center for supercomputing applications from the high performance computing Act of 1991. Popularly known as the Al Gore bill. A good candidate for popularizing the Internet would have to be Marc Andreessen who wrote Mosaic the first popular web browser for Windows and eventually Macintosh. Mosaic includes images in line with text, first at the time that started very early web design but being compatible with Windows and Macintosh computers. Mosaic also helped to bring the Internet into the homes of average people. Mosaic proved to be such a success that the company Spyglass Inc. licensed some of the source code from the University of Illinois to build and commercialize their own web browser. Marc Andreessen also saw the commercial potential of this web browser and in 1994 with several members of his Mosaic team broke off from the University of Illinois and created Netscape Communications. Their new browser Netscape Navigator was a complete rewrite and eventual competitor to Spyglass's Mosaic. It was named internally Mozilla a combination of the words Mosaic Killer. Netscape Navigator quickly became popular to the public with many ISPs and computer magazines distributing it for free. With well over the majority of the web browsing market share by 1996 Netscape soon found itself in a powerful position for the future of the web. Any design changes or new features included in Netscape like JavaScript, frames, cookies and others were soon copied by other browsers in an effort to stay compatible. This would quickly become standards without ever having to go through the World Wide Web Consortium, the organization responsible for standardization on the web. Not only was this helpful to Netscape for allowing it to lead the way for online content being the first browser to get a new feature but it also left all other browsers in the continuous game of catch-up devoting more time to copying Netscape's new features. Rather than creating their own and becoming more competitive. It would take massive developmental resources from a huge company with lots of money to topple Netscape's throne.

Microsoft had quickly realized the potential of creating a web browser and decided to create their own web browser off of the same source code of Mosaic licensing from Spyglass Inc. The first two versions of this new browser called Internet Explorer weren't very impressive. After setting a massive development team loose Internet Explorer version 3 was about functionally identical to Netscape Navigator with the Edit pert from Microsoft the Internet Explorer was conveniently included with Windows operating system. Leaving many users diverted to Internet Explorer browser. Tensions between both companies were unsurprisingly rising. The release party for an Internet Explorer for Microsoft's employees constructed a massive metal sculpture version of the blue IE logo and placed it on the lawn of Netscape's Offices. Not wants to be outdone the Netscape employees knocked it over and placed the sculpture of their mascot Mozilla on top for the sign that read Netscape 72 Microsoft 18. A reminder that even though ie market share was growing Netscape was still on top. Microsoft was still growing quickly and certainly through suspicious means in 1998 the dominance in the browser market became one of the central points in an antitrust case against them United States v Microsoft. Initial ruling threatened to split Microsoft Company into two. But in the end Microsoft was able to keep Internet Explorers part of Windows. By the end of the trial in 2001 Netscape's market share had been all but decimated. It was later bought out by AOL to then up-and-coming Internet Service Provider.

later Netscape was made open-source. After several failed attempts to win back its user base AOL pulled the plug on Netscape Navigator in 2008. The dominance of Internet Explorer during the early 2000s was incredible and with near total control of the industry. Microsoft's Internet Explorer ruled the web much like Netscape Navigator had done in the past.

Internet Explorer version 6 was released with Windows XP in 2001. This was essentially the final nail in the coffin for Netscape Navigator. Within a year of its release Internet Explorer accounted for 95 percent of all web traffic. Microsoft no longer seeing competition from Netscape; began to slow down their update schedule and decided to synchronize updates for the browser with updates to the operating system. This meant that the next update to IE wouldn't come out until over a year after its initial release. It would take two years for the next one after that. Considering that at one point to catch up to Netscape Navigator, Microsoft had been pumping out updates as frequent as two months apart. It was evident that Internet Explorer wasn't competitively innovating for rather surviving off of an already massive install base. All that it would take was a browser willing to innovate faster than Microsoft. Right before Netscape had been bought out by AOL, the code was made open-source and released as the Mozilla application suite. At first it met with strong support but it became apparent that the code was pretty messy from being written for various platforms and a stronger focus on including features rather than writing elegant and efficient code. Going after the codes initial release, Mozilla planned a roadmap to completely rewrite the code-base to be much more efficient. Part of this rewrite also included an ongoing project from the days of Netscape called NG layout. A web rendering engine which was eventually renamed Gecko. Compared to other browsers at that time; Gecko was faster and took up nearly a tenth the required memory. Being able to fit on a single floppy disk. While the introduction of a new engine along with a complete code rewrite delayed the release of Mozilla's new browser. Version 1.0 of what was called Phoenix meant to be symbolic of the browser rising from the ashes of Netscape was completed in 2002. The name phoenix didn't stick though since Mozilla received complaints from the BIOS manufacturer Phoenix technologies. In response the name changed to Mozilla Firebird. At least until the Firebird project then known for their database software of the same name complaint. Mozilla argued that as long as the browser was referred to as Mozilla Firebird the two applications wouldn't be confused. But they eventually relented and came up with the name Firefox. A nickname for the red panda. At first only slowly eating away at IE's user base; Firefox has new features and improved security compared to the data browser helped to gain popularity online. Nearly the same time of Firefox with development; Apple had been working on a browser of their own based on the KHTML engine which was eventually worked into a new engine called WebKit. Since 1997 an agreement with Microsoft had ensured the Internet Explorer was installed as the default browser on Macintosh machines; yes there was actually a time when Internet Explorer was on Mac. This time of year agreement lasted all the way until the release of Mac OS 10.2 and was it no longer in effect. Apple released Safari in 2003 and for Mac OS 10.3 onwards. Apple included Safari as the default browser rather than IE. In fact just like how Internet Explorer for a time was released on Macs as well as Windows. Apple reciprocated the Macs and Windows living together mass hysteria with releases of Safari for Windows from 2007 to 2012. At the time of its beta release Safari was actually shown to be the fastest web browser available for Windows. With the support of Mac and iPhone users by being the pre-installed web browser Safari also took off as a capable competitor to Internet Explorer. The success of Mozilla Firefox cut the attention of other companies as well. Most notably Google. Who is early as 2004 began to hire former browser developers from Microsoft and Mozilla. Originally mixed up about joining in the fierce browser market then CEO Eric Schmidt was so impressed by an early prototype that he changed his mind. The primary focus of this new browser for being fast and minimalist compared to other bloated browser at the time led to its name Chrome. Since its release in 2008 Google Chrome has risen to be the most popular web browser online today. Surpassing Firefox in early 2012 and IE a few months later. Currently Chrome comes for well over the major whole web traffic and it still appears to be growing. This growth can mostly be attributed to Chrome's clean user, interface Google's massive web presence and its inclusion with the Android OS for mobile devices. Internet Explorer may have been popular in 2002 but a combination of too few updates, rapidly changing web standards, focusing on multimedia content, and the introduction of three incredibly competitive browsers created a perfect storm that uneven a 95 percent market share could save. Korean and Microsoft even reached a point where they awaited the prolonged death of IE6, but the decline of Internet Explorer 6 usage didn't necessarily mean that users were transitioning over to a new version of Internet Explorer. Given the incredible age of Internet Explorer and the stigma carried from being supported out of date; Microsoft completely rewrote the browser. Now called Edge which is included with Windows 10. Currently IE still maintains larger market share than edge, which holds anywhere from one to five percent. But the days of the ones ubiquitous IE are numbered with even as creator Microsoft turning its back on the project.

4.8.1   Web Browser terms and Features

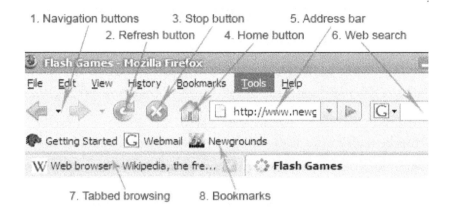

Navigation button: Browser has a back and a forward button to for navigation through web-pages. If user had clicked a link by mistake, he can simply click back button to go back to the webpage that initially was on. Back button takes user one-step back in browsing history, to the page user was on before the current page. The forward button is grayed-out (disabled) most of the time, but it becomes available if user has used the Back button. It allows users to move forward through browsing history, to where user was before the Back button was used.

Refresh button: It is used to force web browser to reload webpage. Most major web browsers use caching mechanism (store local copies of visited pages to speed up performance) that sometimes prevents seeing the most updated information; by clicking refresh, latest version of the page is forcefully reloaded.

Stop Button: (X) Cancels web browser's communication with a server and stops page loading. This will be found either just inside the Address bar or just next to it. It only appears when the page is currently in the process of loading.

Home button: Displays the Home page setup within the browser settings. This is also the first page that shows up when a browser is opened up. Many organizations', offices have their own company web page setup as a home page.

Address Bar: This is a component of an Internet browser where user can enter the website address or URL he wish to visit. Address bars have been a regular feature in most Web browsers since their early versions. They are usually located at the top of the browser and can be hidden with the help of settings in most Web browsers. In some browsers Address bars also offer features like auto-completion and at times a list of suggestions based on addresses in a browser's Web history. Now a day in most browsers Address bar also support searching functionality.

Search Bar: There are two different places to search from in a web browser; there is the address bar and the search bar. Users can type in the URL directly into the address bar. But if the user is not aware of the URL or wants to search like hotels/ restaurants, he can search that using the search bar. In some browser the address bar itself acts like a search bar. It analyses the text put into the address bar. If the text does not look like a URL, the search engine takes over and displays the search results. This function is really helpful. If user misspells the URL he might be re-directed to incorrect and some shady website, but browsers like Google chrome displays the correct website link at the top of all the searches.

Bookmark: It's not easy remembering the web address and complicated URLs of every site users like to visit. Thankfully, bookmarks make it simple to save and organize specific websites so user can revisit them later. Several web browsers have different methods to bookmark a website; but the most common is the Star symbol present in the address bar. As soon as user clicks on the star symbol, the browser offers to save the current URL to bookmark.

History: Every time users use a browser to go online, the browser saves a copy of every page that is displayed. Every browser keeps a track of where user has been and a history of what pages user has seen. This is also knows as Browsing history. Browser application designers realized that people needed a way of knowing where they'd been and what they'd read or seen online over a long Internet session. The history feature on web browsers is there to make users' online experience simpler and to provide convenience. But it can feel a little strange, knowing that someone can peek into users' browser history to see what user have been up to. Most of users wouldn't like that.

May browser have default setting to delete the web-browsing history after certain period. For example, last 30, 60 or 90 days. Any information which is older than the configured days is deleted. User also gets a choice to delete the web-browsing history manually.

Pop-up Blocker: Now a days Pop-up blockers is a hidden feature within most common browsers. They are built into common web browsers to prevent unwanted pop-up windows from interfering with and cluttering users browsing experience. Most pop-ups are ads, malware, and other unwanted windows. They are annoying and most of the times degrade the browsing experience. Pop-up blocker feature of the browser prevent small pop-up windows from interfering with user web browsing. The browser provides some kind of notification when a pop-up is blocked from showing up. But some websites required pop-ups, so the user may have to unblock or whitelist a website to allow the website to show these pop-ups. Similarly sometime the pop-up blocker may fail to disable the pop-up. In such scenarios user may have to Black-list the website manually to stop the popups from showing.

Tabbed Browsing: Tabbed browsing is a Web browser feature in which several websites may be opened in one browser window, versus the traditional method where each website is opened in an individual browser window. Tabbed browsing is a relatively new feature; now days found in almost all Web browsers. Tabbed browsing is a function of some Web browsers that allow uses to surf and view multiple pages by loading the Web sites into "tabbed" sections of one page, rather than multiple pages. This allows the user to open multiple pages at the same time, either in different browser windows or in different tabs of the same window. This allows the user to view a selection of favorite sites in one window, view multiple search results at the same time, and would allow users to set several pages as a home page, rather than just one. The first browser to offer tabbed browsing was *InternetWorks* in 1994, but the feature did not become popular until Mozilla incorporated the function into their browser in 2003. Now tabbed browsing a common feature of almost all web browsers.

Tabbed browsing is a useful Web browser feature as multiple website tabs may be opened simultaneously. Because tabs are neatly arranged, tabbed browsing reduces desktop clutter. Also a slow-loading Web page or website may be opened and loaded in the background, which allows a user to remain engaged in another tab.

Private Browsing: At a basic level, privacy is the state of being free from being observed or disturbed by others. In the cyber world, information privacy relates to users right to have control over how his personal data is collected and used. Users' privacy is important, because users personal information has value, Identity thieves and other cybercriminals who can sell that information to malicious actors. But when a user goes online using a web browser, browsers can store data about users' searches and online activity to make it easier for user to revisit websites. Browsers can store web-based content like usernames and passwords to speed up the log-in process and to improve browsing experience. This can be helpful in the short-term, but users likely don't want this information shared with other users or organizations without their approval.

To avoid this many browsers have a feature knows as Private-Browsing. It is a feature that major web browsers offer to help keep users temporary browsing data private. When using a private browser, such as incognito mode, users browsing history, search records, and cookies aren't retained by the browser. Private browsing is a privacy feature present in some Web browsers that disables Web cache, cookies, browsing history or any other tracking feature that the browser may have. This allows the user to browse the Web without leaving traces such as local data that can later be retrieved. One major feature of private browsing is disabling data storage through cookies, which is a way for websites to track and record a user's activities. With private browsing settings turned on, they help keep users Internet sessions private from other users of the same computer or device. Some private browsing modes can erase files that user have downloaded or bookmarked. Some browsers also offer tracking protection and help hide users location.

Private Browsing Myths: Although private browsing brings users with a bit of privacy; it does not ensure true privacy. Private Browsing does not mask user identity or activity online. Websites can still gather information such as source IP address and other information about users visits, even if user do not signed into the website. Internet Service Providers also can track the websites visited by user. If user uses his device at work or uses a free Wi-Fi, the network provider can track the websites user visited. Also private browsing will not protect user from any malware that may be present on the user machine, such as key –loggers or track wares. Private browsing only hides the browsing activity on the device, not from the network. The network that is used for browsing can still track user activity.

Different web browsers: When it comes to web browsers; users have a variety of browsers to choose from. As of year 2020 AD; there are more than 25 different browsers users can choose from. Some users even prefer to use two or more browser in a single device for various activities. A decade ago Microsoft's Internet Explorer (IE) was the dominant browser on the internet. But as different browsers started to emerge, people quickly adopted them and left IE. In fact, IE was so slow that many people made memes on it.

1) **Google Chrome:** The first beta version of Chrome was released on September 2, 2008, for personal computers (PCs) running various versions of Microsoft Corporation's Windows OS (operating system). Chrome is based on the open-source code of the Chromium project, but Chrome itself is not open-source. Its one of the most popular browser irrespective of platform. Whether it's a PC, or Mac or Smartphones. The main reason for Google chrome's popularity is its speed. It's a fast browser. It opens quickly and loads multiple tabs and pages in just one click. It's probably the fastest browser available today. Another reason for using Chrome is its simplicity. It

combines the address bar and Google search bar in one Omni box and lets the users have an easy browsing experience. Users can sign into Chrome browser using users Google account. This will sync all browsing data across all users Google devices, such as search history, bookmarks etc. Some people avoid it for privacy concerns as users browsing habits and information is tracked by Google.

2) **Apple Safari:** Apple first released Safari browser on desktops in 2003 with Mac OS X Panther. Later a mobile version was bundled with iOS devices since the iPhone's introduction in 2007. Now it's pre-installed as the default browser for Apple product such as Apple PCs, Tabs and iPhones. If a user uses multiple Apple products, the built-in integration and sharing are convenient features such as iCloud, Keychain lets one access saved passwords on iDevices. Safari may be popular among Apple users, but outside this realm Safari is not as popular. One of the reasons is that this browser is not easily available on Linux and doesn't always work well on Window and Lack of openness on Apple's part means fewer customization options.

3) **Mozilla Firefox:** Popularly known only as Firefox, is one of the oldest and still popular web-browser on the internet. The Mozilla project was created in 1998 with the release of the Netscape browser suite source code. It was intended to harness the creative power of thousands of programmers on the Internet and fuel unprecedented levels of innovation in the browser market. Community members got involved and expanded the scope of the project's original mission — instead of just working on Netscape's next browser, people started creating a variety of browsers, development tools and a range of other projects. Firefox was created by Dave Hyatt and Blake Ross as an experimental branch of the Mozilla browser, first released as Firefox 1.0 on November 9, 2004. Tracking has become an epidemic online: companies follow browsers every move, click and purchase,

collecting user data to predict and influence behavior. Most users prefer Firefox over Google chrome as it provides better privacy from online tracking.

4) **Internet Explorer:** The iconic browser was initially released in 1995 by Microsoft. Since then, it has been changed completely with the newer version of Microsoft Windows. However, it is still used by millions of users because of the application compatibility and limitation of the operating system. It offers all the necessary security and privacy-related features. After beating Netscape Navigator Microsoft did not took concrete efforts into the development and up keeping of the browser. As a result its performance degraded over time. In fact, IE was so slow that many people made memes on it. Later, Microsoft launched the Edge browser which had the backward compatibility of Internet Explorer with the earlier version of Windows 10. The new Microsoft Edge is based on Chromium and was released on January 15, 2020. It is compatible with all supported versions of Windows, and macOS. Since then, Edge got many updates and additional features with an advanced user interface for touch screen devices. The Edge browser is comparably fast and consumes fewer resources.

5) **Opera:** Opera is a freeware web browser for Microsoft Windows, Android, iOS, macOS, and Linux operating systems developed by Opera Software. It was first released on 10 April 1995. One of the biggest and most attractive features of Opera that is missing in other browser is that Opera is the only browser that includes a built-in VPN. Web browser users who are concerned about their privacy like to use a VPN (virtual private networks) to hide browsing activities from ISPs and any other intervening entities between them and the site they are visiting.

6) **Tor:** The Onion Router or as its popularly known as TOR, is a web-browsing tool used to surf the web anonymously. There are many ways the Internet can track users. By using users IP address, websites are able to use identifying information to target advertising and collect data about users browsing habits. So it's no surprise that journalists, activists, and privacy advocates have turned to Tor for a more anonymous browsing experience. In a normal Internet connection users are directly connected to the website they're trying to visit. This website, and any other prying eyes on the network, can see who the requestor is and what that user is trying to access using users IP address. The Tor network however is made up of countless nodes, or relay points, that pass user data along using layers of encryption - hence the Onion metaphor. Each node that users data passes through peels off another layer of encryption, showing the previous node's IP address, as well as where it's being sent to. The last node users data passes through is known as the exit node, and it peels off the final layer of encryption and then delivers users data to the intended server. The point of origin, and the intermediary nodes, is completely unknown. Besides browsing the Internet, Tor users can utilize it's hidden services to create private websites and messengers that can only be found using the Tor browser. These private sites, which are part of the dark web, are where pages like the Internet black market Silk Road can be found. However, not all activity on Tor is for nefarious purposes. Anonymous Internet usage can be important for journalists who are reaching out to sources, activists who live in countries that censor or block Internet usage, and even law-enforcement officers who use it for undercover operations. But nothing is perfect, and while onion routing makes it harder for hackers and spies to track user activities, it doesn't make it impossible. There are still ways attackers can view activity on the

network and extract data from vulnerable entry and exit points, especially if Tor users are not diligent.

Browser Plug-ins / Extensions: Since its inception the Web browser, it has progressed a lot. Browsers in itself have a lot of features. But adding more and more features increases its footprint on the device. Along with additional features also comes with additional vulnerabilities. Apart from that many of the users' needs some features which may to be desired by other users, hence adding them could adversely affect the performance of the browser itself. In order to meet the variety of user needs and requirements many browsers provide an option of adding a "add-on" software to the browser. This add-on software are known by various names such as Browser plug-in, Browser add-on or Browser Helper Objects, but commonly known as Browser extensions. A web browser extension is a set of "Add-on" software components that can be added to a web-browser to increase its capabilities. The functionality of a browser extension can range from something simple like giving the user the ability to enlarge images on a webpage or something more complex such as scanning for viruses or blocking advertisements. A browser extension can be created by the company that developed the web browser, a third party company or more often than not the users of the browser. Most of the common browser extensions are free to download and use but some browser extension require one-time or monthly fee. But the vast majorities are free for everyone. A browser extension could quickly become unusable if the browser is regularly updated to newer versions. For some popular browsers such as Google Chrome, Mozilla Firefox there is thousands of browser extension available for free. The most popular browser extensions are usually created to block advertisements, help the user download or manage music or customize a website. Other frequently downloaded browser extension help the user customizes or her browser theme, translate websites into the users desired language or manage and accelerate downloads. Significant portions of browser extension are user created. These browser extensions are usually hosted on the browser's own website and categorized so that users can search for browser extensions that are popular. Sometimes the developer of a user created browser extension asks for a small donation to pay for his or her time creating and keeping the browser extension updated. A browser extension must be maintained by the developer to work with new versions of the browser developers often download the beta version of the browser to ensure that their browser extension still works. If it does not the developer fixes the code and uploads a new version for users to download.

Popular Browser Extensions: The browser extension offers variety of features. But there are some extensions which are more popular than others. Below are some of the most common features and types of extension.

Ad-Blockers: Ad blockers – sometimes known as content blockers – are simple software programs that prevent advertisements from being shown on websites. A vast majority of websites on the Internet exist thanks to online advertising. Millions of websites, from tiny blogs to huge corporate-owned magazines, depend on online advertising revenues in order to operate. Although the most obvious reason that people use ad blockers is to eliminate ads from their web browsing experience. There are actually several other benefits of using them. By removing ads from the web pages users are served faster, page load times are often decreased considerably, and can also reduce data usage. Another reason is that some advertisements make use of scripts, self-contained snippets of code that perform specific functions on a web page – that can be easily exploited to gain access to users' sensitive information or for Drive-By infection attack.

Download Manager: A download manager is a browser extension that makes downloading files faster, easier, and more reliable. A download manager facilitates downloading of files from the Internet. A download manager can download huge files for users even with a poor connection. It can resume broken downloads, limit downloading capacity, browse a site automatically to download specified content, and do regular updating of downloads. It can also be schedule downloads for a certain time, or resume downloads that have been interrupted by a system restart or a power outage. Some download managers also have a feature that let users download music files like Mp3 or wav files from popular websites such as YouTube.

Password Manager: Most web-browsers offer user to save their login information in the browser itself so that the user don't have to log in again and again. But many of the browsers do not save the username and password safely. If compromised, all the users' credentials can be lost. Also if password is changed or modified on one device, it does not sync on the other devices. To avoid this many users install a Password manager browser extension. This extension saves the entire users credentials safe by encrypting before saving them safely, either locally or on cloud. This helps to sync a password change across all the devices. This extension also offer "fill-in" feature where in the extension monitors the website user is browsing to and fills in the credentials when requested by the website.

Notes Manager: This browser extension works like pocket notepad. This helps user to easily copy certain text, image, graphs and other media for later use. It can also help organize the different content downloaded from a browser. It helps users to create quick portable document format for sending quickly via web messenger or email. This also helps user save the web content for late review and use. Web Clipper excels in the ability to pick parts of an article or page to save. Some extension extends the capabilities to include spreadsheet functionality.

Translate and dictionary: The World Wide Web has reached every corner of the globe. Although English being de facto language used globally, but there are millions of web pages which are created in other regional languages. If a user is from some county where English is a foreign language then the Translate and dictionary browser extension can help translate the webpage or a portion of it in users desired language or vice versa. The dictionary component of this browser extension can also suggest words while writing emails or documents online.

Anti-Tracker: Almost every site users visit tracks user to try and link users browsing history to users interests and, in turn, show user targeted adverts. Websites track this user behavior and then choose advertisements suitable for that specific user. This is in a way privacy breach. To avoid that Anti-Tracker extension tracks all the elements of web pages user visits – including plugins and ads placed by external companies. If it sees these appearing across multiple sites user visits then the extension tells users browser not to load any more of that content. The organization says it doesn't keep lists of what to block but discovers trackers as user browse the web and is more effective as time goes on.

4.9 DATA BACKUP

Data backup is the last line of defense. Performing a data backup refers to the action of copying files and information to a secondary location. The data backup process is critical to successful disaster recovery plan. Enterprise's backup data they deem vulnerable to software or hardware malfunctions, data corruption, malicious hacking, user error, natural disasters or other unforeseen events. Backups provide a means to restore destroyed deleted or overwritten files. On the consumer side this process might look like backing up smartphone contacts or photos to a computer, or media files to an external hard drive. In the enterprise, backups can be stored locally on hard disk drives or magnetic tapes, remotely at another physical location, or remotely in cloud storage, which could be public, private or hybrid. For many businesses, best practices include a full data backup once a week during off hours. Additional data backup jobs can be scheduled as necessary.

Some may only backup new or changed data, including incremental backups, differential backups, hot backups, and more. Most enterprises use a combination of backup methods and technologies, as well as multiple backup copies, to ensure complete data availability.

Backup is a copy of data that is created and retained on a backup device for the sole purpose of recovering lost or corrupt data. Organizations also take backups to comply with regulatory requirements.

Backups serve three purposes.

1. **Disaster Recovery:** The backup copies are used for restoring the data at an alternate site when the Primary site is incapacitated due to natural disaster.

2. **Operational Recovery:** These backups are used to restore the data if data loss or data corruption occurs during routine processing. In most organizations the majority of restore request fall into this category.

3. **Archive:** Backups are also performed to meet archival requirements of regulatory compliance.

Backup / Restore Window: A backup window is the time slot/window when it is most suitable to back up data, applications or a system. It is a predefined/prescheduled time when the backup software is permitted to start the backup process on a computer system. A restore window is a predetermined amount of time in which specific data must be restored to avoid any negative or damaging effects on the systems or applications that use the data.

Backup Architecture: A backup system commonly uses client server architecture with a backup serve installed centrally and multiple backup clients installed locally on endpoints on system from where the data needs to be backed up. Below are the three main backup system architecture types

Standalone backup: In this type the backup storage device is directly connected to the device from where data is being backed up. The backup software installed on the machine, such as Time machine on Mac OS or Windows backup software that backs up data to backup storage device. This is suitable for a single user or standalone system.

Two-tier backup architecture: Two machines are involved in this setup. The backup client software installed on the endpoints reads from the source, while the backup manager writes to the data to the backup device. Backup server also manages the storage device.

Three-tier backup architecture: This type is most suitable or large organizations. A dedicated Backup manager has the backup catalog which dictates what needs to be backed up and restored; if necessary. It also collects backup status info. The backup storage node back up the data and writes to the data to the backup device.

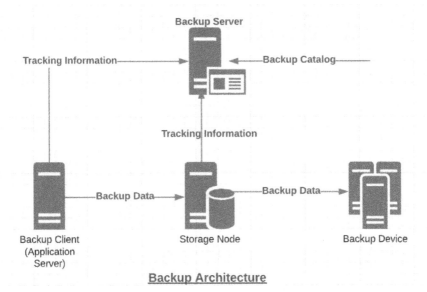

Backup Architecture

Backup Server: This server is responsible to manage backup operations and maintains backup catalogs. This backup catalog contains backup configuration details and backup metadata. Backup configuration is information such as the schedule to run the backup, volume name or partition to backup etc. Backup metadata is the information about the data to be backed up such as type of data to be backed up e.g. file type, data based on time stamps etc.

Backup client: This is installed on the endpoints from where the data needs to be backed up. It is responsible to gather the data that is to be backed up and sends it to storage node. Backup client also sends tracking information to the backup server.

Storage Node: Also known as media server is responsible for writing the data to the backup device. It is also responsible to manage the backup device where the data is backed up. The storage node also sends tracking information to the backup server. In a Two tier backup architecture the backup server and storage node both are installed on a single physical server. Whereas in three tier architecture; Backup server and Storage node, both are installed on separate servers.

Backup Device: It's the physical storage device where the data resides after a backup. This could be physically connected to the storage node or placed on a network connecting it to the storage node platform. As the backup device or media is managed by storage node, it's also referred as media server.

Backup Types: The most common backup types are a full backup, incremental backup and differential backup. Other backup types include synthetic full backups and mirroring.

Full Backup: This is the most common types of backups. As the name suggests this backup type include the entire data. Full backups copy all of an organization's files. Full backups are considered the most reliable, secure method and provide fast restore and recover times. But full backups can be time consuming and require high bandwidth and storage capacity, since it's copying almost the entire data. Full backups are typically scheduled once a week for that reason.

4.9.1 Differential Backup

In backup this method only data changed since the last full back up is backed up. So if a full backup is done on Sunday, a differential backup on Monday should back up all the files changed or added since Sunday. A Tuesday differential backup also back up all the change files since Sunday's full backup, including the files changed on Monday, and so on.

4.9.2   Incremental Backup

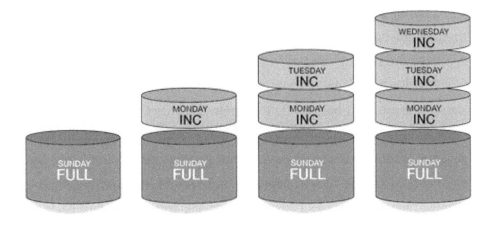

An incremental backup copies all the data that's been changed since the last backup activity of any kind. Like differential, incremental first starts with a full backup. Unlike differential, incremental will only copy data changed since the last incremental backup. So if a full backup was performed on Sunday, Monday's incremental backup would only copy anything changed since Sunday's full backup. But Tuesday's incremental will only backup files changed since Monday's incremental backup, and so on.

Performing a Full backup requires the most amount of space, and will also take the most amount of time. The benefit of an incremental backup is that it copies a smaller amount of data than a full backup. Thus, these operations will have a faster backup speed, and require fewer medium to store the backup. Backup software typically uses the modified time stamp on files and compares it to the time stamp of the last backup. Backup applications track and record the date and time that backup operations occur in order to track files modified since these operations. Differential and Incremental backup methods are used to save space and time when protecting sensitive information. But alternatively, will be more time consuming to restore and search for individual files.

Hot and Cold Backup: Back is also classified as Hot backup and cold backup.

Hot Backup: This is also known as dynamic backup. It is performed in near real-time when the systems are up and running, and new data is continuously generated or captured. There is a time parameter involved as to when to perform a hot-backup. This can range from seconds to minutes. Hot backups are a bit resource intensive as there are multiple repetitions stored at a time. This allows the user to restore the backup to a required point. The most important advantage of Hot Backup is the capability to continue business operations while the backup is in progress. For example databases needs to be available at all times, and hence the business can continue as usual. As a result Hot backup method is chosen to backup database.

Cold Backup: Cold backup is also known as static backup. During this type of backup the normal operations are entirely stopped, and then the backup is performed. This requires the data access to be completely shut off before the backup process can be launched. While the backup is in progress, no business operations can be performed. This is mostly accomplished before the beginning of the day or at the end of the day or over weekends. Cold backups consume fewer resources but have a limitation.

Both Hot and Cold backups have their pros and cons. Organizations must understand which works for them the best. An organization with business operations working around the clock and cannot afford any disturbance or downtime usually go for the Hot backup. If any organization that has fixed working hours, then cold backup is better suitable. The data which has been updated through the working day will be easily copied over without any hindrances. Moreover, since there are no active backups taking place during working hours, the server does not have to handle any extra performance load of the backup operation.

Backup Operation: Backup operation is typically initiated by the Backup Server, but it can also be initiated by the backup client. The backup server coordinates the entire backup process with all the components in a backup environment. The backup server maintains the information about all the backup clients reporting to it in a two or three tier backup architecture setup. It also holds the information of the storage node and backup devices to be used during a backup operation.

The backup server initiates the backup process for different clients based on the backup schedule configured for them. The backup schedule might be different for different clients. When backup is initiated, the backup server retrieves the backup schedule from the backup catalog. Based on this information the backup server instructs the storage node to load the appropriate backup media in the backup device. Simultaneously it instructs the backup clients to collect the data to be backed up and send it to the storage node over a physical connection or over a network. Once the backup client sends the data to the storage node, backup client sends the backup logs (meta data) to the backup server. This includes the name of the files, number of the files, the amount of the data, details of storage node etc. This information is then updated into the backup catalog. Once the storage node receives the data from backup client it organizes it and sends it to the backup device. Similar to the backup client, the storage node also sends logs and metadata to the backup server. This may include the location of the data stored on the backup device, time of the operation, etc. The backup server also updates information received from the storage node into the backup catalog.

Recovery Operation: The restore operation is mostly initiated from the backup client. Some backup client have separate component to perform the restore operation. When a backup is initiated from the backup client, a request is send to the backup server. The backup server refers the backup catalog to check which client is requesting a restore. The backup client can request to restore the data locally on the same backup client or a separate device or node. The backup server selects the data to be restored and the time from which it has to perform a restore. This information is retrieved from the backup catalog. The backup server instructs the storage node to mount the requested backup media on the backup device. Once the backup device loads the backup media and it is ready, the storage node reads the data from the backup device and sends it to the backup client. The storage node sends the metadata to the backup server. Once the backup client receives the data it performs the restore operation and also sends logs and metadata to the backup server confirming success of restore process.

Backup Vs RAID: Backups and redundancy schemes are both data protection methods, but they are not interchangeable. RAID stands for Redundant Array of Independent (sometimes Inexpensive) Disks. There are a number of different types of RAID available. The most common arrays are RAID 1, RAID 5, and RAID 10. The basic purpose of RAID is to provide redundancy, if one disk fails, the other drives essentially take over until the failed drive is replaced. RAID 1 and RAID 10 can both survive multiple drive failures; RAID 5 can survive a single disk failure. While redundancy is the main benefit of a RAID array, it is also one of the cons because in the case of data corruption, the corrupted data is written to all drives on the array. Redundancy is a data protection method intended as a real-time fail-safe measure against hard drive failure.

Backups on the other hand protect against data corruption and loss, but don't provide true redundancy. A backup doesn't provide real-time protection, but it does provide protection against a greater set of problems, including failed drives, device theft, fire, or even just accidentally deleting files.

4.10 CONCLUSION

Just a couple of decades ago, who would have imagined that the internet will become an inseparable part of our lives? Since its inception, the internet has transformed the business and society at all levels. Whether we are at work or on our morning commute, whether we are travelling or shopping, all the time we rely on the internet and the instantaneous access to unlimited information. The internet has embraced our daily routine in such a way that we may not even remember what life was like before the internet. We are at the beginning of a new era which will be characterized by digitalization and the constant interconnection of everything. The internet has become an integral part of our lives. People at large seem to have let the internet take over the helm of their lives consensually and happily. At the same time, it is also impacting the lives of people who are not even connected to it.

With the growing number of internet users across the globe, the threats of breach of privacy and cyber crimes are also on the rise. On one hand, people are happy with the convenience and benefits of staying connected and carrying out online transactions. However, very few can understand that the convenience comes at the cost of being exposed and vulnerable at times. Protecting important information, such as financial data, personal health records, identity revealing information, etc. has become a dire necessity in the world of the internet. Along with the positive impact, the internet has also made it easy for the cyber criminals to commit various types of cyber crimes. For example, it has become possible for any individual to threaten the entire world from the comfort of their home. It could take up the form of website hacking or breaking into the systems of banks and corporate companies.

As we ride the unavoidable tide of the internet, we cannot afford to ignore the necessity of a life jacket known as Cyber Security. The invention of new technologies brings with it new ways of attacking the users and disturbing the system. The complexity of the attacks also increases over time. Therefore, it is imperative for everyone accessing the internet to know the online threats and the preventive as well as corrective measures to avoid or recover from such attacks. It has indeed become the need of this hour. The Cyber Security awareness is going to play an important role in the modern world. This realisation inspired me to venture into the field of Cyber Security and pour my knowledge and skills into this book. I hope this book has given you enough insight on how the cyber crimes can affect you as a user. The tools and techniques elaborated in this book are intended to help the readers prepare their defence against most of the common and even some of the uncommon cyber attacks. This will also help those looking forward to making a career in the field of Cyber Security. Overall, this book will help strengthen the base knowledge of Cyber Security.

www.ingramcontent.com/pod-product-compliance
Lightning Source LLC
LaVergne TN
LVHW041203050326
832903LV00020B/432